JOHN D. CAPUTO

Hermeneutics
Facts and Interpretation in the Age of Information

A PELICAN BOOK

PELICAN
an imprint of
PENGUIN BOOKS

PELICAN BOOKS

UK | USA | Canada | Ireland | Australia
India | New Zealand | South Africa

Penguin Books is part of the Penguin Random House
group of companies whose addresses can be found at
global.penguinrandomhouse.com.

First published 2018

002

Text copyright © John D. Caputo, 2018

The moral right of the author has been asserted

Book design by Matthew Young
Set in 10/14.664 pt FreightText Pro
Typeset by Jouve (UK), Milton Keynes

Printed and bound in Great Britain by Clays Ltd, Elcograf S.p.A.

A CIP catalogue record for this book is available from the British Library

ISBN: 978-0-241-25785-2

Contents

A Conclusion without Conclusion

ACKNOWLEDGEMENTS

My thanks to Ananda Pellerin, my editor at Penguin, and to James Risser and Nancy Moules, who read earlier versions of this manuscript, all of whom gave me invaluable advice for which I am deeply grateful.

A Matter of Interpretation

A PRIMER ON POSTMODERN HERMENEUTICS

'That's a matter of interpretation.'

That observation is an excellent way to make mischief, if you are so inclined. But, mischief-making aside, it also makes a sound philosophical point.

Still, a fact is a fact, yes? It's as clear as the nose on your face. Maybe not. Ask yourself, how many facts are there around you right now? You see the problem. We have to specify the terms, the framework. Are you counting noses or chairs or subatomic particles – or what? We need an interpretation before we can start counting. The theory that *everything* is a matter of interpretation is called hermeneutics. This may sound like making mischief in the extreme, but it also makes perfect sense. Hermeneutics is cold, sober theory, and it lies at the basis of all our inventiveness in the sciences and the arts, of our democratic freedoms in politics, and of innovative institutions and living traditions. Without it, things would come to a grinding halt.

So, every time a well-known speaker insists, perhaps accompanied by a bit of table-pounding, 'The fact of the matter is . . .', well, whatever interpretation it is that the speaker means to pound in, the right philosophical response is that there are no uninterpreted facts of the matter. Every matter of fact is a matter of the interpretation that picks out the facts. Hermeneutics is the theory that the distinction between facts and interpretation bears closer scrutiny, which is what we intend to undertake here.

To get these issues on the table, let's start with a short FAQ about postmodern hermeneutics, an imaginary dialogue in which I defend hermeneutics against an inquirer who treats the distinction between facts and interpretation as sound dogma. We'll resume this dialogue in the Conclusion of the book to see what we've managed to accomplish in the meantime.

Hermeneutics: FAQ

What is hermeneutics?

Hermeneutics is the theory of interpretation. It is the theory that everything is a matter of interpretation.

But aren't certain things just facts?

In hermeneutics, we defend the idea that there are no pure facts. Behind every interpretation lies another interpretation. We never reach an understanding of anything that is *not* an interpretation. We can never peel away the layers to get to some pure, uninterpreted, naked fact of the matter. No matter how loudly you proclaim you are just sticking to the facts, you are only raising the volume of your own interpretation. In hermeneutics, I like to say, interpretation goes all the way down.

Does this go for what you just said?

Of course. I am presenting an interpretation of hermeneutics, which I am prepared to defend against the alternatives, which I will point out as we go along. Interpretations go all the way down *but* some interpretations are better than others (which I will also explain as we go along). It is important to hold both those thoughts in our heads at the same time.

So, you're saying facts don't matter. How can you deny that there is a distinction between a neutral fact and an interpretation?

Facts matter quite a lot. That's why it really matters that we understand what facts are. To understand anything at all requires having an angle on it, a perspective, an interpretive slant, in the absence of which we would just not understand, period. A neutral and disinterested understanding is pretty much a blank, unknowing stare. It is the look you see on the faces of students with a writing assignment without the least idea of what they are going to do. Their problem? No slant, no angle of entry, no interpretation. The facts you find are a function of the interests you have, and disinterested interpretations are nowhere to be found. A disinterested understanding has never got a term paper written, or anything else.

Are 'hermeneutics' and 'interpretation' interchangeable terms?

The word 'hermeneutics' comes from the Greek, and 'interpretation' from its Latin translation. But it is more useful to distinguish between them by saying that interpretation is an art, and hermeneutics is the theory of that art. An interpretation is a first-order *act* or process – like an analysis of a film by a critic, of an X-ray by a radiologist, of the causes of the First World War by a historian, of an economic recession by an economist, or of the testimony of a witness by the jury. Hermeneutics is a second-order *reflection* upon such acts, upon the concrete work of interpretation carried out in art, in science, in classrooms and courtrooms, and in general.

So, in hermeneutics we show these people how to make interpretations?

We would never presume such a thing. Concrete interpretations are the business of the specialists in these particular fields. Hermeneutics does not pretend to be a know-it-all and it is not a how-to manual. It a *philosophical* theory. We show people how to understand what is going on in interpretation.

Why philosophical?

Because hermeneutics is a theory of *truth* – it describes the nature of truth as something that is acquired only through interpretation – and of *being human*, because it claims that interpretation lies at the heart of who we are as human beings.

Why add 'postmodern' to hermeneutics?

Hermeneutics has a long history, stretching all the way back to Aristotle.[1] We're dividing that history into two parts, the first of which we call the modern era, beginning in the biblical studies brought on by the Protestant Reformation and culminating in the nineteenth century. In the twentieth century, everything changed, and culminated in what we're calling postmodern, which is the version that really interests us here.

So, what's the difference?

In the modern era, the humanities were put on the defensive in the face of the rising prestige of the new natural sciences and the success of the scientific method, which was threatening to take over everything. So, the people who worked in the humanities said, Look, in the humanities we also have a method, and we also attain truth and objectivity, but it is different. The natural sciences give us *causal explanations* of mathematically measurable phenomena, while in the humanities we reach an *interpretive understanding* of works of art or historical events, phenomena which have a non-mathematical *meaning*. The humanities are different but just as legitimate.

That makes a lot of sense. What was wrong with that?

First of all, let me be clear that 'postmodern' does not mean *anti*-modern or returning to the *pre*-modern. It passes *through* modernity, allowing itself to be instructed *by* modernity, and then comes out the other end with a new twist, continuing what was started in modernity by another means. In the twentieth century, two important things emerged which changed the course of traditional hermeneutics. First, the postmodern philosophers said that there is no such neat divide, that *every* act of understanding is *already* an interpretation, not only in the humanities but also in the natural sciences, and, as a matter of fact, not only in the academic disciplines but in everything we do in daily life. Second, they said that we should take some of the air out of this word 'method', a favourite of the natural sciences, and realize that truth is wider and deeper than method. Method can be very wooden and it can even be a positive obstacle to finding the truth. So, we have to see that interpretation is a more flex-ible, inventive process than any method will allow – scientific or otherwise.

I can see that in the humanities but not in the natural sciences.

That's the nineteenth-century mistake. We learned from twentieth-century historians of science, who were studying the people on the ground in the sciences, researching real scientists actually 'doing' science, that science is a much messier business than the modern philosophers had led us to believe. There's a great deal of interpretive skill in-volved – proposing speculative hypotheses, interpreting evidence, reading data, devising experiments, dealing with anomalies for which the method is unprepared, passionately sticking to an idea even when the evidence is slim and every-one in the scientific community thinks you are mad. This proved especially true when the historians studied revolu-tionary changes in science, which look a lot more like polit-ical or artistic revolutions than the modern philosophers and scientists wanted us to think.

But what happens to objectivity in all this interpreting?
Especially in the sciences?

Objectivity is redescribed, not discarded. It is understood in a more cautious and circumspect way, with all the appropriate conditions, complications and restrictions. We deconstruct the idea of pure objectivity or pure facts and replace it with the distinction between good interpretations and bad ones.

What do you mean by 'deconstruct'? What's that?

Deconstruction is the particular version of postmodernism that we are using here. There are other versions, which are better fit for other purposes, but this is the one that works its way into hermeneutics in the most felicitous way. For the moment, let's just say that deconstruction is the theory that all our beliefs and practices are constructions, and that whatever is constructed is de-constructible, and that whatever is de-constructible is also re-constructible, which would mean that all our beliefs and practices are *re-interpretable*. So, deconstruction backs up the idea of endless reinterpretation and rejects the idea of ready-made truths that drop from the sky. There's a lot more to it, but that should get us started.

I don't quite get the difference between hermeneutics and deconstruction.

Hermeneutics, which comes from German philosophy and has a theological provenance, is focused on the law, the historical tradition and the classics, and so tends to be a bit more interested in mainstream culture and canonical great works. Hermeneutics stresses that we do not begin from scratch; we begin from an inherited situation which is already up and running. Deconstruction, which started as a French movement of the 1960s and has a background in contemporary linguistics, tends to be of a more radical stripe, more suspicious of inherited traditions. Hermeneutics takes *conversation*, not *critique*, as its model of inquiry, while in deconstruction the model is a scrupulously close, the-devil-is-in-the-details *scrutiny*. My argument here is that each one requires the other. Without deconstruction, hermeneutics risks being naïve; without hermeneutics, deconstruction risks running off the rails. That is why I call this postmodern approach 'radical hermeneutics'.[2]

What do you mean by 'radical'?

In radical hermeneutics, we take the point of view of the outliers, the outsiders, the ones whose views have been neglected or excluded. Postmodern – radical – hermeneutics takes the view from the margins. Deconstructors are disposed to dissent, to point out alternative explanations, to bring up anomalies, to question received interpretations, to suspect unquestioned assumptions. They are not against conversation, but they worry about those who cannot get into the conversation, either because they are excluded or because they don't have the requisite linguistic skills or are speaking in a new way. Deconstructors cultivate a congenital disposition to look at things *otherwise*, to pick up views that have fallen out of favour or dropped through the cracks of the tradition.

Why should the rest of us care about any of this? Isn't this just all academic stuff?

Not at all. As a life-long academic, I would be the last one to treat academic studies lightly, but these are not just arcane debates. Hermeneutics provides our best protection against the threat of tyranny, totalitarianism and terror in politics, and of dogmatism and authoritarianism in ethics and religion. Indeed, these threats can be found anywhere – including in the sciences, the art world or that of economics – anywhere that the quiet dictatorship of a rigid orthodoxy takes root. Orthodoxy discourages dissent (alternative interpretations) and tries to impose a privileged interpretation.

Are you saying that hermeneutics is crucial to democracy?

That's one of my claims. Postmodern hermeneutics, in which we reserve the right to ask any question, is constitutionally anti-authoritarian and democratic. Without hermeneutics, you would never to be able to explain what a democracy is. Without democracy, you would never be able to practise hermeneutics; you would end up in jail, or worse.

But if everybody has their own opinion and we leave it at that, isn't that just inviting chaos? Isn't that just as bad as authoritarianism?

That's an excellent point. That's the opposite extreme, and it is a particular problem today.

What's so different about today?

That's another part of what 'postmodern' means – the high-tech, mobile, globetrotting, multicultural, polyglot, cosmopolitan world we live in. In postmodern culture, things are more de-centred, democratic, pluralistic, multifocal and bottom-up. The mainstream is interrupted by the voices and the faces from the margins. Consequently, we are today far

more likely than we have been in the past to appreciate that
an interpretation *is* an interpretation, to see that there are
other interpretations, to recognize that it has not fallen from
the sky, that it is not an eternal truth handed down from on
high.[3]

But don't philosophers deal in eternal truths?

Ah, but eternal, absolute truths are interpretations that
we have forgotten are interpretations. Hermeneutics is the
'inconvenient truth', to borrow an excellent phrase from Al
Gore which reminds us of what truths themselves are. In
the modern era, things were taken to be more orderly and
methodic, more centred and stabilized – science here, the
humanities there, subjectivity here, objectivity there; all
things tidily in place. Postmodernism, like democracy, is
messier. We have acquired a sensitivity to the diversity of
cultures and the multiplicity of lifestyles, to difference –
ethnic, gendered, sexual. Difference is our watchword. So, we
also have to worry about the opposite problem, not absolutism or authoritarianism but sheer relativism.

What do you mean by 'relativism'?

In its pure state, relativism means 'anything goes'. There
are as many truths as there are opinions. We all have our
own truths, the way we all have our favourite flavours and
colours.

Relativism insinuates itself into postmodern thinking in
subtle ways, some of which could prove lethal. For example,
it is one thing for the conservatives to be shocked by young
people who simply reject the marriage game, who assert that

they are responsible adults who are going to live with whomever they want to live with and break up with them whenever they are of a mind to. On this point the conservatives have to realize that they don't get to tell other people how to live their lives. That's not relativism, that's different points of view, which is a fixture of life in postmodern times. But it is quite another thing when relativism takes hold and people enlist hermeneutics in the service of dangerous and destructive causes.

Like what?

Like the climate-change deniers, who argue that the looming ecological disaster is just a theory, that it is only an interpretation, or, worse still, the conspiracy theorists who say it is a left-wing fiction meant to enhance control by the state over private enterprise. Or religious fanatics who question the theory of evolution on the grounds that it is just a theory, or who reject the findings of contemporary physics in favour of their interpretation of Genesis. In a democracy, such people are legally entitled to their views, but the danger is that such thinking will infect public policy and undermine efforts to control climate change, or affect how science is taught in schools.

Right. Facts matter. So, we should hit people like that with the hard facts.

Not so fast. We cannot pick and choose when we think hermeneutics applies. Even our firmest truths are matters of interpretation, but that does not mean that anything goes. *Some interpretations are better than others.* Some are arbitrary, frivolous and contrived, and some are serious and well tested. They are 'proven' not in the sense of becoming an Absolute Truth but in the sense that we say that someone is a person of proven experience in the field. That is why we prefer the 'opinion' of a respected physician over that of our crazy uncle about this nagging pain we are having. While there may not be this thing the moderns called Pure Reason, which is plugged into Absolute Truth, there are *good reasons* to believe one thing rather than the other – like the things the climate scientists are telling us – and, consequently, we have a moral obligation to our children and grandchildren to listen to their warnings.

Then are you admitting that there are 'alternative facts'?

'Alternative facts' is a cynical political ruse aimed at undermining good interpretations. 'Alternative interpretations' is good hermeneutic theory, and also, we might say, a fact of life.

So, climate change is not just a matter of interpretation?

If we truly understand what an interpretation is – which is what we do in hermeneutics – we would never say '*just* a matter of interpretation'. A good interpretation is a blessed event, a wonderful thing, a *tertium quid*, the 'third thing' that shows the way out of the loggerhead that results whenever the fruitless and destructive war between absolutism and relativism breaks out.[4]

You said this word 'hermeneutics' comes from the Greek. Is there a story there?

A great story. The word comes from the myth of the Greek god Hermes, who was a very colourful god indeed, famous for his cunning and thefts, his tricks and deceptions. For Hermes, telling the truth is human, but lying is divine. On his first day on Earth, he caused a terrible row on Mount Olympus by stealing fifty cattle from the great god Apollo. Hermes was a loveable rogue, sweet talking, ambitious, shrewd, inventive, and bold as brass, a deity with the devil in his eye.[5] The word first came into modern terminology when it was used by Protestants during the Reformation for the study of the Bible.

But why would the Reformation theologians invoke a god like that?

They were drawing on the later Homeric tradition. By then, Hermes had become a safe character, the winged messenger (*angelos*) of Zeus to mortals. The devilish divinity of the earlier versions of the legend had been confined to an entirely respectable function, reduced to a kind of divine postman or instant message system. This downgrading was the doing of the followers of the cult of Apollo, upper-crust, aristocratic Greeks who were of a mind to keep this trickster god in check. Hermes the deceiver was denounced as a downright disgraceful deity by Plato and Aristotle, who expected better behaviour of a god. So, the powers that be consigned him to the post room in the Olympian basement. Then the biblical scholars conveniently forgot Hermes the cunning rogue, an independent deity and nobody's messenger boy, more likely to steal the post, or tamper with it, than to deliver it. The earlier Hermes was a rabble-rouser.[6]

So, the first myth of Hermes had a political slant?

Precisely. Hermes gave voice to a rising middle class tired of being pushed around by the aristocrats, who clearly preferred the status quo. He saw from his cradle that all the wealth and power had been concentrated in the upper 2 per cent of the population, and that the time had come for a change. He was more a Robin Hood than a common thief, more a freedom fighter than a criminal – distinctions that clearly depend on your point of view, on your interpretation, which is hermeneutics 1.0.

It sounds like Hermes himself requires a hermeneutic.

That should not be surprising. Greek myths, biblical myths – myths in any tradition – give us something to think through, and that means to interpret. One of my main ideas is that, in the ancient story of Hermes itself, we can divine the difference between *two interpretations of interpretation*. The one you follow depends upon on your interpretation. Hermes the Straight Man, favoured by the mainstream, the theologians, the more tradition-bound, or Hermes the Trickster, favoured by the marginal, the outliers. Mainstream and marginal hermeneutics. Insider hermeneutics and outsider hermeneutics. Hermeneutics straight up and exorbitant hermeneutics. The view from the centre and the eccentric view. The one figure is more hierarchical, conservative and subservient to the gods on high, representing a kind of law-and-order, top-down hermeneutics. The other is a god of the people, a voice of the *demos*, a divine disturber of the peace who made the higher-ups nervous because he would not conform to the established order; in short, a more radical hermeneutical type intent on shaking up the system and making unpredictable things happen.

So in postmodern hermeneutics, we follow the lead of the impious Hermes?

My idea is to give Hermes the rogue a hearing, to pay more attention to the hell-raiser and the trouble-maker, and to defend a more mischievous, radical, devilish art. But with one qualification: I do not want to abolish the pious Hermes. I am not trying to *abolish* interpretations (it's the absolutiz-ers who abolish) but to *multiply* them. I affirm throughout the *two* faces of Hermes, both traditional interpreter and interloper, both messenger and trickster, both courier and corruptor, both god of caution and god of risk-taking. The two interpretations of interpretation are deeply intertwined, the way hermeneutics and deconstruction are intertwined. The very idea of the postmodern is to cast doubt upon tidy, ordered and settled distinctions. Interpretation worthy of the name takes place in the distance between the two and is nourished by the tensions of an optimal disequilibrium. Without *both* faces of Hermes, hermeneutics not only has no name, it has no heart, no life.

Itinerary

I will look in again on this conversation in the Conclusion but, before we get started, let's get an idea of the path we will be following in this book. In the first part (Chapters 1–6), we will introduce the leading figures in postmodern hermeneut-ics, and in the second part (Chapters 7–10), we will take up some pressing issues in the postmodern world where we can see hermeneutics at work.

We'll start with Martin Heidegger (1889–1976), who was the game-changer in contemporary hermeneutics. To be sure, the first thing anyone says these days when they hear his name is that he was a card-carrying member of the Nazi Party, and that's the first test hermeneutics faces in this book. How do we interpret the thought of a man whose personal politics were so odious? Does the corruption of the man corrupt the work? I defend the view that *Being and Time* (1927),[7] his magnum opus, is the most important work of continental philosophy in the twentieth century; after it, nothing was the same (Chapter 1).

Even after the Second World War, Heidegger published a whole new wave of books, which received a surprisingly warm reception in France. That altered the course of hermeneutics *again* and contributed to the emergence of postmodern theory in the second half of the century. So, we'll have to look into the post-war Heidegger, too (Chapter 2). Heidegger had a number of important students, the most important of whom, from our point of view, was Hans-Georg Gadamer (1900–2002), whose own magnum opus, *Truth and Method* (1960),[8] represents *the* magisterial exposition of hermeneutics in the twentieth century, which clearly merits a careful look (Chapter 3).

Next (Chapter 4) we turn to Jacques Derrida (1930–2004), the founder of the movement called deconstruction, and his major work, *Of Grammatology* (1967).[9] So, without pretending to cover everything, I will highlight how this book, along with *Being and Time* and *Truth and Method*, changed everything in hermeneutics, mutating the modern into the postmodern. I should warn you that the most controversial feature of my presentation is the inclusion of Derrida, one of the '68ers', as in 1968, the year of the student protests in Paris and something of the unofficial roll-out year of post-modernism. In the standard renderings of hermeneutics, Derrida is regarded as the devil himself, as a critic of hermen-eutics and one of its itchiest antagonists. If hermeneutics is the theory of interpretation, its critics deride deconstruction (Derrida's game) as a theory of *mis*interpretation, as if the great works of the tradition can mean anything you want them to mean. For his part, Gadamer was worried that Derrida's emphasis on difference was so strong that it would end up making conversation impossible.

Derrida himself avoided using the word 'hermeneutics', which he confined to its conservative theological side. He reduced it to the interpretation of *the* meaning (as if there were but one) of *the* tradition (as if there were but one), which finds the *key* which unlocks the authentic and authori-tative interpretation. But that of course is to restrict it to the mainstream interpretation of interpretation – not interpret-ation from the margins, but from the centre, from the heart of the tradition. So, what I do in this account is to allow Derrida to play the part of a Parisian Hermes, to be a crucial player who shifts the backdrop of hermeneutics from German theologians to an odd assembly of atheistic trouble-makers on the Left Bank. I am saying, if Derrida bedevils her-meneutics, the result is a devilish hermeneutics. Derrida is said to be a post-structuralist, so to see how all this works, we will also have to follow his critique of structuralism (Chapter 5), which is where deconstruction started.

This is not to say that all the big names in postmodern hermeneutics are German and French. It has a very colourful representative in the United States, Richard Rorty (1931–2007), and in Italy, Gianni Vattimo (1936–), who became friends later on in their lives, and to whom I devote a separate treatment (Chapter 6). This isn't everybody, to be sure, but they are the main modern hermeneutic players.[10]

In the second part of the book (Chapters 7–10), I try to catch hermeneutics in the act, to observe it in action in the postmodern world, in the workplace, in the vocations and professions, in concrete institutions and real life. I start with the question of justice and the interpretation of the law, where hermeneutics has never been more important (Chapter 7). I then look in on a group of Canadian nurses who have taken Gadamer to heart in a fascinating way, which shows the bedside manner of hermeneutics in contemporary healthcare (Chapter 8).

The main challenge for hermeneutics today, in my view, is to address what is becoming of the professions, of our institutions, of our world, in the age of 'advanced information technologies', which have brought about a sea change in everything we do. Here we see a mutation from the postmodern to what is called the 'post-human', to indicate the ways in which the human is being invaded and taken over by the technological. Here I come to the question of the 'program' – of Big Data, of the Algorithm – which would bring the play of interpretation under its rule. Today, in what I will call the 'post-human imaginary', we are left to wonder, 'Have we ever been human?' (Chapter 9).

I edge towards a conclusion by going back to where

hermeneutics started, in religion and theology. The reason that religion finds itself in crisis today – it is becoming increasingly unbelievable among educated people – is a hermeneutical misunderstanding, a failure on the part of religion to understand its own character as a *symbolic* practice. My idea is to see not whether religion can save us but whether hermeneutics can save religion – from itself. I bring up the interpretation of religion not only because it is so much in the news but also because there is something religious about interpretation, something which taps into the deep structure of our lives, a certain proto-religion, which will, however, provide little consolation to the pious (Chapter 10).

After a brief summing-up (Chapter 11), I bring everything to a head in a 'Conclusion without Conclusion', a kind of concluding postmodern postscript which describes the possibility of a God even Nietzsche could love. If that all sounds a bit mysterious, let's just say it is the mystery implied by saying that interpretation goes all the way down.

CHAPTER 1

How Heidegger Changed Everything

READING *BEING AND TIME*

1. The Heidegger Affair

I begin with Martin Heidegger (1889–1976) because with Heidegger begins everything that we mean by contemporary or postmodern hermeneutics. But before I begin, I have to acknowledge the elephant in the room. Heidegger is one of those people who did not need enemies. No one could have done a better job of smearing his name and tarnishing his reputation than he did through his own unaided efforts. It is his fault that, before discussing his groundbreaking work as one of the most important philosophers of the twentieth century, I have practically to apologize for bringing him up. Interpreting Heidegger himself is a dicey business and a testy example of the very business of hermeneutics.

A good case can be made that Heidegger's masterpiece, *Being and Time* (1927), is the single most important book of continental European philosophy in the twentieth century, and that, after the Second World War, Heidegger published a new line of work that dominated the better part of the second half of the century. Heidegger is arguably the greatest continental European philosopher since Nietzsche. Even if you prefer your philosophy to be of the Anglo-American variety, Heidegger is the Chunnel, the most interesting link with

Ludwig Wittgenstein (1889–1951), who enjoys a similar guru status this side of the Channel (let's ignore the fact that Wittgenstein was an Austrian immigrant).

I was drawn to Heidegger because, like him, I was born into a pre-Second Vatican Council Catholic world where the air was filled with as many absolute truths as you could count (so long as you could count in Roman numerals), and, like him, my initial interests in philosophy were the Catholic Middle Ages. So, for a Catholic college student like me, fed an austere bread-and-water diet of medieval scholasticism, *Being and Time* was electrifying, and I was far from alone. By introducing a whole generation of Catholic philosophers (not to mention every other type of philosopher) who came of age in the middle of the twentieth century, inspired by the *aggiornamento* (the 'bringing-up-to-date' of the Church) announced by Pope John XXIII at the Second Vatican Council (1962–5), to phenomenology, hermeneutics and existentialism, *Being and Time* was emancipatory, breathing new life into the works of Catholic philosophers and theologians from the old scholasticism.

So where's the elephant?

Heidegger was a Nazi.

No one suspected that he was a particularly political person before the Nazi era. No one suspected that he was anti-Semitic, including Hannah Arendt (1906–75), his brilliant and eventually world-famous Jewish student, then political theorist, with whom he had an affair back in the 1920s. But there it was. He was a member of the Nazi Party even though he himself had altered one of his post-war publications to read 'movement', not 'Party'.

WHAT WE THOUGHT WE KNEW

Of course, I knew then – in the 1960s and 70s – about Heidegger's 'Nazi affair'. I knew what we all 'knew', that he was involved in the Nazi movement during the time that he served as Rector of the University of Freiburg (1933–4), and that he got out of the job and the movement after ten months, having seen what the Nazis were up to. Or so we thought. That was one interpretation. The one that Heidegger and the people close to him put out. Most of us thought that was all there was to it. Let him who has never done anything genuinely stupid in his life throw the first stone. But in the late 1980s and thereafter, a series of damaging disclosures revealed the ugly truth.[1] His involvement with the Nazis went deeper. He remained a member of the Party throughout the war, had great contempt for Western democracy and was anti-Semitic. There had been plenty of evidence of the latter before now. But the recent publication of his *Black Notebooks* – a journal he kept from 1931 to 1938 – has dispelled any lingering doubts.[2] Wave after wave of punishing revelations peeled away the cover-up. Ironically, if one of Heidegger's strong points as a philosopher was his analysis of truth as 'un-concealment', it was not one of the strong points of his personal or professional life.

DEMYTHOLOGIZING HEIDEGGER

So, Heidegger is not only the beginning of contemporary hermeneutics, he poses the first hermeneutic problem we have to solve: how much weight does the author's personal biography have when interpreting their work? Long before the *Black Notebooks* was published, I gave my answer in

Demythologizing Heidegger[3] – you could fill a library with the interpretations of Heidegger that are out there – where, after venting my frustrations with him, I tried to reach a balanced judgement about his thought.

In 1933, he was a politically active Nazi with an interest in the Nazification of the university and in becoming the intellectual *Führer* of the movement, but his ambitions were quickly doused. He was invited to step down from the rectorship because the Nazis judged him an inept administrator who was doing more harm than good to the movement. He in turn became disillusioned with the people around Hitler and harshly critical of the Party, but not of the 'inner truth and greatness of the movement',[4] which he thought he understood and they did not. This, he said, lay in the spiritual kinship of the Germans with the ancient Greeks; genuine and deep thinking could be conducted only by pondering ancient Greek and speaking modern German, which authorized the German nation to lead the world. The Party was totally baffled. It was glad to have a famous professor on their side, but the link between National Socialism and the ancient Greek (pre-Socratic) philosopher Heraclitus, between *Mein Kampf* and Heraclitus' *Kampf* (*polemos*), was lost on them.[5] In a photo of Heidegger giving his inaugural lecture as rector, with Nazi officials on the stage behind him, you can almost see them leaning over to ask one another, 'What is this guy talking about?'

After the rectorship, he began the inner migration to a spiritualized private version of National Socialism. Heidegger had a great love of the Black Forest landscape – in those days, the conservatives were the conservationists – and a deep concern about the destructive effects of modern technology on the environment. He rather foolishly thought that the architects of the Nazi military machine shared his distrust of technology, which he associated with the Jews and Marxists in Berlin. After the war, he was suspended from teaching, nearly lost his pension and had a nervous breakdown. But he published a series of evocative meditations upon the natural world (*physis*) and a provocative critique of technology in the name of what he called not hermeneutics but 'poetic thinking'. Ponderous and pompous, pensive, perplexing and profound, the post-war works changed everything again. They contributed importantly to what was called 'deep ecology', and invited comparison with the mystics. Deep, and often at odds with the existentialist views he had held before the war and written about in *Being and Time*, they set off a whole new wave of thinking that fed directly into what we today call postmodernism.

SO, SHOULD WE STOP READING HEIDEGGER?

This situation is so bad – and it keeps getting worse as scholars continue to root through his unpublished manuscripts – that the political values of many people of goodwill lead them to refuse to read his work. Some even suggest relocating his books from the philosophy section of the library to that of the history of National Socialism. I understand the anger, but that is a mistake. Here's the hermeneutical lesson: scrutinizing the author's biography for clues to understanding what was in their books is a useful place to start, even when it uncovers an inconvenient truth. But if it is a place to start, it is not a place to finish. Ultimately, what matters is to understand not the authorial subjectivity but the author's subject matter. You ignore Heidegger at your peril. His influence reaches into nearly every corner of contemporary arts and culture. As maddening as this is to many, he remains the dominant figure of twentieth-century continental philosophy – and there is no way around him.

2. The Early Freiburg Period (1919–23)

When the young Heidegger came home from the First World War, he was a new man, or at least a new philosopher. Abandoning his student interests in late-medieval logic, along with his Catholicism, he converted to Lutheranism and took up a thorough study of the New Testament, Luther and Søren Kierkegaard (1813–55). At the same time, he began a series of courses on what he called 'the hermeneutics of facticity', which galvanized students like Gadamer and Arendt. The word rapidly spread around Germany that a new philosophical star was rising in Freiburg.[6] Heidegger promised a radical renewal of philosophy. Instead of the business as usual of bloodless concept-building, philosophy would plunge straight away into the 'blooming buzzing confusion' of everyday life, as the American pragmatist philosopher William James (1842–1910) put it.[7] Where once philosophy was conducted in the agora, where Socrates debated with his fellow citizens over the nature of the good life, philosophy today had been reduced to anaemic academic debates. But unlike Kierkegaard and Friedrich Nietzsche (1844–1900), who undertook their critique of philosophy from outside the university, Heidegger wanted to revolutionize the university, to remake it into a place where one could actually philosophize and raise radical questions. This he did in a vocabulary that was so odd and idiosyncratic that he had an article turned down for publication and was passed over for a teaching job at Göttingen – but a vocabulary so provocative that Gadamer thought this was Heidegger's finest hour.

THE HERMENEUTICS OF FACTICITY

By facticity, or factical life, Heidegger meant not the *fact that* but *how* we live, not the factual, as in pure facts, but the actual, the impure and messy business of our everyday life, not abstract constructions but concrete experience.[8] When, for example, the New Testament speaks of the way of the 'world', this does not mean a cosmological entity but the *how* of the world, a way of living that has turned away from God. Or when Paul speaks of the 'flesh', he is not speaking of bodily tissue but the rule or regime of sin as opposed to the rule or reign of God, which he called the spirit.[9] Like this, factical life meant a form of life, a way of living in the world, a mode of 'being-in-the-world', as the young philosopher put it.

Even so, why call this hermeneutics? Because 'factical' does not mean a matter of fact but a matter of interpretation. The hermeneutic 'how' refers to *how we interpret* our lives and our world and our 'being-with' one another in the world. Interpretation is not an isolated act, one thing among many that we *do*; it is what we *are*, the pivot, the crux of our being. Interpretation adjusts the settings of our being-in-the-world; it tunes the way we are attuned to the world. Interpretation is a world-making where the world is where and how we dwell. We are not 'in' the world the way water is in a glass but by living and dwelling there – and it is sometimes a warm and embracing place and sometimes dark and foreboding. That is what interpretation meant in the premodern world, from Aristotle to Augustine to Luther. For Aristotle, hermeneutics meant the articulate expression of our life in the *polis*, where our lives are shaped and nourished. For Augustine, interpreting the Scriptures – his hermeneutics – is a soul-searching and soul-shattering exercise, to be undertaken in fear and trembling, not a bit of reading for an idle afternoon.[10]

But in modernity, hermeneutics has been corrupted. Take that as a general rule for Heidegger: modernity is always the corruption of the ancient. That is pretty much what he means by modernity. Corruption means something more than a mistake, an error in calculation. It means decadence, life in decay, a cultural rot of which modern philosophy is the sallow spokesperson. In modernity,[11] hermeneutics is reduced to a pallid methodological reflection upon interpretation which supplies the method of the humanities. In modernity, the concretely situated living historical being has degenerated into 'consciousness', a 'thinking thing', a disengaged 'critical' self, of which there is nothing greater. The world is reduced to the grey-on-grey of an 'object' to be passed in review under the gaze of the thinking 'subject'. Even God is hauled before the court of modernity, his very existence henceforth requiring proof if it is to be taken seriously. Instead of tapping into deeper roots, the modern ego is a rootless, deracinated consciousness, a judge submitting the world to a ruthless critical review under the name of what it called 'pure reason'.

Against all of this, Heidegger amasses all his resources,

which he advances under the name of hermeneutics. Because, for him, hermeneutics means life: whenever I open my mouth, it is not just I myself doing the talking but rather something greater than me; it is life itself coming to words. Hermeneutics taps into a deeper, prior self-interpretation.

THE ONTOLOGY OF DASEIN

To get at this lush and fluid life which precedes the arrival of the philosophers, the young philosopher kept the calcified vocabulary of modern philosophy at a distance and took up a series of tongue-twisting formulations, the most important of which was Dasein. This is the ordinary German word for 'existence', literally meaning 'being-there' (as opposed to *Sosein*, being such-and-such), which Heidegger turned into a bit of a mind-bender: the being we intend to interpret in hermeneutics is itself the being who interprets, the being whose very Being[12] is to interpret itself – and consequently to interpret others, with whom it is bound, and the world in which it is embedded.

Hermeneutics is interpretation interpreting itself.[13] So the 'hermeneutics of factical life' can be read in either direction: both the interpretation of factical life and the factical life of interpretation. We are all self-interpreting beings, and in this we differ from everything else – the rock, the plant, the animal – which for Heidegger are beings which are *simply* present, simply *there*, without making their presence (their 'there') a matter to interpret. If the rock is simply there (present), our being-there wavers in interpretability, questionability. We are the beings who make our Being a matter of interpretation, who put our Being into question. The beings which we ourselves are are the beings whose task is *to be (zu sein)* our there *(da)*, to take it over and interpret it, to 'be' it (taken as a transitive verb), Dasein.[14] The locution is a circumlocution, a way around speaking of 'human' being. It is not a neologism but a literalizing and energizing of a familiar word which drives translators to despair, and who nowadays have wisely capitulated and simply use the untranslated word Dasein. Heidegger's idea is to adhere rigorously to the 'Being' of human beings. Since, in philosophy, talk of Being is called 'ontology', hermeneutics is to be conducted on an ontological plane (as Being-talk), not an anthropological plane (as human-talk).[15] So the full title of his 1923 course is 'Ontology: Hermeneutics of Facticity'. This means:

> The doctrine of Being;
> The interpretation of the beings whose Being is to interpret their Being.

The students were both confused and excited. Either way, they knew something radically new was breaking out.

THE HERMENEUTIC CIRCLE

Heidegger would thereby give a new twist to the 'hermeneutic circle', a familiar trope in traditional hermeneutics, where it had a completely methodological significance as a technique of reading. It went back to Luther, who said we should read each part of the Scriptures in the light of the whole and the whole on the basis of the parts, going back and forth between the two until the text snaps into place. Heidegger did not so much reject the methodological circle as rework it into an ontological circle.

If our very Being is to interpret our Being, then, obviously, we are always doing it. Our Being is being interpreted all the time, whether we realize it or not, and whether we interpret ourselves or misinterpret ourselves. We move around within this interpretation without even appreciating that interpretation is going on, that the world in which we live, and we ourselves, have *already been interpreted*. When we arrive in the world, the interpretation of the world is already up and running before we open our eyes. It is like the air we take for granted, something we do not notice unless it is cut off or fouled by some odour. It is given by simply being taken as *a given*, without our so much as giving it a thought. Interpretation is always running in the background while our attention is taken up by what is going on in the foreground. So, the work of hermeneutics is to *work out* our 'always and already being interpreted', to bring it to the forefront or to the surface.

How are we to do that? *Not* by way of the 'critical consciousness' cultivated in modernity, which tries to disengage itself from all presuppositions, but by keeping our hermeneutic ear close to the ground of life, pressed against the breast of lived experience. *Not* by setting in advance the terms that life must meet, but by allowing life to speak on its own terms in the categories of factical life. Hermeneutics 'reads off' our Being from our Being, thereby spelling it out. But this is not a simple matter. It requires a certain ability to read between the lines of life and track down what is being presupposed, what is not being said explicitly. It's a tricky business and it requires a hermeneutic ear, hermeneutic tact.

So, there is no need to build a bridge to reach this implicit sphere, as we are *already* there. We already *have* it because we already *are* it. Interpreting is our very Being. Still, while we have it, we have not articulated it. We have not expressed it. Our pre-interpreted Being is always just assumed, presupposed, implicit. That means the hermeneutic circle is not just a piece of methodological advice about how to read a book. Nor is it a vicious circle, which assumes what it wants to prove. It is a virtuous ontological circle, which explicates (unfolds, works out)[16] or makes explicit the implicit interpretation we *already have*, which we 'fore-have'. In a hermeneutic circle, the preconceptual pre-interpretation is turned into a concept; the vague pre-understanding is articulated.

ASKING QUESTIONS

So, interpreting Dasein is not a matter of simply undertaking an inspection and making an inventory of what we observe. We cannot simply look at ourselves and make some notes, the way a geologist might look at a rock or a botanist might look at a plant. Why not? Because it is a basic tendency of our being that this pre-understanding remains concealed, in the background, while we busy ourselves with what is going on right under our nose in the foreground. We are beings whose deeper Being tends to withdraw from view. We are not simply there, period, not simply present, like a rock or a plant which has certain properties. Our Being is more evasive, more self-evasive, so a hermeneutic investigation is more like detective work, looking for clues.

Like good detectives, hermeneuts have to ask a lot of hard questions about who we are, and not be satisfied with ready-made answers.[17] The philosophers take it as axiomatic that we are 'rational animals', and the theologians take it as a matter of faith that we are the 'image of God'. But in hermeneutics, we have to put these prepackaged interpretations on the shelf and ask this question of our Being more radically. We have to interrogate the standing interpretations that have always been around, and thereby radicalize our own Being – because we are the beings whose Being is to raise the question of the interpretation of our own Being.

BEGINNING WHERE WE ALREADY ARE

But does not all this radical questioning end up sounding a lot like the 'critical consciousness' of Descartes, who is the villain of the piece for Heidegger, the very man who, by trying to doubt everything in order to find the absolutely indubitable, to obtain absolute certitude, launched the project of modernity?[18] Not a bit. It is the very opposite. Descartes wanted to put all of our presuppositions into question in order to *start from scratch*, to start from nothing, philosophizing *ex nihilo*, finding something absolutely *presuppositionless*. In hermeneutics, we are doing the opposite: we begin where we *already are*, in the world, up to our ears in an inherited culture, native language, etc. (factical life), not in order to root out but to get to the roots of our presuppositions, back to the living heart of our factical life.

Hermeneutics does not seek to find some pure, eternal *ahistorical essence* but rather to tap into the deepest roots of our inherited *historical existence*. It does not seek to begin with nothing but to begin with how the world presents itself to us from day to day and then try to burrow deeply into the hidden springs from which our world has sprung. It is not a matter of *freeing* ourselves *from* presuppositions but of *renewing* our presuppositions, *revitalizing* our deepest resources. Hermeneutics is not a matter of making a presuppositionless beginning but of rethinking the beginning with which we originally began. Hermeneutics does not mean beginning with nothing but beginning with the beginning, beginning *again*, which means it is always a certain *repetition* of the beginning. Repetition is crucial; it does not mean repeatedly covering the same ground but digging deeper into a more originary ground. Hermeneutics is like digging down to a wellspring that has been blocked off and unblocking it. (Descartes, by contrast, wanted to get water by striking a rock.)

The real problem with Descartes and his desire for pure reason was not that he failed to get as far as a doubt-free presuppositionless beginning (which was inevitable) but that *he did not presuppose enough*. He did not appreciate the rich and fertile nature of the presuppositions that nourish life – like the French and Latin languages he was *trusting* in order to *distrust* everything! Hermeneutics does not begin with nothing; it begins with everything – which it seeks to renew radically. In the hermeneutical circle, we already have what we seek to know, but the task is to recover, clarify and renew it. We are already *there*, but the task is to clarify *how* we are there. The *how* is called our factical life and the work of explicating (interpreting) it is called hermeneutics.

GETTING HELP FROM ST PAUL

To borrow an expression from the apostle Paul, we might say that 'we live and move and have our being' in an understanding of our Being – and ultimately of Being itself – and the task of hermeneutics is to work out this understanding. St Paul was preaching to the Athenians on the 'unknown God', for which the Greeks had prudently provided a statue, lest they anger any divinity they omitted. Paul seized on this and said that that was the only god they got right. You constantly seek for God, Paul told them, 'though indeed he is not far from each one of us. For "In him we live and move and have our being"; as even some of your own poets have said' (Acts 17:27–8).

Paul's strategy in addressing these gentiles is strikingly hermeneutic. Gentiles though they may be, the Athenians are seeking what they *already have* but do not yet know – and he has come to Athens to tell them what that is, namely, to *interpret* for them what they already, if only vaguely, understand. Alienated as they may be from God, God is nothing alien, for God is closer to them than they are to themselves. Finding God is not finding an alien being, but overcoming self-alienation. This model shaped the spiritual search recorded in St Augustine's *Confessions*, and, later on, Christian existentialist philosopher and theologian Paul Tillich (1886–1965) would say that is the basic model of theology.[19] The alternative, which tries to start from scratch (as Descartes did), from a world without God, from no-knowledge of God, in order to get to knowledge of God, has cut the lifeline of theology and will never reach God. If we substitute 'Being' for 'God', we can see what hermeneutics means for Heidegger.

HEIDEGGER'S TABLE

To show what he means by a hermeneutics of factical life, Heidegger gives his students an example from – where else? – everyday life: a table in his house. What could be more commonplace than that? How does this table present itself to us in daily life? How is it habitually interpreted? We might be tempted to start by saying that the table is a three-dimensional extended mass occupying a point on a space-time grid. But while we might, later on and for special purposes, take it that way, that is not how it is originally given, not *how* it is *taken* in factical life. Perhaps, then, Heidegger suggests, we should fill in this description and add that it is also a thing of use. Over and above the basic stratum of the neutral material object, there is a second layer of utility, its use-value. But that is to falsely imagine that our concrete experience is a composite of two abstractions, a neutral object to which a use-value has been added, neither of which is given, lived, experienced. Such constructions pass over the characteristic *how* of factical life.

What then *is* the table? What it *is*, Heidegger will say, is what it is taken *as*. The *is* is the *how*; the *is* is the *as*.[20] Heidegger's evocative language, in this case not so obscure, is worth citing in full:

> What is there in *the* room there at home is *the* table (not 'a' table among many other tables in other rooms and houses) at which one sits *in order to* write, have a meal, sew, play. Everyone sees this right away, e.g., during a visit: it is a writing table, a dining table, a sewing table – such is the primary way in which it is being encountered in itself . . .

This and that about it is 'impractical', unsuitable. That part is damaged. It now stands in a better spot in the room than before – there's better lighting, for example . . . Here and there it shows lines – the boys like to busy themselves at the table. These lines are not just interruptions in the paint, but rather: it was the boys and it still is. This side is not the east side, and this narrow side so many cm shorter than the other, but rather the one at which my wife sits in the evening when she wants to stay up and read, there at the table we had such and such a discussion that time, there that decision was made with a *friend* that time, there that *work* written that time, there that *holiday* celebrated that time . . .

Then, he adds, after many years the table is disassembled and ends up in the basement, no longer usable:

> . . . it is found lying on the floor somewhere, just like other 'things', e.g., a plaything, worn out and almost unrecognizable – it is my youth. In a corner of the basement stands an old pair of skis . . . That book over there was a gift from X . . .[21]

The table links us to other people who also sat at it, is marked by the times of the day, by the time of life. Were the boys to come upon this table long after he and his wife are dead, their parents, the whole *world* of their childhood, would come rushing over them.

THE HERMENEUTICS OF HEIDEGGER'S TABLE

We should notice a number of things about this very fertile example, all of which are brought out in the early sections of

Being and Time – and which are clearly drawn from the 1923 lectures.[22]

Firstly, there is no pure, uninterpreted fact of the matter which is then layered over with an interpretation. What is given right from the start is not a pure fact but the table, and it is given *as* a place to work or eat or play. The table is *for* sitting *in order to* have a meal. Its 'in order to' is inscribed in it from the start, not *added on* to a neutral fact. Being-in-the-world is not a matter of pure, disinterested consciousness which neutralizes the world into a set of pale, impersonal objects. It is a matter of *being deeply engaged with the world of everyday concerns*.

Secondly, the table is not an isolated thing but part of a whole, belonging to a holistic and concatenated system – of chairs and cutlery, stoves and windows, the other rooms in the house, the road that leads up to the house, the houses of neighbours, the nearby town, etc. The system is localizable and datable (there is no television running in the background nor any mention of a microwave, for example). The table belongs to an interpretive framework, outside of which it cannot be understood. The whole makes sense (has 'significance') in terms of the parts, and the parts in terms of the whole. They form a 'hermeneutic circle' of part and whole. When archaeologists unearth an ancient artefact, their first question has to do with its *for which* and *in order to*. The concatenation is the 'world' to which the item belongs (the prehistoric world, the modern world, the art world, the world of household life, etc.).

Thirdly, knowledge of this totality is implicit, not explicit. It is the sort of thing we take for granted, except perhaps when we visit a foreign country, where everything is different and we lack the right background knowledge. Or when the system breaks down. When the electricity fails we suddenly realize how everything is connected. When the hammer breaks at a crucial moment, we hastily look about for other things to hammer with.

Fourthly, the table links us to other persons: the carpenter who made it, the neighbour who visits us. Being-in-the-world is always and already *being-with* others. The social order is not a sum total of isolated egos but beings whose Being is being-with from the start.

Fifthly, the three-dimensional, measurable object located at a point on a space–time grid is not an interpretation-free thing-in-itself. It is the fruit of *another interpretation*, the result of suspending the movements of everyday life and taking the table differently, *as* a measurable spatio-temporal object. Dasein, to get back to this term, is never purely neutral; it is always interested in the world, but it has different interests. For instance, in the scientific attitude, we neutralize our practical interest in the table – suspend the world of everyday interests – in order to accentuate our scientific interest. Striking the scientific attitude is a *modification* of our *primary* being-in-the-world, which is always running in the background and resets as soon as we break off the scientific attitude – scientific pursuit is not an endgame or a final, objective way to look at something; it is one of many different ways, all of which have their own truth. Nor is the objectivizing-scientific interpretation illegitimate; it is founded upon and a modification of the prior experience of the table. Whichever way the table appears, its 'how' or 'as', is a function of the task in which we are engaged. The physicist at breakfast sits at the table; in the laboratory, the interpretive framework shifts and the scientific attitude is struck. But the everyday attitude will instantly reset at the first interruption of the world – the phone rings, the equipment breaks, etc.

Sixthly, the *how* of the table, what it is taken *as* – an item of use, the occasion of the remembrance of things past, a beautiful work of craftsmanship from a bygone world, a complex of subatomic particles – all this goes back to Dasein. It is a function of the task in which Dasein engages, the interest it brings to bear, which Heidegger summarizes under the expression 'projection'. Dasein projects the totality within which items *in* the world are taken *as* the things they are. The urinal in the Gents and the one sitting on a stand in the art museum labelled 'Fountain' belong to different worlds. These worlds go back to Dasein, not in the sense that Dasein creates them *ex nihilo* but in the sense that their *how*, the way they are taken, their hermeneutic *as*, is projected by Dasein in view of Dasein cares and concerns. Dasein's being-in-the-world comprises multiple interests, cares and concerns.

Seventhly, the chosen example of interpretation is of a practical activity – knowing how to use the table – not a theoretical one, like interpreting an ancient manuscript. Dasein has both theoretical and practical cares and concerns. The work of interpretation crosses over the distinction between theory and practice, the humanities and the sciences, the religious and the secular. That is because interpretation is not something we do. Interpretation is what we *are*.

3. *Being and Time*

When *Being and Time* was published (1927), it struck like thunder. Ironically, to those who had attended the early lectures on the hermeneutics of factical life, the text actually seemed a bit tame. Compared to the rawness of the early post-war lectures, they thought Heidegger had to some extent succumbed to the German academic demand for system and architectonic.

THE HERMENEUTICS OF EXISTENCE

Heidegger's 1923 lecture course was the basis of the first chapters of a larger project entitled the 'existential analytic', whose task it was to make the vague and implicit understanding Dasein has of itself as *existence* into an explicit interpretation (here, 'existential' means related to existence, which is the word made famous by the group of French thinkers that would come to be known as the existentialists). It begins with a twofold stipulation: 1. The essence of Dasein lies in its existence (*Existenz*), which is to be taken not in the traditional sense of *existentia*, simple presence, but in the Heideggerian sense of having-to-be-the-there; 2. Such Being is *in each case mine*, the being that I myself am uniquely called to be. I can hire a lawyer to represent my case in court, but no one else can do my *existing* for me (if I am found guilty, it is not the lawyer who goes to jail).[23]

Heidegger had adopted the notion of existence from the Danish philosopher Søren Kierkegaard, a Lutheran in the Augustinian tradition, a hugely influential proto-existentialist and arguably the greatest religious author of the last two centuries. Kierkegaard was a brilliant polemicist whose arrows were directly aimed at what he called 'Christendom', the nineteenth-century Christian bourgeoisie. These Sunday-morning Christians pay lip-service to Christianity, he said, nodding their heads in church when the pastor says that without God we can do nothing, but spend the rest of the week showing everyone just how much they are capable of doing with no thought of God at all. Against this farce, he posed the task of becoming a genuinely 'existential' Christian, where existence is defined as 'being-possible', meaning that our being is a being-able-to-be, not a finished product off an assembly line but an ongoing work of freedom and decision. For the 'existing individual' to be a Christian is not just a matter of being baptized but of labouring in fear and trembling, standing one to one 'before God' (*coram deo*). Existential truth is the truth that is true *for me*, by which he meant not any vicious relativizing of the truth but the truth of the 'single one', of the existential self, alone before God, where the truth, as St Augustine said, is never neutral. We either love it, when it is on our side, or we hate it, when it punishes us and declares us guilty. For Kierkegaard, as for Augustine, God is truth, and God is not deceived.

What Heidegger's 'existential analytic' did with Kierkegaard in *Being and Time* can be variously described as *secularizing* Kierkegaard's Christian-existential analysis by dropping the *religious* element, *formalizing* it by dropping the Christian *content* and *ontologizing* it by turning existence or being-possible into a feature or structure of our *Being* – regardless of what the particular content might be.

Our Being is a possibility for Being – whether that means the possibility of becoming a Christian, an artist, a teacher, a social worker, or whatever possibility is held out before our freedom. These *particular* possibilities Heidegger called 'existen*tiell*' inflections of the *general* or fundamental 'exist-en*tial*' structure of our Being.[24]

FALLING

Part One of *Being and Time* begins at the beginning, where we are from day to day, in the swarm of everyday concerns. Interestingly, Heidegger omits the more touching side of the description of the family table – the boys, the remembrance of things past – and concentrates on the table as 'equipment', an item of everyday use. He emphasizes that we tend by a natural inclination to be 'fascinated' with the world; the world in which Dasein dwells (being-in-the-world) holds Dasein in its grip *to the exclusion* of deeper (existential) matters. Everydayness exerts a kind of suction on Dasein which draws it in, and Dasein tends to 'fall' into this world, lured by the ease of accepting the 'public interpretation' of itself. That is the interpretation of the world contained in what 'they' say and think and do, where everything is immediately understood, a matter of obvious common sense, and nothing needs to be questioned. Dasein in its average everydayness is no self in particular, no one self. The they-self is not my own self; indeed, at bottom, it is no self at all, a condition Heidegger calls 'inauthenticity', a word that in German literally means not-my-own-ness (*Uneigentlichkeit*).[25]

In falling into everydayness, Dasein goes with the crowd and takes the easy way out. This theme of the 'easy' is found in Johannes Climacus, the most famous of the pseudonyms employed by Kierkegaard. Kierkegaard was, as Heidegger points out, an essential 'impulse' for his own work in these early years. Climacus mused that, since everyone (in the nineteenth century) is making things easier – the philosophers are proposing systems that explain everything, and everywhere the telegraph and railways and newspapers are making life easier – the sole remaining project for Climacus, if he is to have any prospects as an innovator, is to make things harder. Climacus reminds us that making everything easy robs life of its depth and substance. We are everywhere just as busy as busy can be, but we ignore the ultimate business of life. We are making expeditious progress, but we have no idea where we are going. We are everywhere swept up in our daily concerns but neglect our 'ultimate concern' (Tillich), which is to raise the question of being true to the being which we ourselves are. Like Nietzsche, Kierkegaard presciently described the 'public', the 'they', as a new phenomenon of nineteenth-century life. This new category for philosophy – if this is to be called philosophy at all, a new existential philosophy – is a function of the newly emerging media, the newspapers and the telegraph. Today, with social media and the internet, the power of the 'public interpretation', of the 'they', has been unleashed with unprecedented power, an important point we will revisit in Chapter 9.

THE CALL OF CONSCIENCE

If Part One of *Being and Time* deals with Dasein in its average everydayness, Part Two takes up the 'authenticity' (own-ness, *Eigentlichkeit*) of Dasein. Here Dasein is *called back* from its dissipation in everydayness to its deeper self. The strategy turns completely on an existential version of the hermeneutical circle. The fall into the everyday interpretation of Dasein does not *extinguish* its pre-understanding of its Being as existence, as the being who has its Being to be. That would be impossible, for this pre-understanding is what we are. So, however mute or mutilated, repressed or forgotten, vague and alienated it may be, it is always there. What is there? It, the 'it' which 'calls' to us, which declares us 'guilty' of falling, the call of existential conscience. In *Being and Time*, Heidegger is rehearsing the movements of a highly Augustinian-Lutheran-Kierkegaardian self, but here in a completely ontological key. The call of conscience is not the call of God but the call of the self to itself, calling the (inauthentic) self back to its (authentic) self. The call of conscience restores the circulation of the hermeneutic circle: it arises *from* ourselves (from the depths of our self-understanding), is addressed *to* ourselves (in our drift towards everydayness) and calls upon us to *come back to* or *become* ourselves. What does the call say? Nothing. It does not give any specific advice – it simply summons the self before itself, tells it to be itself.[26]

The ever-stirring, inextinguishable *pre-understanding* each one of us has of ourself as an *existential* being disturbs the tranquillity of everydayness, haunts us with a vague uneasiness, a deeper, indefinite 'anxiety' more disturbing than any definite 'fear' – we fear the dentist but are anxious over our very being-in-the-world – reminding each one us, in our singularity, of what we each know but will not say: that our life is a misunderstanding, a misinterpretation, that we know better and that we are, each one of us, solely responsible for our being. We always and already know that, but we are inclined to suppress it. We know that we are not like rocks or tables (*existentia*). We know we are not imprisoned within a fixed essence; we know that existence means freedom. We know we are not a finished actuality but a being-possible. We know that the meaning of our Being has not been assigned from all eternity, that our Being is to interpret our Being, to *be* our Being, to *exist*. The pre-understanding summons the misunderstanding before itself and calls upon it to assume its authentic potentiality for Being.

That is the existential-hermeneutical circle: to be true to the being we always and already are. The idea is not to get rid of the circle but to enter it in an authentic way, to penetrate our deepest presupposition, our truest pre-understanding of ourselves. St Augustine again! I went out in search of You and all the time You were within. *Noli foras ire*, don't go abroad, go within, where the existential truth dwells.[27]

AUTHENTIC RESOLUTENESS

In order to secure an authentic interpretation, the hermeneutic analysis must bring Dasein into view: 1. as a whole – it must not confine itself to its day-to-day being-in-the-world but embrace the whole of life, from birth to *death*; 2. authentically – it must come back from its falling fascination with the world to its authentic self. To take Dasein *as a whole* is to see that, over and beyond its day-to-day possibilities, what ultimately lies ahead for Dasein, its uttermost potentiality-for-being, is *death*.[28] Hovering in the background, like a spectre, the ultimate being-possible of Dasein is the possibility of no more possibility, no-more-being-there, the possibility of impossibility. The prospect of death wrenches Dasein back from the they and brings it back before its authentic itself, death here playing the role of the being formerly known as God. In Augustine and Kierkegaard, the individual soul stands alone 'before God', before the white light of God's truth. In *Being and Time*, the existing individual stands alone before death ('being-unto-death'), before the black depths of no-more-being-there.

Having steeled ourselves by confronting the prospect of death, the scales of everydayness drop from our eyes, the authentic being of Dasein is disclosed and Dasein resolves upon its ownmost proper way to be. To be sure, this does not mean that in *Being and Time* Heidegger will identify the one true choice each one of us should make. That is none of his business. That is for each one of us to decide, our own existenti*ell* business. But what he can do as a philosopher is to spell out the formal, onto-logical, existen*tial structure* of authentic Dasein. (As one commentator quipped, after reading *Being and Time* he felt an urgent need to do something, but he did not know what to do.)

TEMPORALITY

This implicit pre-understanding of existence is explicated when it is worked out as existential 'temporality'. That is, authentic resoluteness has the tripartite structure of time itself:[29]

   (a) Dasein casts itself *ahead* toward its own possibility to be, actualizing the potentiality which is uniquely its own to be (the authentic *future*);

(b) This it does not do out of the blue, but out of the concrete hermeneutic situation in which Dasein already finds itself, now viewed not as the dead weight of the past but as a set of possibilities (an authentic *past*);

(c) Resisting the pull of the 'present age', the temptation to go along with the they, Dasein resolves in an *instant* of decision, in a *moment* of existential truth and authenticity.[29]

Fully interpreted, Dasein understands its being temporally, not merely as a being *in* time, but as a being whose Being it is to *temporalize* (towards the future, from out of the past, in the moment). If we could treat the noun 'time' as a verb, we could say that Dasein understands its being as time-ing, temporalizing (*Zeitigung*).

The task of becoming a self is not some kind of *creatio ex nihilo*, not an exercise in pure freedom – which is the mistake made by Jean-Paul Sartre, who emphasized freedom to the point of absolutizing it – but of *situated* freedom, of an authentic as opposed to an inauthentic repetition. In the existential-hermeneutical circle, the meaning of my past is always up ahead, and the meaning of my future is somehow already there. I draw from the possibilities the past hands over, I am not weighed down by them, and I am turned to a future which is not absolutely wide open. The future is the future of someone who has a particular past – a culture, a language, a history, etc. I project upon the possibilities that I have inherited; the range of the future is fixed within parameters set by the past. Great as he was, Alexander the Great was never going to conquer Alaska or set foot on the moon.

THE EXISTENTIAL DYNAMICS OF MODIFICATION

In virtue of the dynamics of the existential-hermeneutic circle, an authentic self-interpretation does not happen in a vacuum, like a bolt of lightning out of the blue. The existential individual is not a *solus ipse* (as in 'solipsistic'). Instead, Heidegger says, authenticity arises as a 'modification' of inauthenticity. Being-oneself is a modification of being-with others. We begin where we are. We are born into and grow up in a world that is already running before we arrive on the scene, and we are formed by that world, draw all our resources from that world – *but* at some point we make our own distinctive mark (or fail to do so). We 'appropriate' the common world we inherit, which literally means we inflect it in our own way, make it our *own* (*propria*). Think of the way great pianists start out by being taught to play the classics without making any mistakes until, eventually, at a crucial point, the playing becomes their own; they achieve their own style, their own unique *interpretation*. Authenticity is always an inflection, an appropriation, a repetition, of the average inauthentic everydayness in which we first find ourselves in the world.[30]

DESTRUCTION, VIOLENCE AND RETRIEVAL

But appropriation is not just wine and roses; an authentic modification or appropriation also demands making a break, which Heidegger called, quite controversially, a 'destruction' of the inherited interpretation.[31] We should note, at once, that Heidegger adopts this notion from Luther, whose lifelong task was to retrieve the original sources of Christianity in the New Testament, to release anew the original Christian impulse. Luther called upon Christianity to *re*form itself or *re*new itself, not to make something absolutely new but to go back to the oldest of the old. This, Luther said (in Latin), required a *destructio* of the medieval scholastic metaphysics by which primitive Christianity had since been covered over, a term which Heidegger took up in *Being and Time* when he spoke of the 'destruction (*Destruktion*) of the history of ontology'. Mistaken by his critics to be an exercise in nihilism, a *destructio* is a desedimentation, stirring up the sedimented forms a tradition has taken which now block off the source. When Derrida coined the word *déconstruction*, a word which would really have legs in contemporary theory, this was a gloss on Heidegger, who was glossing Luther, who was himself glossing St Paul (1 Cor. 1:19), who was citing Isaiah, who had the Lord say, 'I will destroy (*apollo*) the wisdom of the wise.'[32] Talk about a history of repetitions and interpretations!

Heidegger also says that authentic interpretation requires a certain *hermeneutic violence*.[33] In hindsight, given Heidegger's later Nazism, this choice of words was particularly unfortunate, and if I were Heidegger's director of public relations I would have advised him to look around for another word. But by this he does *not* mean ethical, political or military violence, nor does he mean that 'anything goes', that we can say anything we like, however arbitrary. Hermeneutical violence means pushing back against the pressure of received readings to make contact with the original, in just the way that authenticity requires the existential strength of character to stand up to the crowd, to brush against the grain of what they say. Authentic interpretation moves against the tendency of the public interpretation to trivialize, to cover things over with a veil of thoughtless superficiality; it uncovers what has been covered up. Any great innovator knows exactly what this means.

Creativity in hermeneutics is not creating *ex nihilo* but *retrieving*. It takes place by way of a repetition, not exactly of the past, which is something done and over with, but of what 'has been' stirring all along, as an authentic recovery of what has been there the whole time. Authentic repetition does not reproduce past actualities; it actualizes inherited *possibilities*; it goes back to what *has been* as a wellspring of the possible. That is why Heidegger says the possible is higher than the actual. The possible is the ultimate resource of the *future*, of the re*new*able. Hermeneutics is driven by 'the quiet power of the possible'.[34] A hermeneutic retrieval goes back to the origins, to the sources, and releases their deepest, hitherto untapped energies.

HISTORICALITY, THE STUDY OF HISTORY, AND THE HUMANITIES

In *Being and Time*, this fundamental hermeneutic schema – authentic interpretations are modifications of inherited interpretations – holds true for everything from our personal life to our institutional life to our collective life as a nation, for the humanities *and* for the sciences. The circular dynamics of existential temporality of Dasein have several important implications for hermeneutics.

Dasein's *temporality* is the foundation of Dasein's *historicality*.[35] Beyond *my* being-possible there is *our* being-possible, the collective possibilities that our generation has inherited, possibilities which constitute the 'we' of our historical being.

This is a matter of returning to the deepest deposits of Dasein's historical heritage and making them its own, engaging in a historical repetition or reappropriation of our collective legacy. This Heidegger calls Dasein's 'destiny', in German, *Geschick*, what has been collectively 'sent' (*schicken*) our way by our tradition, what we have been sent to do.

As a strictly ontological matter, there is nothing ominous about that. Unfortunately, the collective Heidegger had in mind was not humanity at large but our 'people' (*Volk*). In retrospect, this passage serves as a flashing signal warning us of Heidegger the National Socialist who, in 1933, would speak of the collective 'destiny' of the German people to assume the leadership of the world. But no one suspected this at the time and, more importantly, even if that is where Heidegger would take it, that was his (*existentiell*) business – even if it was odious. That was his *interpretation*. But as an existent*ial* structure, the text is no less applicable to the collective 'destiny' – that is, what is genuinely calling and being called for – of democracy, or of civil rights, where a world-historical shift takes place in establishing the rights of women and people of colour. Martin Luther King is a man of destiny in this sense, and Rosa Parks a woman of destiny. Right now, our generation has a collective historical duty to future generations to stem climate change.

Dasein's *historicality* (*Geschichtlichkeit*) is in turn the foundation of Dasein's *historiography* (*Historie*), that is, the basis of the writing of history, of historical interpretation.[36] We study history because we *are* historical. For Heidegger, historical research is, at bottom, an attempt to understand our historical being by exposing it to its originating powers.

It seeks to recover the life-giving sources of our tradition, and to do so by repeating not past actualities but the existential possibilities handed down to us by the tradition, and so make new possibilities real. Historical research is the searching of existentially engaged investigators, not bloodless, disembodied minds rooting through dusty archives, a point that will be developed in detail by Gadamer (Chapter 3). When, for example, we today go back to the impulse that was pulsating in the Enlightenment idea that 'all *men* are created equal', we experience the possibility, the power of the possible, let us say the 'possibilizing' of women and of slaves and of the unpropertied who also lay claim to that same equality – even if they were not included when the statement was first uttered. This gives birth to contemporary research programmes, like Feminist Studies, which set out in search of the forgotten women of the past. Such work does not undermine historical research or historical objectivity; it drives it.

Furthermore, this holds true not only for the study of history but, more generally, for what is called in German the *Geisteswissenschaften*, including both the humanities and social sciences. This does not mean that Heidegger's hermeneutics supplies the 'method' of the humanities (Wilhelm Dilthey) but that it offers a way to understand *what is going on in* the humanities, the *existential truth* of the humanities.[37]

THE HERMENEUTICS OF THE NATURAL SCIENCES

Finally, one of the most interesting, and frequently overlooked, features of the hermeneutic turn taken in *Being and Time* is found in Heidegger's hermeneutics of the natural sciences, which provides a remarkable anticipation of Thomas Kuhn's landmark *The Structure of Scientific Revolutions* (1962).[38]

For Heidegger, an interpretation projects the horizon within which things can appear *as* the things that they are. So, the family table appears *as* the table because it is situated within the horizon or world of factical life, within the framework of its distinctive mode of being. It *is* its *as*; it is *as* we understand it. That is true of *all* the various disciplines. The various fields of study are each set within an interpretive framework (an 'understanding of Being') which sets or fixes the horizon of appearance for entities in that domain. Each field is staked out in advance by its own 'fundamental concepts' – like 'life' in biology, 'language' in literature, 'space-time' in physics, etc.

It is important to see that this happens in *both* the humanities and the natural sciences, with the result that, in Heidegger's hermeneutics, the sharp distinction between them is weakened. Natural scientific thinking is not horizon-free; it simply makes use of *another horizon*. Scientists project things on the horizon of mathematical measurability. By suspending the default mode of everydayness, the table shifts from being a household thing and is taken *as* measurable mass located at a point on the space-time grid, but this does not negate its existing as an everyday thing. Working scientists remain existing beings. These fundamental concepts do not arise out of the blue but are drawn from *pre*-scientific life. Biologists are making thematic in scientific terms an experience of being alive we have all had since long before there were any biology laboratories.

Science for Heidegger is something to 'do', a practical

mode of being-in-the-world that requires the ability to conduct experiments, make measurements, read meters, etc., and cuts beneath the distinction between theory and practice. Natural scientists have not dropped from the sky like avatars; they are not Vulcans, like Mr Spock, but concrete historical beings with historical interests who bring to bear upon their experimental work a host of presuppositions, intuitions and hunches and hands-on feeling-around for clues. Whether they research this (men's diseases) rather than that (women's diseases, diseases in poor nations) is a function of who they are, of politics and purse strings. The ideas of 'value free' science, of presuppositionless scientists, of purely disinterested, dispassionate minds, are dangerous myths.

SCIENTIFIC CRISIS

In the day-to-day work of science, these horizons are tweaked and corrected by the ongoing course of experience in that domain, gradually confirming and correcting the existing horizon, the prevailing models, in the discipline. For the most part, Heidegger says, research 'leans towards' collecting its results in manuals, increasing the information in that field, and passing that knowledge on to apprentices. But, he points out, 'real progress' lies elsewhere: the real 'movement of the sciences takes place when their basic concepts undergo a more or less radical revision . . . The level which a science has reached is determined by how far it is capable of a crisis in its basic concepts.'[39] This happened, he says, when Luther changed everything in theology, and Einstein in physics – and, we can add, Copernicus in astronomy or even Picasso in painting, and so on. Progress then is not linear but revolutionary, a shift in the hermeneutic horizon. At this point, the previously stable disciplines 'begin to totter'. The 'fundamental concepts' (horizons), then, are not eternal or atemporal forms but historical-temporal projections. These transformative changes 'run ahead' of the positive work done inside the sciences.

That, in Heidegger's view, is where *philosophy* can play a role in the general culture – an idea that we find hard to imagine today – by showing that, up to now, the work of all the sciences has been blocked by an underlying and un-questioned understanding of Being as *presence*, rest, *stasis*, stability, while movement and becoming are denigrated as imperfections. Just as Aristotle thought that, while individu-als come and go, the biological species were eternal, Kant thought the table of categories he proposed was unchanging and eternally true. But Heidegger thinks that he can provide an impetus for scientific progress by raising the question of the meaning of Being in general, which will show that all our categories are temporal and given to unforeseen mutations.

COMPARED TO KUHN'S SCIENTIFIC REVOLUTIONS

Remarkably, the basic elements of the Kuhnian distinc-tion between 'normal' and 'revolutionary' science, and of a 'crisis' occasioning a scientific 'paradigm shift' which crosses the borders of the natural and human sciences, were already in place in *Being and Time*, thirty-five years before Kuhn. Instead of pursuing this insight, Heidegger became increas-ingly alarmed by the growing power and prestige of the complex of the natural sciences and technology in the 'atomic age', and even of the 'information' age – a word he presciently singled out in 1956[40] – which threaten to turn the earth and human life itself into raw material for techno-science. The result was that Heidegger came to be regarded as a hostile and antediluvian critic of techno-science, which was not entirely false but also not entirely true. Not only were his concerns legitimate – as the threat posed by climate change and the destruction of the environment illustrate – but there is also a fertile opening for a hermeneutics of science in *Being and Time* that he did not pursue and has not been sufficiently pursued by others.[41]

In *Being and Time*, Heidegger undercut the rigorous divide between the natural sciences and the human sciences and, more generally, between the scientific-rational-objective and the non-scientific-emotive-subjective, which is the keystone of modernity. This dichotomy is replaced with a hermeneutical distinction between a relatively stable, conventional (normal) order (horizon of expectation) in *any* discipline, and its possible disruption, not by something irrational but by something different, Kuhn's 'anomaly', something unforeseen which forces a change in the framework of received, conventional concepts. The rogue element on the margins may be simply a passing irregularity or it may end up sparking a total revolution, and science does not have an algorithm, a rule, a *method*, that enables it to rule out one or the other.

Heidegger's hermeneutics breaks the grip of the dichotomy between the absolute and the relativistic, the rational and the irrational, objectivism and subjectivism. Destabilizing events, anomalies and unassimilable differences, which not without confusion and consternation provoke new configurations, may occur anywhere – from quilt-making to quantum physics, from James Joyce and Picasso to Einstein. As Jean-François Lyotard puts it, using Wittgenstein's notion of language games: sometimes we make new moves in an existing game; and sometimes we invent a new game altogether.[42] (And sometimes a new game is invented completely by accident.) That's postmodern hermeneutics in a nutshell.

THE FAMOUS MISSING PART

In Part Three of *Being and Time*, Heidegger was to undertake the hermeneutics of Being itself, making our implicit understanding of Being explicit. There, Heidegger promised to show that the pre-understanding Dasein has of its Being as existential temporality is itself rooted in a pre-understanding of Being as time, which explains the title of the book. But Part Three was never published. Why not? you might ask. The honest answer is that he had been offered a job at Marburg and needed to get the book out in a hurry, finished or not. But on a more philosophical level, he did have some hesitation about what he was going to say, and that proved prophetic of all the controversy surrounding how to interpret the post-war Heidegger.

CHAPTER 2

Heidegger Strikes Again

HERMENEUTICS AND HUMANISM

Something Bigger Than Us

Like a lot of people nowadays who have vaguely religious feelings, Heidegger always thought that 'there is something bigger than us'. He always had the idea of something more powerful than we are, something deeper and weightier,[1] and the various ways he named this something are telling markers of his path of thought. This conviction explains his original interest in hermeneutics, which was set in motion by a vague and implicit *pre-understanding* of a deep, underlying experience which philosophy seeks to articulate or *interpret*. Even in *Being and Time*, for all its emphasis on the authentic individual, the point was to bring a deeper pre-understanding of *existence* and *Being* itself to the surface and give them words, just as in the early 1920s he had focused on the implicit sense of *factical life*. From the mid-1930s on, the matter more powerful and weightier than us bore the name of *Being* and, increasingly, of various surrogates for Being, chief among them truth, language and, finally, event (*Ereignis*).

This concern with something greater than you or me also explains why, right from the start, Heidegger kept his distance from the word 'human'. The very thing that allowed the word 'hermeneutics' to get into his pen also kept the word 'human' out. So, when a debate broke out in France in the 1930s and 40s about the true humanism – was it Christian or Marxist? – and Jean-Paul Sartre argued it was existentialism, Heidegger intervened. Existentialism may very well be a humanism, Heidegger said, but *Being and Time* is decidedly not existentialism, regardless of what Sartre thought. In *Being and Time*, Heidegger was not interested in humanism, whether it was the tradition stemming back to the Renaissance, or any modern-day permutation which put human beings each at the helm of their own individual craft. The task was to work out the Being of human beings (as Dasein), *not* to identify the human as such, which he considered a matter of anthropology, not ontology. As it turned out, after *Being and Time* he distanced himself from humanism altogether, from any possible reading which would take our eye off Being and let it rest on human being. That also drove him to drop the word 'hermeneutics' – having concluded that hermeneutics, too, was tainted with the traces of subjectivity, with the interpretive human subject. In a sense, Heidegger was retrenching, conceding that modernity had done so much damage to this word, had made it so much a matter of human subjectivity, that its premodern sense could not be rescued. The task of 'thought' – the word he chose to replace not only hermeneutics, but philosophy itself – required that he move on without it.

That story, and its consequences for postmodern hermeneutics, is what we want to explore here.

The Question of Humanism

If *Being and Time* struck like thunder, it is no exaggeration to say that, after the Second World War, Heidegger's thunder struck again, once more transforming the landscape of continental European thought, where it proved to be a crucial provocateur of what came to be called postmodernism. Even the French philosophers, both Christian and atheistic, far from rejecting a German thinker whose fortunes had been so closely tied up with the Nazis, were in fact deeply interested in Heidegger. In 1946, Jean-Paul Sartre published an immensely popular essay meant to demonstrate to both the Catholics (who thought he was a heartless atheist) and the Marxists (who thought he was a bourgeois individualist) that *Existentialism is a Humanism*, the true one.[2] Sartre could have been excused for concluding that *Being and Time* represented a kind of 'existential humanism', a powerful account of the drama of human authenticity in the face of death and the faceless 'they'. That interpretation was a large part of Heidegger's success in 1927. Sartre, who was a member of the French Resistance, and French readers generally, could also have been excused for not dropping in on the lectures Heidegger was giving in Freiburg during the Third Reich, in the course of which Heidegger was – unbeknown to the wider world – changing everything.

Heidegger's intervention, the *Letter on Humanism* (1947),[3] pulled the rug out from under Sartre. *Being and Time* is about Being, he said, not human being; its emphasis is not on us but on *Being*, which is bigger than us. So before we can take another step forward, we have to make clear how Heidegger's use of the word 'Being' changed after the war.

What is All This Stuff about 'Being'?

In *Being and Time*, Heidegger spoke of Being in terms of Dasein's horizon of understanding, a framework of interpretation, something like a light Dasein projects in order to let particular beings appear as the things that they are, tools as tools, artworks as artworks, etc. Think of the light on the miner's cap which illuminates things otherwise in the dark as the miner moves about. The word echoes with Kant's idea of the 'transcendental', where human understanding supplies the conditions under which things are understood. In fact, Heidegger published a book on Kant in 1929 (which was actually a section of the unpublished part of *Being and Time*).

But when he used the word in the mid-1930s, 'Being' is not like a miner's cap but more like the sun which greets us when we step outdoors, the light already there *in* which we stand, which rises and sets, lights and darkens, arrives and withdraws, *on its own*. Furthermore, he shifts the focus from the Kierkegaardian existential individual to the historical world, the age or epoch in which individuals are situated, a perspective Kierkegaard would have repudiated as shameless Hegelianism. For Heidegger, the age of the Greeks, the Middle Ages, modernity, the atomic age (1940s–50s) – today, as Heidegger predicted, we would say the information age – are stages not of human history but of the 'history of Being'. These epochs, these worlds, are not *our doing* but what Being is *doing to* us, how Being is presenting or disclosing itself to us. So now the word 'Being' echoes not with Kant but with Hegel's notion of the *Zeitgeist*, the 'spirit of the age', which also happened to be the focal point for Dilthey's hermeneutics. When the later Heidegger speaks of Being, most of us would just say 'the force of history', but with this difference: for Heidegger, this meant the successive ways that Being has revealed itself to us. Being, of course, is not a being that resides somewhere; it is the look taken on by beings as a whole, the look of the world, in any given epoch. Dasein remains a being-in-the-world but now on the receiving end of Being's historical movements.

What has happened is that the deep, implicit pre-understanding in which we 'live and move and have our being', is now being described as the movement of Being itself, which, after all, was what *Being and Time* had set out to interpret. Beginning in the mid-1930s, Dasein's projective understanding of Being is rethought as Dasein's standing-under Being's own advance, and Dasein's authenticity, being-its-own-self, now looks more like being-owned by Being, and its being-in-the-world is being-in the historical world that Being sends its way.

Receiving Messages from Being

Going back to Dilthey, hermeneutics for him means the interpretation of the 'spirit' or 'world-view' of an age, which is a concatenated whole of which the religion, art, politics and philosophy of the age are particular but integral expressions. The later Heidegger's view is actually similar to Dilthey's but, instead of speaking of spirit, he speaks of

Being, and instead of our view-of-the-world he speaks of the way that the world views us, the way Being looks in on us or comes to us (like the sun rising) or withdraws (like the sun setting). Heidegger is thinking of Being as a deeper truth-event, as a total world-disclosure, deeper than any particular proposition which we form about this or that item in the world. Being is a way that an entire historical period is disclosed, penetrating and conditioning the way individuals living in that world think and act. Heidegger takes the emphasis off creative artists producing works of art or individual philosophers coming up with interpretations of the idea of Being, and he shifts it to human beings on the receiving end, accepting the truth of Being from Being itself. Truth is not something we conceive but something we receive, something granted. It is like the way conservative theologians say that the Scriptures are not our words about God but the words God has given us, God's word about God.

In the *Letter on Humanism*, human beings are positioned on the receiving end of messages from Being. They are called upon to provide a place for Being to arrive, to let Being be, to let it come into appearance. The circle between Being and beings is still spinning but in the opposite direction. Instead of us spinning out (projecting) an understanding of Being, we are called upon to open ourselves to Being's own spin (advance). Along with 'hermeneutics', Heidegger also drops talk of the 'meaning' of Being – that's too epistemological, anthropological and psychological – in favour of Being's 'truth', which means Being's un-concealing of itself, where we are called upon to get out of its way and let Being be. Even the 'question' of Being is too subjectivistic. Questioning

Being is like questioning God: not recommended. The task of thinking was not to be interrogatory but gratefully receptive of Being's advance. Thinking is thanking Being for its arrival. Hermeneutically speaking, instead of us doing the interpreting, we are receiving Being's messages in the post. Instead of the call of conscience taking place in our authentic self, now Being calls upon us as from afar and asks us to respond.

Beyond Existential Subjectivity

We, along with Sartre, might have thought that, even though the word Dasein in *Being and Time* had a strictly ontological sense, not an anthropological one, Dasein was still an *existential* subject. Not a Cartesian thinking subject, to be sure, but a Kierkegaardian 'subjectivity', an engaged subjective agent. Not so, Heidegger insists. The *Letter on Humanism* is a sustained effort to extinguish every trace of human subjectivity that clung to *Being and Time*. Although with different ends in mind, Heidegger after the war and the French structuralists and post-structuralists of the 1950s and '60s (see Chapter 5) had a common project: to shed the anthropological and the psychological standpoint, which they called in philosophical shorthand 'humanism'.

Beyond Objectivity

It's important to note that it would be equally misleading to say that shedding subjectivity was aimed at gaining objectivity, since objects are the correlates of subjects, and both belong to the modernist framework. Being is not an object but the prior light in virtue of which both subjects and objects make their appearance in modernity, which is a stage in Being's history. Being is not more 'objective' but more *sachlich*, referring to the motto of Husserl's phenomenology, 'back to the things themselves', back to *die Sache selbst*, where *Sache* means the matter of concern, the matter more powerful and weightier, the very stuff which concerns us the most, somewhat like the way we say in English, 'the thing of it is . . .' The antecedent figure for Heidegger's version of phenomenology is Aristotle, whose deepest concern (*Sache*) was the question of being as such. The antecedent figures for the phenomenology of Husserl – and Sartre – were the great modern philosophers of subjectivity and consciousness, Descartes and Kant.

So, if human beings cease to look like Descartes' *ego cogito* in *Being and Time*, from the mid-1930s on they also cease to look like Kierkegaard's existential subjectivity, and they start to look and sound like mystical poets. 'Existence' no longer means being existentially engaged in seeking personal authenticity; it now is redescribed as ek-sisting ek-statically open to the coming of Being. Authenticity does not go out of the window, but it is dramatically reinterpreted. Phenomenology appears at this point to have mutated into mysticism. The word Dasein no longer means to be actively engaged in being our own there but to patiently be the 'there of Being' (*das da des Seins*), the place or open clearing where Being is revealed. Think of the way the Romantic poet is pictured as the lyre on which nature plays.[4] So 'hermeneutics', were that word to be used here, would now mean being a messenger of Being (not God). Now 'Being' is a verbal noun, not an infinitive. In short, the thing that is bigger than us, the matter to be thought (*die Sache des Denkens*), is Being. That in contrast to 'humanism', where the matter to be thought is human being, be that the 'rational animal' of classical philosophy, the *imago dei* of theology, or – he now adds – the existential subjectivity of Kierkegaard and Sartre.

A Higher Humanism?

Still, one might ask, does this not betoken a *deeper* care for the being of human being, for the *humanitas* of human beings, after all? Yes and no, Heidegger says.

No, not if, as Jean-Paul Sartre says, 'we live on a plane where there are only human beings'. On the contrary, Heidegger says, we live on a plane where there is something greater than human beings, where 'there is' only Being.[5] Heidegger here exploits the German idiom *es gibt*, translated as 'there is' but literally meaning 'it gives', in order to say that Being is not projected by us (the miner's cap) but given to us (the sun). It is given, it gives and withdraws itself, on its own terms. We live on a plane where 'it gives Being', where Being is given, in its truth, and we are the place where Being is given.

Yes, if we see that the failure of philosophical humanism is not to go *far enough* in estimating the true worth and dignity of our genuine *humanitas*, which lies in being claimed by Being, needed by Being, for Being's own revelation. The true dignity of the human is to be found not in lording it over beings as their master – later on, this would get the attention of the ecologists – but in serving as the shepherd of Being.

So, in that sense, there is a kind of higher and ec-centric humanism, where the human has been de-centred in favour of Being. Still, he adds, there is a *strategic* value in criticizing 'humanism' – in the name not of an inhumane anti-humanism but of something bigger, higher, deeper, weightier, in just the way Heidegger risks a stand against logic, and even God, in the name not of the illogical or of a godless atheism but of something higher, viz., the openness of Being.[6] The true humanism lies in affirming something greater than humans.

Leaving Sartre Holding the Bag

The problem for Sartre was there was a message in the *Letter* for everyone. The tide went out on the word 'humanism', its market price plummeted and Sartre was left holding a worthless equity. Lutheran ears perked up at the 'call of Being', which sounded like the Word of God. And it did not go unnoticed by the Catholics that the new Heidegger sounded a very great deal like the critique of human hubris in medieval mystical theology. It had the same meditative tonality, the same valourizing of stillness and silence. When he used the word 'Being' with a cross through it (B̶e̶i̶n̶g̶), signifying that this word was a human construction, that looked a lot like 'apophatic' (negative) theology, in which any affirmation made about God had to be corrected by a negation which inscribes a zone of respect around God's transcendence. It even sounded a bit like Buddhism, and provoked a number of comparative studies.

Personally, my ears perked up at his mention of the

fourteenth-century mystical theologian Meister Eckhart. My first project as an academic scholar was to sort out the 'mystical element' in Heidegger's thought, given that one of Eckhart's central terms, *Gelassenheit*, 'letting-be', had become a touchstone of the later Heidegger's vocabulary.[7] Just as Eckhart called upon the soul to let go of the ego and let (*lassen*) God be God in the soul, Heidegger speaks of letting go of our subjectivity in order to let Being be Being. When Heidegger added that he wanted to think in the 'dimension' in which Being yields the holy, and the holy yields the Godhead, and the Godhead is the dimension of the appearance of God, and so the thought of Being is neither theistic nor atheistic, the Catholics jumped on board.[8] Like the mystics moving beyond theology to an ecstatic openness to God, Heidegger even became a critic of 'ontology', a word that held pride of place in *Being and Time*, and of 'onto-theology', in favour of an ecstatic openness to Being.

There was even an olive branch to the Marxists, where Marx was associated not with spiritless materialism but with Hegel and hailed as a genuinely historical thinker.

There was more. Sartre loved the city, did his writing in cafés, and he thought that the great outdoors was for animals. But Heidegger had a life-long affection for the mountains of the *Schwarzwald*, where he kept a rustic cabin (*Hütte*) to which he beat a hasty retreat at every opportunity and where he did most of his writing. So, Heidegger linked his critique of humanism with a critique of technology, not only because the new technologies looked like they were about to blacktop the Black Forest, but also because of what he called the 'essence' (Being) of technology. By this he meant that technology was infecting our very conception of our Being – our self-interpretation – and of the world (that is, our relationship with Being). Ironically, in the second half of the century, when the environmentalists criticized the unbridled capitalist greed which was destroying the environment and decimating other animal species, Heidegger became a leading resource for 'deep ecology' and its critique of – what else? – humanism. Heidegger was to become a darling of the left.

When the structuralists then launched their own attack on humanism, all the stars were lined up against Sartre and his star was destined to go out. He remained a popular public figure until his death (1980) but his philosophical significance would evaporate.

But what happened to the star of hermeneutics?

Hermeneutics after *Being and Time*

It does not take much to see that in the framework of the later Heidegger the word 'hermeneutics' would have a short shelf life. Taken in its traditional sense, the word is held captive by the subject–object schema: as creators give their inner, subjective experiences an outer, sensuous, objective expression, hermeneutics traces the opposite path, tracking (interpreting) the objective expression back into the inner, subjective experience, be it of the individual author (Schleiermacher) or the spirit of the age (Dilthey). Even in Heidegger's radical rethinking of the word 'hermeneutics' in *Being and Time*, interpretation was a matter of *our* working out *our* pre-understanding, and to that extent it still smacked of a subjective achievement. So Heidegger rarely used the word again and it would fall to Gadamer to save it from the flames.

But Heidegger did discuss hermeneutics one last time, in a text composed in 1953–4, which takes the form of a dialogue between a Japanese thinker (Tezuka Tomio) and an 'inquirer' (Heidegger himself), where the two try to capture what Heidegger was saying about hermeneutics back in the 1923 lecture course we discussed above, and why Heidegger had stopped using the word.[9] Tezuka had come to Germany with the hope that German 'aesthetics' (the philosophy of art and beauty) could illuminate his own experience. But right from the start Heidegger expresses a fear that the Japanese philosopher will allow the very meditative and non-conceptual experience of the art and poetry of Japan to be distorted by the dualistic conceptuality of European philosophy, above all by its subject–object framework.[10] The conversation quickly focuses on how this experience is embedded in *language*, which, in Western philosophy, has been reduced to an outer, sensuous sign of an inner, super-sensuous meaning – the very same notion of language that the structuralists will want to displace but for completely different reasons (Chapter 5). So, Heidegger warns the Japanese not 'to chase after European conceptual systems', or the latest fad in European philosophy.[11]

Bearing Messages from Being

Heidegger says words like 'hermeneutics' and 'meaning', and even the word 'Being' itself, proved to be of less and less use to him, in his attempt to avoid injuring the matter to be thought. He and his interlocutor agree that genuine thinking is close to the Japanese experience of art and language, a point seized upon by many commentators to reveal a crack in Heidegger's Graeco-Euro-centrism and an opening-up to an East–West dialogue. Heidegger then invokes Hermes, the pious message bearer of the gods – but significantly *not* the impious prankster and thief. The poets, as Plato's Socrates said (*Ion* 534e), are 'the interpreters of the gods', and Hermes is their patron divinity.[12] The essence of the hermeneutical is then described as the 'bearing of a message and tidings', which shifts it away from 'interpretation', where it is the work of a human subject. No longer interpretively projecting the horizon of Being, hermeneutics – a word Heidegger no longer uses but is here willing to use just this once to explain how it should be understood – would now be taken to mean that the 'truth' of Being itself, the way Being opens the space in which beings appear as the beings that they are, is *sent* to us, like a message sent by the gods to mortals and borne by Hermes.

So, the operative figure in the word 'hermeneutics' in this dialogue is not interpretation but the postal figure of message-bearing and receiving. Being *sends*. Being is what is sent. Being is the self-sending, and the thinker/poet is stationed on the receiving end, passing these messages along to (other) mortals, like the prophets in the Scriptures. Being is our *Geschick*, 'destiny', here meaning that the task of thinking is to open ourselves for what is sent (*schicken*) our way to say and think, for our 'mission' (from *mittere*, to send). To have a destiny, we should recall, is to be open to inherited possibilities, not a deterministic closing; it is freedom, not fatalism.

Language

In this post-humanistic view, language is taken not as human subjects expressing their inner thoughts but as Being bringing itself into words. What is essential is the 'relation', the link between Being sending itself to language and human speakers opening themselves to what Being sends us to think and say. 'Language defines the hermeneutic relation.' So, the something greater than us is language itself, which is weightier and more powerful than us. Language speaks (*die Sprache spricht*), not us. But if humans do not command, they are still in demand, needed 'hermeneutically', namely, as the ones who receive and preserve the message from Being.[13] Humans do not 'have' or 'take on' that relation; that relation is what they *are*. Their Being is to be the beings entrusted with maintaining the difference (*Unterschied*) between Being and beings.

Poets and thinkers in particular are commissioned (sent) to bear Being's message, to take their stand within the new sense of the hermeneutical relation.[14] Poetry is not versifying; it is revelation, world-disclosure. This means, Heidegger says, that, ultimately, we are not to speak *about* the nature of language, as if it were an object of scientific study, but *from out of* our experience of the essence of language. In speaking, we stand already in language, presupposing language, in order to speak. 'I once called this strange relation the hermeneutic circle,' Heidegger adds, but now, he cautions, rather than a hermeneutic circle he would speak of a 'hermeneutic relation', the movement back and forth between language 'itself' speaking to us and humans speaking in response, between addressing and responding. Each side is needed by the other, in a dialogue between 'language' and us.[15] This is the third version of the hermeneutic circle: we live and move and have our being in an implicit understanding of a) factical life (1923), b) existence (1927) and c) language or Being (1953), which becomes explicit in our words.

Has Heidegger Overcome Interpretation?

So, the one time the later Heidegger addresses the word 'hermeneutics', he adapts it to the top-down Apollonian model, where Hermes is a messenger boy, not a roguish disturber of the peace, and 'interpretation' is consigned to being merely the work of human subjects who interpret. However, without rejecting Heidegger's life-long concern with letting something bigger than us, some deeper, prior or weightier preunderstanding, come to words, I do think that his post-war attempt to brush off 'interpretation' falls short on several levels.

First of all, I would argue that the *Letter on Humanism* is an interesting example *of* interpretation, of what Heidegger called in *Being and Time* hermeneutic violence. In it, this man, Martin Heidegger rattles the timbers of European philosophy by *re-reading* his own book, *Being and Time*, in an unexpected way, one that is not bound to the original intentions of its author, which in this case is himself, since he has changed his point of view. No reasonable exegesis of *Being and Time* could conclude that the *Letter on Humanism* is an exegetically, philologically faithful account of the 1927 text.[16] It is instead a hermeneutic *re*interpretation or 'retrieval' (*Wiederholung*) of nearly all the major terms in *Being and Time* – Martin Heidegger's own, over and against Sartre's, which stressed the existential subject. The two retrievals are to be judged on their intrinsic merits, and not on the basis of what the historical author of the 1927 text, which bears his name, wished to say (*vouloir dire*). The entire debate about the later Heidegger is basically a hermeneutical debate about the violence of hermeneutics. In it, this man named Martin Heidegger argues for changing the switch of the hermeneutic *as* and sending the book down a different track. Do not interpret this 'as' *as* a function of how human beings project but *as* the way that Being is given. Hermeneutics, Heidegger argues, is to be hung from another hook. He has stopped using the word 'hermeneutics', but the *Letter on Humanism* is an exercise in interpretation from top to bottom.

A Chap Named Heidegger

Second, as I said above, I maintain that what Heidegger means by the 'sending of Being' is what most other people would call the tides of history. A world-disclosure, he holds, is not the achievement of individuals, of larger-than-life historical agents who shaped their world. It is a collective formation, the effect of a kind of collective spirit. So, despite other underlying differences, the way Heidegger interprets an 'epoch of Being' compares to the way Hegel and Dilthey interpret the 'spirit of an age'.[17] Consequently, history is being *interpreted* by a chap named Martin Heidegger *as* the history of world-disclosures keyed to the way Being is understood by the selected poets (always German) he has read and the philosophers (Spinoza, a Jewish philosopher, never appears) he has selected from that epoch. He concentrates on poets and ignores the role of prime ministers, generals, economists, the Anglo-Americans, etc. This highly edited, selectively rendered (interpreted) historical period is then *interpreted* by him *as* the successive ways the 'truth' of 'Being' (the age) is opened up. An 'epoch of Being' means *how* the historical-factical life of that epoch is disclosed to the writers the later Heidegger has chosen in advance. *The* history (in the singular) of the West is monogenetic – its origin is Greek, no mention of the Bible – and nationalistic – its deepest streams can be thought only in contemporary German.

His Greeks, His Germans, His Poets

This also explains the trouble Heidegger brought down on his head in the 1930s. The call of Being turned out to be a pretty particular interpretation, namely, Martin's own highly tendentious rendering of the history of the West, as if there were just one thing that could be named that simply. That could only end badly. 'Greece' – not just any Greece but *his*

Greece, specifically tailored to be the spiritual fatherland of the Germans; *his* Germans, making use of the poets, *his* poets (Hölderlin, especially), are called upon to supply the spiritual depths of *his* strange version of National Socialism (in 1933), or, after the war – when he criticized nationalism as a form of humanism – more generally, of the 'West'. The historical sending of Being that Heidegger had in mind stands precisely in need of being *demythologized*, that is, interpreted with hermeneutic discernment. Nothing illustrates the need to *interpret* the 'call of Being' better than its invidious interpretation by Heidegger himself in 1933 *as* Being's singling out of Germany and National Socialism as its favoured spokesman. Even after the war, this Graeco-German privilege persisted, albeit more discreetly.

Should We Ban the Call of Being?

So, should we ban Heidegger from the philosophy section of the library and relocate him to the history of National Socialism, as his most severe critics insist? No.

Should we drop the later Heidegger and just stick with *Being and Time*? Not exactly.

Then what? Let's *interpret* the call of Being differently. What Heidegger calls a 'call of Being' is neither more nor less than a call for an interpretive understanding of the times, for understanding the times *as* calling for this rather than that, for taking something *as* one thing and not *as* another. The call of Being is a call for hermeneutic discernment, in just the way that what Heidegger had to say in the 1950s about the 'atomic age', the triumph of the 'information' society, and the unchecked fury of environmental destruction unleashed by technology really did prove to be discerning, prescient and very timely insights.

Something of importance is going on in the later Heidegger's delimitation of the lingering existential subject-ivism in *Being and Time*. It brings out a deeper structure of hermeneutics as the hermeneutics of the call, or what I am calling the interpretive imperative. In *Being and Time,* the hermeneutic imperative was the call of individual con-science, and in the later Heidegger it has become a historical imperative, the call of the 'history of Being'. Furthermore, the call is lodged still more deeply as a call that cannot be captured by any ontology, as he held in *Being and Time*, or any theology, or onto-theology, all of which are too tied up in conceptual thinking (let's add nationalistic mythology to this list). Instead, it is given to us in a moment of non-conceptual, meditative stillness that evokes a comparison to mysticism. This will turn out to be important, but, any way you look at it, the call still stands in need of *interpretation*.

Being and Time is a monument to hermeneutics, and the *Letter on Humanism* is a contribution to another dimension of hermeneutics, regardless of whether Heidegger had lost interest in the word. For both, interpretation is inescapable, first, last and constant. At this stage, when Heidegger was distancing himself from the term, it was crucial that some-one come along and put the house of hermeneutics in order and restore this word to its proper place. That task fell to Gadamer.

CHAPTER 3

Gadamer's *Truth and Method*

PHILOSOPHICAL HERMENEUTICS

Hans-Georg Gadamer (1900–2002) kept both the word and the notion of hermeneutics on the table. If Heidegger made the radical breakthrough, Gadamer sealed the deal and helped us see the point – but this time without the extravagant language, mystical leanings and the disastrous politics. Gadamer made Heidegger make sense to a wider audience of readers in the humanities by turning Heidegger's insights, both in *Being and Time* and the later writings, into a comprehensible and comprehensive account. If Heidegger was the trail-blazing genius who put hermeneutics in the postmodern sense on the map, Gadamer, who was a genius of a different sort, saw that it stayed there.

Gadamer was of a different disposition from Heidegger. Erudite, urbane and elegant, Gadamer was the very epitome of a gentleman and a scholar. A lover of Plato and Aristotle, of the Renaissance and of the golden age of German philosophy from Kant to Hegel, he also loved a good conversation, especially if lubricated by a good wine. He lived every one of his 102 years with no little personal grace, though he didn't achieve philosophical celebrity until he was in his sixties, with the publication of *Truth and Method* (1960). This book translated and extended Heidegger's more tortured analyses into an elegant German prose, waded deep into the history of hermeneutics and made a head-turning presentation of the new direction in hermeneutics that Heidegger had first staked out.

Philosophical Hermeneutics

In order to get a feel for what is going on in *Truth and Method* – after *Being and Time* itself the most important work of hermeneutics in the twentieth century – allow me to first tell you a personal anecdote. Once, when I was taken to the hospital emergency ward after a bad fall, the doctor said that he wanted to keep me overnight for further observation. When I protested that I wanted to go home and sleep in my own bed, he said to my surprise, 'All right, go home.' What he meant was, let's see you get yourself off the examination table. After nearly collapsing in a heap on the floor in the effort, I agreed that the doctor was right. When Gadamer describes his work as 'philosophical hermeneutics', that is a bit like my doctor. Gadamer is not telling the historians and students of literature how to go about their work; he is not giving them methodological instructions. So, if the historians insist, against Gadamer's advice, that their idea is to produce a work of pure, disinterested objectivity, Gadamer replies, 'All right, go ahead. Do it.' Inevitably, the patient falls off the table. The result is always a timely but datable interpretation which, if it is really good, will assume a place in the ongoing history of datable interpretations. Like my doctor, Gadamer is not trying to be cynical. He is interested in the historian's well-being. He is trying to help the people working in the humanities to understand their work, to provide them with a *philosophical understanding* of what is going on in the humanities.

Hermeneutics is Not the Police

In *Truth and Method*, Gadamer focuses on the tendency of method to get too big for its boots. That is so true that commentators sometimes quip he could have entitled the book *Truth against Method*. If modern thinkers like Descartes sought a method for discovering the truth, Gadamer sought the truth that eludes method. But hermeneutics as Gadamer presents it is not the police of the humanities, it is a warning about *misunderstanding the understanding* that takes place there. Hermeneutics itself is a neither a *method* nor a meta-methodology that monitors particular methods but a philosophical meditation upon the sort of *truth* that emerges in the various humanistic disciplines, whatever methods they employ and with whatever success. I have often had students say that for their research paper they want to 'apply' hermeneutics to some historical or literary movement, and I tell them that's a misunderstanding. Any historical or literary study already *is* hermeneutics *in the act*. The hermeneutics is already there – it couldn't not be. What we are doing in philosophical hermeneutics is clarifying in a second-order way what humanities scholars are already doing in a first-order way, but with varying degrees of self-understanding. Hermeneutics does not supply a template that can be transcribed into a particular discipline. It is a *philosophy* of how understanding is reached in the humanities and the sort of *truth* that is at stake there. Of course, Heidegger had shown in *Being and Time* that the same thing is going on in the natural sciences, too, but that is not the side of hermeneutics Gadamer pursues (he lived a long time, but he couldn't do everything). Beyond that, the helping hand hermeneutics extends is not limited to the academic disciplines but embraces the length and breadth of human experience, inside or outside the academy.

Truth and Method is divided into three parts: 1. The truth of the work of art; 2. the truth of the human sciences; and 3. a hermeneutic analysis of the experience of language. Let's take up each in turn.

1. The Work of Art

WHY CHILDREN ARE RIGHT TO HATE MUSEUMS

Every year, countless students are marched off by their teachers on school trips to art museums, which the students regard as only slightly less painful than staying confined to their classrooms. *Truth and Method* provides such students with a good argument that they are right, that it is not natural to experience art in a museum, and the villain is a characteristically modern creature called aesthetic consciousness.[1]

Like Hegel and Heidegger before him, Gadamer does not look upon the work of art as a copy (*mimesis*) of life, making it a stage removed from reality, as Plato thought. Instead, they see artworks as an *intensification* of reality, more like a zoom lens that picks out something, sometimes very small or seemingly insignificant, and produces a magnification of it in which reality itself is made to shine in all its depth and beauty. The work of art is not a narrowly artistic 'object' of the 'aesthetic' gaze; it is an event of truth. To experience a work of art is to enter a world of truth, the truth of a world. Beauty is the glow of Being's truth, the glow of the world itself.

Museums are creatures of the age of the pure *ego cogito* of Descartes, or of the Kantian 'transcendental ego', of an autonomous subject passing in review of objects hanging on a wall. In this way, 'aesthetics' – the modern philosophy of art – robs the work of art of its truth. 'Art for art's sake' is a slogan of the aesthetic frame of mind. These works do not belong in a museum, where they can be visited on weekends; they belong in and to daily life itself. Just the way that good mirrors were first produced in the age of self-consciousness (sixteenth and seventeenth centuries), it is of telling significance that, while there are certain prototypes in the ancient world, the museum, like the concert hall, is fundamentally a modern innovation. Gadamer is not recommending that we abolish museums, of course – they provide a way for the general public to access art – but he is pointing out that they are testimony to modern alienation (disenchantment), where life means business, means–end rationality, and art is recreation deprived of cognitive content. Business is business: art belongs in museums, religion in churches, everything in its self-sealing place – that's modernity. But just as there are no temples in the heavenly Jerusalem – where God has finally become all in all and there is no need to go to church on Sunday – there were no art museums in ancient Greece, where art was everywhere to be found, in public life and private life. By the same token, the great medieval cathedrals were not always tourist sites and requiems were not always performed in concert halls.

WHAT THE CHILDREN KNOW

Modern aesthetics reached a conceptual peak in Kant's *Critique of Judgement*. Kant, who was scandalized by difference and particularity, set out in search of a way to reach universal consensus in judging a work of art. This he found in the idea of a purely disinterested aesthetic subject contemplating a purely formal aesthetic object. In Kant, the artwork is shrunk down to an object savoured for its structural properties without regard to any interest we might take in its actual content. Imagine trying to explain that to a Greek entering the temple of Athena or a medieval friar at prayer in a great cathedral – or to a schoolchild. We visit art museums like theologically illiterate tourists in Italy in August, gaping at the great cathedrals of the past.[2] And the modern museum poses the danger of being a kind of cemetery for preserving works of art created by people now long dead – which is exactly what schoolchildren know. From Gadamer's point of view, the bored children are picking up on the structurally alienated situation of the museum, where the work of art has been torn away from its natural life setting. Consider, in contrast, that these same children are not bored by the sheer poetry and ballet-like beauty of a football game and the majesty of a modern athletic stadium, where beauty is integrated with everyday life.

JOINING IN THE PLAY

My example of children and a football game was not chosen at random. The opposite of gaping at an object is joining in the game. So Gadamer sets out a phenomenology of play as a model that dissolves the sharp distinction made between the disinterested aesthetic subject and the pure aesthetic object.[3] Take the example of the teamwork in a good soccer game. The players converging on the goal, passing the ball back and forth among themselves as if they were one body made up of different members, or all fingers of the same hand, each one absorbed in the task and wholly absorbed in scoring a goal, having suspended their sense of being separate individuals. We say these teams have chemistry, but we could also be describing their biology, their symbiosis. Their entire momentum is organized around the magnetizing movement of the ball, negotiating their motions in tandem with one another and with the movement of their opponents.

The ball is given to unpredictable bounces, which adds to the incalculability of the game. The game has rules, and the field has boundaries, which set the tensions of the play. So, by play, Gadamer does not mean 'anything goes' or random arbitrary motion, but rule-governed activity. Without the rules, we would not have more play but no play at all. Play is made possible by the rules, by exercising a spontaneity, innovativeness and creativity within individual situations that do not themselves have rules. The most brilliant players make unexpected moves and can perform magic with the ball. The best coaches devise creative game plans that throw their opponents into confusion. People who cheat at games destroy the meaning of the game.

EVERYBODY'S A PLAYER

Now, in place of the ball, put the work of art. The same thing happens. To experience a work of art is to be drawn into a play set off by the work, where the players shed their subjective consciousness and become entirely absorbed in the game. The player *participates*; the observer merely looks at. The artwork is like a powerful dramatic performance (a play) in which the audience is transported into that world and has been lifted out of its empirical seats in a theatre on a downtown street. The players and audience alike are absorbed in the play. The people listening to a piano recital are playing the piece for themselves, their bodies subtly playing along with the players, having checked their isolated egos at concert-hall doors.

The work of art is not a play of formal properties but a magnetic centre into which everyone is drawn who *experiences* its play, that is, its *truth*. What sort of truth? The truth of a world-disclosure, of a form of life, of a mode of being-in-the-world, a truth it alone is *uniquely able* to open up, and a truth that is visited upon *me* (existential truth). Like Heidegger, Gadamer is attributing exemplary importance to the work of art – its play is very serious, substantive, weighty (*sachlich*) – as it has access to a kind of truth denied to traditional philosophical thinking. By losing myself in the play, I regain myself as transformed by the work. Unless you are willing to lose yourself, you will never gain yourself. No artificial boundaries fence off the beauty in the artwork from truth and goodness. No critique of pure reason polices the borders between art and ethics, religion or science. No dualism enforces a distinction between pure reason and mere feelings, between the epistemological, ethical and the aesthetic, between subjects and objects. In the work of art – think of Athena's temple – the true, the good and the beautiful converge, or rather, were never separated to begin with.

A subject does not stand over an object in judgement; rather, the work of art comes over us as from on high. We undergo the experience, submit to its spell, let it overtake us. The player *submits* to the play, the play *admits* the player and *transmits* the truth at play in the work. We do not observe works of art; we play them and we are played by them. We should not ask what does this work mean but how do we play it? This comes out even better in the German, where *Spiel* does service for both 'play' and 'game'. So, in German, players play the play and are in turn played by the play. In either German or English, the play's the thing, the *Sache* (Heidegger), the absorbing concern, the substantive matter, not a purely formal object of a disinterested aesthetic judgement. We do not judge an object; the artwork stands in judgement of us and puts us in the accusative. Like the later Heidegger on Being, the circle is moving in the opposite direction.

THE *POLIS* NOT THE POLICE: ARISTOTLE, HEGEL, HEIDEGGER, GADAMER

Gadamer's analysis is a transcription of Aristotle through the lens of Hegel and Heidegger. When Aristotle described human beings as 'political animals', he did not mean the dog-eat-dog partisan politics of today. He meant that a Greek citizen is not an autonomous ego who has chosen to enter into a social contract but a participant born into a substantial unity, in a sustaining, supportive and embracing form of life. The *polis* is a matrix which engenders human life, a living unity of the true, the good and the beautiful, which utterly pervades and forms the individual's being – the articulation of which is the original meaning of hermeneutics, according to the young Heidegger. A purely apolitical being, a being outside the *polis*, is inhuman and monstrous. When Hegel criticized the autonomous liberal subject of the Enlightenment in favour of the substantial community, he had Aristotle's *polis* in mind.

HOW IS CRITICISM POSSIBLE?

This has huge implications for understanding artistic creativity, artistic reception and artistic criticism. If the art lover is not a critical observer who stands above the artwork and subjects it to judgement, free from its spell, *is art criticism even possible?* Of course it's possible, because it is actual. Hermeneutics begins with that fact, with the actual existence of concrete acts of interpreting, like the things that art critics do for a living, but the question for hermeneutics is to *understand* what it is. Criticism is a work of a second-order *reflection* upon the prior participatory experience. It is an act of strategic conceptualization that must acknowledge that the pre-objectified world (being-in-the-world) is first, last and always. To criticize is to interpret, and to interpret is to explicate, to make explicit the implicit experience of truth in the work, but hermeneutics demands that criticism confess that its reflection is an artefact and that it can never catch up to the lived participation.

Furthermore, the work of criticism will ultimately be absorbed into the play; it will extend the play of the work, contribute to the subsequent history of the reception of the work and render the critic into something of a second-order creator. *The critic is a player, too.*

The work of art is not, as in modern philosophy, an illustration of a truth that has been independently established by philosophy, simply supplying philosophy with examples it can use for expository purposes. For Heidegger and Gadamer, *the artwork discloses the world in a way that cannot be otherwise accessed.* It opens up the world to which we always already belong, about which criticism can at best form second-order reflective propositions, an always lagging indicator of what is going on in the work of art, trying to piece together analytically what pre-exists in a unity in the experience of the work of art.

2. Tradition and the Human Sciences

THE PLAY'S THE THING, NOT THE AUTHOR

This analysis is of the utmost importance, not only in the interpretation of works of art and literature but in the interpretation of laws and constitutions, institutional statutes, ethical codes, religious scriptures and traditions and in the humanities and social sciences generally.

If the subjectivity of the disengaged spectator is undermined, even more shocking and controversial is the displacement of the subjectivity of the author or creator. If the play's the thing, then, for Gadamer, the 'intentions of the author' are no longer *normative* for the interpretation of the work. Gadamer's argument here is directed against the attempt by Friedrich Schleiermacher (1768–1834) to define hermeneutics in terms of the reproduction of what was in the 'mind' of the original producer by reconstructing or retracing the steps from the outer expression to the inner intention of the author or the historical agent.[4]

First of all, it would in fact be impossible to reconstruct what is in someone's mind, not to mention the problem posed when, as sometimes happens, the authors themselves later on change their mind (as happened with Heidegger). Second, it is not their mind that matters but the matter of the world they had in mind. It is the work which they have produced that constitutes the only real evidence that we can analyse. These works do not have an absolute sense but a contextual sense whose meaning is fixed by being fitted to a changing context. What something means is not completely relativistic but it is context-dependent; it is a function of both the works themselves and the context in which they are repeated.

Once again, Gadamer is not trying to destroy every vestige of the author or the agent, no more than he is trying to destroy every trace of objectivity. The intentions of the author are not nothing; they belong to a *first* reading which tries to reconstruct the original context. We typically begin to interpret by proceeding reproductively, by learning the original language, studying the original culture, ascertaining the original audience and the original purpose that was being served by the work. There is no other way to avoid misunder-standing the work and distorting it anachronistically. This is the mistake of people who think they can simply sit down, pick up the Bible, or any ancient text, and start reading. Gadamer's point is not to prohibit such a reconstruction (as far as this is actually possible) but to situate it. This is the first stage of interpretation, the best way to start to read, but it cannot be the *normative* interpretation and, in actual fact – as history is our witness – it never is the *final* reading, not, at least, if the work is of any substance. We normally begin by reconstructing the original context; but it belongs to the very structure of the text to be *re*contextualizable, again and again – if it is any *good*.

The original author's authority is limited. The real life of the text depends entirely upon the *death* of the author, be it structural or physical. In the same way that senior members of the faculty or the firm need to have the grace to retire in order to breathe new life into the university or the institu-tion – and sometimes death is the only way we can get some people to retire – the author must withdraw, let go, symboli-cally if not physically, in order to let the text live on. When this does *not* happen, it is because texts are so dependent upon their times, so completely bound by the intentions of the original agents in the original context, that the writing is written off as 'time-bound', completely 'dated', no longer to be of any interest to anyone. Let the dead bury the dead.

It is the texts that are *not* time-bound, *not* restricted to the original intentions of the author, that have a shot at becoming a 'classic'.[5] What is a classic if not a text that is indefinitely recontextualizable, able to speak again and again to ever-new audiences, in ever-new contexts the author could never imagine? How about a play by Shakespeare, or the story of Alexander Hamilton, told in rap music? But to make it as far as a classic – as the work of Aristotle is for Heidegger and Gadamer – it is not enough for a text to be structurally repeatable, which is a formal feature of every text, including a laundry list. A classic is a work that makes itself *worthy* of repetition, and this because it speaks from the *depths of truth*. So, in hermeneutics, we say things do not have an essence, which would spell death to them, but an ongoing, living history.

AVOIDING MONSTERS

If the words of the founders of the nation and the writers of the American Constitution were confined to the intentions of their authors, then slavery would never have been abolished, and women and unpropertied men would never have gained the right to vote. Laws have to be structurally appealable and repealable, constitutions amendable, codes of conduct revisable, religious myths demythologizable. Our understanding of marriage has evolved, once excluding interracial marriage, while today we are witness to the breakdown of the barriers against same-sex marriage, which nobody would have predicted even a couple of decades ago. Even marriage has a history, not an essence. The misguided attempt to be literally loyal to the past makes the past into a monster, closes down the future and deprives tradition of its inherent ability to renew itself. That leads to Gadamer's next point.

TEXTS GROW UP AND LEAVE HOME

Texts are like children – they grow up, leave the nest and lead a life of their own. That's not a complaint. As any parent can tell you, that's what is supposed to happen. When it does not happen, that is something to complain about. Just so, that is the point of writing – to preserve what is being written down for the time when the author, the original audience (and in the case of a current event, the subject matter) of the writing, is no longer around. A text, a musical score, a work of art, all are like a will that can always be broken by the court. There is nothing the author can do to ensure that their will (what they 'mean', in French, will or wish-to-say, *vouloir dire*) is always observed, nothing to monitor the process so that interpretation happens according to the will or wishes of the author. All that is as it should be. The author is dead, as a structural matter, whether the author is standing beside us large as life or long since dead and gone.

The philosophical point Gadamer is making here is that the text has a *potential* meaning.[6] What does this book say? Not a thing. Sit there with it in front of you as long as you like, listen very carefully, and it won't say a word. It does not actually say (or mean) anything until someone reads it, just the way a score does not make music until someone plays it. So, the reader is also a player, just like the critic. What the Bible says is *nothing* – until someone reads it (almost always in translation) and says what it says; even if they are reading on their knees, they are knee-deep in interpretation. So, when authors write something down, they produce a set of inscriptions, written signs, which are so many potentialities that can be actualized again and again (so long as the language and the text are not lost).

When I was a young philosophy department chairman, the academic vice-president said something to me that was not only useful administrative advice but good hermeneutical theory: Don't write anything down if you don't have to. If you don't want it to follow you around your whole life, if you don't want it to live for ever, don't write it down. (Nowadays, don't post it on Facebook.) Once things are written down, they are given out for public consumption, where they lead a life of their own. The author does not own the language, cannot control the rules of the language, the associations that have been set off by the words, and certainly and above all cannot control the sense these words will take on in *new contexts* long after the author is gone. The very idea of writing means the author enters into the play of a language that was already running before they arrived, deploying denotations and connotations that will run off in new directions when the text finds itself in a new context. The author may be playing the keyboard of the language, but the language is also playing the author, and all kinds of things are happening in the language behind the back of the author.

THE FUSION OF HORIZONS

In turning to the experience of the truth of history, Gadamer is making trouble for Leopold von Ranke's (1795–1886) famous claim that the task of the historian is to tell it like it really was (*wie es eigentlich gewesen*). While Gadamer does not propose telling it like it wasn't, he does think von Ranke is trying to dodge the hermeneutic circle and is chasing after the moon of empirical objectivity, where the truth is nothing but the facts – pure, uninterpreted facts – of the matter. So Gadamer opposes this objectiv*ist* point of view by way of what he calls the 'fusion of horizons'.[7] By this he means that historical understanding occurs in the sparks that are given off when our horizon, which we cannot shed, encounters the horizon of the past, which shocks us with its difference. At first, they collide – they are shocked to meet each other – and then fuse, failing which, there is a misunderstanding, and the distance between the past and the present proves unbridgeable. Gadamer is describing the *experience of truth* in historical studies. Truth for him – as for Heidegger – is not primarily a matter of forming concepts, propositions and arguments about past historical objects. The deeper experience of historical truth requires putting our being into question and letting it be exposed to the shock of the other time, in such a way as to let it affect us, lay claim to us and transform us. We learn something about ourselves, about the meaning of being human, when we study history; indeed, when we study any of the humanities. The fusion of horizons is a third thing, neither the past nor the present but something new, something that has not and could not have existed before. It represents an extension of the tradition, its ongoing truth-event, a new form or figure in which the tradition continues to happen, not the last, not necessarily even the best, but the latest figure. Truth, for Gadamer, as for Heidegger, is thus both existential, since we are personally engaged with the tradition, we belong to it, and phenomenological, since it is a new configuration of the world, a new figure of life, a new configuration of our lived experience.

Think of the ancient Greek *polis* – compared to which we are deracinated, overly mobile beings always on our mobile phones. The distance of the tradition from us is not a matter of disinterest but a pressing concern, and the distance is productive. We come away from the world of the Greeks transformed, the horizons of both their world and ours expanded.

HAVING A CONVERSATION WITH THE PAST

In criticizing objectiv*ism*, Gadamer is not being a cynic about objectiv*ity*. In criticizing the objectivism of 'historical consciousness', he is not advancing the cause of a vicious subjectivizing of historical knowledge. He is not licensing historical revisionists to deny the Holocaust, as his most hysterical critics complain. He is trying to understand what historical understanding *is*. He is not discarding objectivity but redescribing it more sensibly.

The experience of truth arises from the shock of the different, of the hitherto unknown coming to us from the distance of the past. Here is where the model of conversation comes into play in a crucial way: we require the capacity to put our own presuppositions into question in order to enter into a dialogue – just as with another person – with the tradition. *Conversation, the play of the dialogue, the plasticity of discourse, is the central operative model of hermeneutics for Gadamer.*[8] We address the past with questions, and the past answers back in such a way as to put *us* into question, going back and forth in a productive hermeneutic circle, a dialogue and a dialectic. Theologians will be reminded of the method of 'correlation' proposed by Paul Tillich (another serious reader of *Being and Time*, whom we will meet again in

Chapter 10), where we bring contemporary questions to classical theology, resulting in new answers that shock our contemporary sensibility. Theological questions, historical questions, every serious question, puts us in question in return. Gadamer's model of the hermeneutical circle borrows elements from the dialogue method of Plato and from the dialectical method of Hegel, without embracing the metaphysics of Plato's Forms or Hegel's Absolute Knowledge.

Gadamer is not proposing conversation as a methodology but as a way to avoid misunderstanding historical understanding. What historians make of the tradition will inevitably reflect their own interests, their own times and concerns. A good history of the Renaissance begins by reviewing the history of the histories of the Renaissance that preceded it. It is impossible for historians to be fully transparent to themselves, to turn themselves inside out and fully inspect their own presuppositions, impossible for them to neutralize their own presuppositions. Indeed, such neutrality, were it even possible, would make no sense, because the 'historical distance' that separates their contemporary sensibilities from the past is *creative and productive*, which we see in contemporary feminist studies, which brings new questions to bear upon the past. Otherwise, historians would be like people with a tin ear judging a music competition. They must approach the past as a conversation partner looking for answers, and that demands having a living question to begin with, having something that matters, along with a willingness to be put into question by the answer that comes back and takes them by surprise.

THE PREJUDICE AGAINST PREJUDICE

The tendency to distrust all presuppositions, to be drawn in by the lure of the 'ideal' of presuppositionlessness, to moon over the moon of pure objectivity, is what Gadamer calls the 'prejudice against prejudice'.[9] Historically, the word 'prejudice' derives from a legal term *prae* + *judicium*, meaning a preliminary judgement, the result of a preliminary inquiry into whether or not a matter bears further inquiry. It does not distort anything but gives the court a guiding indication about what to do next. Just so, hermeneutic understanding proceeds by means of a preliminary orientation towards a subject matter, certain 'fore-structures' (Heidegger), which are either confirmed or disconfirmed, but lacking which we would be completely disoriented. An authority, accordingly, is not necessarily a bad thing; the only time authority is bad is when the authority is bad. When we need a lawyer or a physician, we seek out recommendations from people in the know. Without reliable authorities, the first thing we would have to do every day before having our morning coffee is to invent a coffee pot.

The tradition then is not a pure 'object' (*Gegenstand*) but a 'matter of concern' (*Sache*), more substantive, weighty and important. The tradition is what concerns us, *sachlich*, that is, deeply, substantively; it is in our bones; it is us; it is greater than us. Gadamer is talking about the only really sensible way to have a tradition, which prevents the tradition from becoming either of purely antiquarian interest, a cemetery housing the bones of history; or a monster that dictates the future. That requires the recognition that we belong to the thing we ourselves are exploring, while exposing ourselves to the shock it delivers in such a way as to allow our lives to be transformed by its very reality, by its being, by its *truth*.

THE HISTORY OF EFFECTS

So, we belong *to* the thing we are trying to talk *about*. We ourselves are one of the moments in the same stream, one of the effects of the history we are studying. We stand downstream in the history of its effects. That is what Gadamer calls our 'consciousness of the history of effects'.[10] That is about the best we can do to translate a word that is unwieldy even in German (*Wirkungsgeschichtebewusstsein*). By this he means a consciousness that understands that it stands in and is formed by the history that it is trying to understand. This is the paradox of reflection: whenever we try to reflect on our consciousness, the act of reflecting adds another moment to that conscious stream which eludes our reflection; it always comes a moment too late and is now a new moment of consciousness. But standing in that flow is how we have access to it in the first place. Our St Paul is delivered up to us by Augustine, Luther and Kierkegaard and, try as we might, we will never quite twist free from that, although we also want to try – since Paul had never heard of these people. But if we try too hard, we will blow up our bridge to that past. The tradition is never what is simply over; nothing is ever simply dead. The tradition is *us*, part of our being, where we have come from, and we are reflecting upon it with the resources it itself has given us. It is like a relative who says to us, 'You are just like your Uncle Sam', when we did not even know we had an Uncle Sam.

3. Language

BEING WHICH IS UNDERSTOOD IS LANGUAGE

In the final section of *Truth and Method*, Gadamer defends his broadest and deepest thesis, that the ultimate hermeneutical horizon, the deepest structure of interpretation and truth, is language – 'Being that can be understood is language',[11] a variation of the later Heidegger's famous line that 'language is the house of being'. By this Heidegger and Gadamer mean that language provides the most overarching frame of understanding, interpreting and applying, of action and production, of experience in the most encompassing and comprehensive sense.

Nothing will be understood without language. Heidegger and Gadamer do not mean that everything is linguistic in the narrow sense, that there are no pre-linguistic bodily experiences, or no non-linguistic arts. Hermeneutics does not confine us to what Fredrik Jameson calls 'the prison house of language'. On the contrary.

Nothing will be *understood* without language. Gadamer and Heidegger are not denying that affectivity is pre-linguistic; they are just saying that when affectivity wants to be *understood*, when our implicit pre-reflective life wants to become explicit and reflective, this will take place in language, which is why people who defend views about the pre-linguistic sphere *write books* about it. Language attains its tidiest form in propositions and arguments, which come after the fact, clearing up the world in neat definitions, explicating the implicit in crisp assertions and forceful arguments.[12]

But it takes its deepest and richest form in world-creative, world-disclosive language-events like poetry, which resonate with the pre-objectified, pre-conceptual and even pre-linguistic world we inhabit.

Naming Sonatas and Silences That Speak Volumes

Gadamer and Heidegger are saying that language is the ultimate horizon of experience, that nothing is untouched by language, that the *pre*-linguistic is pre-*linguistic*, that if and when the pre-linguistic is *understood* that will take place in and through language. We know now that even pre-natal life is not insulated from the world of sound and language of the mother, and that newborn children begin accustoming them-selves to the rhythms and inflections of their native language right from the start. Language is not a prison; the lack of language is. That is why parents are terrified when their child's language acquisition is delayed. A non-linguistic work of art, like music or painting, comes with titles which are hermeneutic forestructures that prepare the listener or observer for what is coming. When an artwork comes with a number, not a name, we cannot resist searching for a pos-sible name. 'Untitled' is still a title, a very taunting title.

Even the precious experience of silence is a phenomenon of language. You can hold your tongue only if you have a tongue. Silence is a gap, an empty space, a caesura that occurs *within* language, the way the empty space in a room is totally shaped by the surrounding wall. A pause in the music is intrinsic to the rhythm; an awkward silence in response to an unwelcome question speaks volumes. A monk in his cell practises ecstatic silence. The mystics are often brilliant preachers like Meister Eckhart, or poets like John of the Cross, whose soaring language sings a song to silence. They fill volumes saying that whatever we say of God is not true (never adequate) and that it is what we do not say (when we admit God exceeds our understanding) that is.

IN A GENUINE CONVERSATION
NO ONE IS CONDUCTING

The fundamental model of hermeneutical activity for Gadamer is linguistic – the conversation – which is the point that will be seized upon by the voluble Vattimo and the ironic Rorty (Chapter 6). In a genuine conversation, both partners are participating and neither one is in control. This is to be distinguished from a didactic conversation, in which the leading questions of an all too clever Socrates in the Platonic dialogues gradually elicit the answer he has known all along (whereas we can imagine that the historical Socrates, who was much more of a sceptic than his student Plato, was genuinely unknowing about the questions that he asked). In a genuine conversation, the 'play' of the talk takes over and the participants are carried along by the flow. We do not conduct a genuine conversation, Gadamer says; we fall into it.[13] The play of the logos, like the bounce of the ball, leads the players down a path neither of them can see in advance, let alone steer. (The reason using the 'Socratic method' in a classroom is often a failure is that the teachers are asking questions to which they already know the answer. A genuine question is lost for an answer and puts the questioner in question.) The separate horizons of the speakers soften and grow porous, finally giving way to a fusion, so that afterwards it is difficult to reconstruct who said what and at what point a threshold was passed and something emerged that neither of the two knew in advance. A committee should work like this but, as anyone who has served on one knows, that's a bigger dream than the dream of pure objects dropping out of the sky, presupposition-free.

THE UNIVERSALITY OF HERMENEUTICS

When Gadamer speaks of the 'universality' of hermeneutical life, he does not mean that there are common universals found across every language and culture that can be reached by intercultural dialogue. He means that, with goodwill, there is nothing we cannot discuss, no difference that we cannot put on the table, no distance that cannot at least be brought to words even if it cannot be crossed, no situation in which we have nothing to learn from one another – even if our understanding of each other will always be incomplete. A foreign language is not foreign to language itself. He means that the model of conversation – exposure to the other and a willingness to put our own presuppositions into question – applies everywhere.

This serves as a fruitful model for what in religion is called interfaith dialogue, when people are willing to put their own faith presuppositions into question, something that is next to impossible for many religious people. It is a model of the conversation that should take place between political parties, instead of the bitter partisan politics, the venomous personalized attacks, the politics of media-savvy personal destruction, we have today. It serves as a model of international dialogue, where the only alternative is bloody war.

The Three Subtleties

Truth and Method represents a felicitous adaptation of a distinction that goes back to J. J. Rambach (1737–1818), according to which hermeneutics requires a threefold *subtilitas*.[14] By *subtilitas*, Rambach means finesse, tact, having a light touch, the right touch, the opposite of being heavy-handed. Hermeneutics is the subtle art of understanding (*subtilitas intelligendi*), of interpretation (*subtilitas explicandi*) and of application (*subtilitas applicandi*), where these are not three different things but one and the same thing in three different stages of articulation. There is no such thing as a pure understanding that can be reached prior to or without interpretation. Understanding is not a base over which an interpretation is laid. Still more surprising, and no less important, there is no explication without application, no such thing as an application-free interpretation. The field of interpretation, we might say, is fieldwork.

Rambach, a Pietist theologian, is thinking of the application of the Bible to personal life. A good sermon leaves me shaken. I feel like the pastor has singled me out in particular, embarrassing me in front of everyone. But, for Gadamer, Rambach's point is general. The work of art, the tradition, the texts of Plato or Hegel, are directed right at us and are meant to form and transform our lives and to put us on the spot. We do not 'understand' in the hermeneutic sense if we are not changed. This model of hermeneutic understanding is akin to Aristotle's idea of *phronesis*, 'practical wisdom', the know-how of a person of seasoned judgement who understands the particular demands of a unique situation. If you can't *do* it, you don't *get* it, or rather it has not got you.

Derrida and the Two Interpretations of Interpretation

In a Nutshell

To summarize what we have said so far, Gadamer put hermeneutics on the map and saved it from the flames of the critique of humanism in the later Heidegger. Deconstruction, to which I turn now, gives hermeneutics a chance to practise what it preaches – exposure to the other – because deconstruction looks every bit like another challenge to hermeneutics, like the 'other' of hermeneutics. While deconstruction gave hermeneutics a hard time, it also – like a good tennis partner – gave it a still sharper edge. Hermeneutics became a more radical hermeneutics, a bit more like the prankster Hermes, not the messenger boy. Deconstruction proved to be a productive challenge to hermeneutics, bringing another dimension to the term, and, it can be argued, in that sense it is a part itself of the hermeneutic process.

I am proposing that Derrida the critic of hermeneutics is better understood as Derrida the author of a more critical hermeneutics. Derrida advanced the cause of hermeneutics in a critically important way, even if he himself, too rashly I think, consigns hermeneutics to its traditional sense, treating it as a kind of code-breaker, a method of finding the one true meaning of a text. Indeed, back in the 1960s, when the very idea of deconstruction was still gestating, he allowed himself to use the word and had clearly caught the spirit of the spritely, slightly roguish Hermes.

Derrida's Day Job

In 1964, when Derrida was still an aspiring young philosopher in the fiercely competitive Parisian academic world, he landed a job at the École Normale Supérieure (ENS), one of France's most elite institutions, where he himself had been a student (1952–6). He was not yet 'Jacques Derrida', one of the luminaries of twentieth-century philosophy, the 'father of deconstruction', a word that became so famous it has worked its way into common parlance. His job was to prepare students for the gateway exam that would gain them entry into the profession and enable them to teach philosophy in the *lycées* and, ultimately, find university positions. The task the students faced was twofold, and not a little tricky. On the one hand, they had to show that they thoroughly understood what Descartes, Kant and Hegel had said. But over and above that, they were duty-bound to be brilliant, to show their originality, that they not only knew how to reproduce what others had said but also that they themselves had something to say. They had to be completely obedient to the original texts and, at the same time, original voices themselves. The two objectives did not sit easily together.

Derrida's solution was to press the students to undertake a reading that would be a punishingly meticulous reconstruction of the original (the first requirement), but so close, so micrological, as to expose the hidden presuppositions in the text, which would in turn expose a conflict. His hypothesis was that the text is implicitly divided against itself, that the presuppositions push against the very positions pursued in the text, which a close reading would make explicit. If you dig deep enough, you will hit conflict, not an underlying unity. That spells big trouble for the hermeneutic circle: the whole (the Bible, Plato, etc.) is not a unity but a multiplicity, and that is a basic distinction between Derrida and the dominant hermeneutic tradition. Even the revised sense of hermeneutics put forth by the early Heidegger and Gadamer, whose *Truth and Method* had just appeared, would not suit him. The close *re*construction issues in a *de*construction. Now, whether Derrida thinks so or not, an exercise in 'close reading' that explicates its implicit and latent presuppositions is hermeneutics at its best. I propose that deconstruction is not anti-hermeneutics but hermeneutics in a more radical mode.

So, according to intellectual historian Edward Baring, who tells this story, deconstruction is the outcome of Derrida's day job at the ENS.[1] That should encourage young assistant professors everywhere who complain that their teaching duties interfere with the research they need to do to get tenure.

Is Deconstruction an Outsider?

The story is even a bit amusing. Derrida is usually portrayed – and he himself is complicit in this portrait – as the consummate outsider, the man on the margins, who was rejected by the powers that be in the academic establishment in France, a good candidate for the other face of Hermes. That picture is not without its truth, and Derrida himself enjoyed portraying himself as the anti-establishment outlier, the

Algerian-born *pied noir*, the 'little black and Arab Jew'. But that is more true of his later career, after he resigned his post in 1984. He had gone to all the best schools as a student and as a young professor travelled in an elite circle of French philosophers and intellectuals. Later on, he would become the *bête noire* of the conservatives in the academy, who regarded deconstruction as their worst nightmare. Derrida, they complained, had undermined the interpretation of texts and shown no respect for the classics; his only principle of interpretation was 'anything goes'. An amusing mistake in view of the fact that deconstruction was born in one of France's most prestigious institutions (its 'Ivy League' is contained within one square mile in the heart of Paris, the Latin Quarter on the Left Bank, which houses the Sorbonne, the ENS and the Collège de France). Widely assumed to be the enemy of all institutions, deconstruction was the fruit of the system that Derrida devised to earn his students a ticket into the mainstream establishment in French academic circles.

I am not saying that deconstruction is not disruptive, a form of interpretation from the margins – a kind of outsider hermeneutics. I would not be interested in it if it were not. But it is not disruptive the way the Vandals were disruptive, by levelling a civilization to the ground. Deconstruction is not a simple destruction. If it causes pain, it does so by undertaking a painfully close reading of a text and shows that the text is at odds with itself, and further, that this is not bad news but a creative opening. As the late Leonard Cohen said, 'There's a crack in everything, that's how the light gets in.' Derrida is not doing anything to it – the text itself is autodisruptive. Don't shoot the messenger.

The Principles of Reading

This throws a great deal of light on a passage – not often cited by his critics – from Derrida's major work, *Of Grammatology* (1967), in which he is discussing his 'principles of reading'. Now, whether he likes it or not, a theory of reading is a theory of interpretation, and a theory of interpretation is what hermeneutics means. That Derrida sold the word 'hermeneutics' short had more to do with Parisian academic politics than with hermeneutics. So, whether he intended to or not, if he is going to put his 'principles of reading' on the table, I am going to call it his hermeneutics. I don't care about his intentions as an author. I care about hermeneutics, and nobody put Derrida in charge of the dictionary. That, by the way, is one of Derrida's own principles of reading that he shares with Gadamer: in hermeneutics and deconstruction alike, we have made a crucial shift in our point of view from the creator to the receiver. Philosophers in the past were more interested in the creative act than in the re-creative one, more interested in authors and artists than in readers and critics, but postmodern thinkers insist that how things are heard and understood, how they are interpreted and reproduced, is an essential ingredient in their history.

An Exorbitant Method

Derrida reluctantly agreed to call the close reading he recommended his 'method', so long as it was called an 'exorbitant' method. To him, the ultimate task of reading is to make a 'productive' reading. A productive reading cannot just be a respectful reproduction of the conscious intentions of the author. It cannot settle for setting out in a plainer or clearer way just what the author intended to say but said more opaquely. But, any productive reading must *start* with a reproductive one:

> This moment of doubling commentary should no doubt have its place in a critical reading. To recognize and respect all its classical exigencies is not easy and requires all the instruments of traditional criticism.[2]

A good commentary is hard to do. The students back at the ENS, charged with understanding the difficult texts of the great philosophers, are throwing their *chapeaux* in the air and shouting, *Oui! Oui!* in enthusiastic agreement. Scholars pass a lifetime in dusty libraries trying to get authors straight, picking up on the twists and turns their thinking takes, learning the original language, reading the secondary literature: all in all, a daunting challenge. Derrida continues:

> Without this recognition and respect, critical production would risk developing in any direction at all and authorize itself to say almost anything.

So, we are not to dismiss the traditional reproductive reading, which at the least is productive of clarity. Without it, the reader could say anything at all about the text. Without it, anything goes. If there is something like deconstruction, it must be preceded by a careful commentary and reconstruction. The irony of this passage should not be missed: here,

Derrida warns us in advance against the very thing of which he would be consistently accused of ignoring by his critics.

Then Derrida adds: 'But this indispensable guardrail has always only protected, it has never opened, a reading.' The first reading is necessary, but not sufficient. It is not enough to reach an understanding of what has already been understood by the author. What is needed is a second, 'critical' understanding, pressing forward into the deeper conflicts embedded in the text. This reads (*legere*) between (*inter*) the lines, representing thus a literally 'intelligent' interpretation (*inter* + *pretium*).

But why make trouble like that for a good book? From simple perversity or mischievousness? Of course not. We seek to tweak what is already understood in order to learn something new, by exposing this text to a world that was unknown to its author, the world around us now, and, still more importantly, to expose it to the future, to which the text ultimately belongs. So, over and above the reading which protects the text, we require a reading that puts it at risk, that exposes its vulnerabilities, that 'opens' it – to what it did not see coming.

Why Readers are Also Creators

By shifting our perspective from the creator to the receiver, and by differentiating a productive reading from a reproductive one, Derrida is now telling us (as does Gadamer) that the receiver is not merely *re*ceptive and *re*productive. The 'productive' *reader* is very much a producer and not merely a consumer, a player in the game, not just an observer. So, one of the marks of contemporary hermeneutics, of what we today call theory or critical theory, is the recognition that the creator is not the only creative one, that the re-creator, the reader, the interpreter, also plays a productive role.

The sound you are hearing now is a roar of protest from a throng of hoary old scholars emerging from their dusty stacks, clouds of chalk dust rising from their wrinkled tweed coats. To a man (usually), they howl charges of heresy, blasphemy. This claim to a productive reading, they loudly lament, is exorbitant!

That's true enough. Derrida just said so himself. A great deal – and, in my view, really everything – in hermeneutics comes down to understanding what is being said here. What Derrida is saying about productive reading is not only right, it is inevitable. As Gadamer shows, it is what is going to happen anyway; it is what has always happened, whenever reading occurs. Reading ends up being exorbitant; even for the soberest scholars. Every new interpretation belongs to a *history* of prior interpretations, which is a history of greater or lesser exorbitance and elliptical renderings. Let the history of reading be our witness; it will testify that reading *has* a history and it tends towards exorbitance.

Exorbitant Does Not Mean Stupid

This somewhat impious and exorbitant reading requires that there first be an orbit. The orbit here is the original context – the original author's intentions, the original language used, the original audience addressed, the historical, social, political, geographical world to which it belongs. In a word, the original context – for there is always a context, be it the original or the current one. Or, as Derrida puts it in the next paragraph, 'there is nothing outside of the text', nothing without a context, nothing that is ever non-contextual; no reference is ever made without or outside of a textual system of references.

Derrida's statement, that there is nothing outside of the text, is my candidate for the most misunderstood sentence of any French philosopher in the second half of the twentieth century. It is not a wise principle of interpretation to assume that an important thinker is saying something patently foolish. The sentence became notorious because it was not read in context, that is, precisely in violation of what it itself was saying! The statement immediately follows upon the paragraph we just read, that is, the one on the necessity of a prior moment of close and respectful commentary, of a reproductive reading, cutting off in advance every wild anything-goes kind of reading – which is exactly what his critics decided they wanted to hear.

So, the statement was wildly misconstrued to mean that Derrida doubted or denied the existence of the world and maintained that there is nothing outside of words (the most stupid reading); or, that he denied that we can know anything excepts words, as if we are locked inside a prison house of words (second most stupid reading). I leave it to you to imagine what it would be like for someone to believe that words exist but to doubt the existence of the real world, or that we understand only words but not what the words are speaking about. As Husserl continually pointed out – and Derrida's career was launched with a ten-year study of

Husserl – to think and speak at all is to think and speak *of* something, viz. the thing of *which* we are thinking and speaking.

What the Author Commands and Does Not Command

Derrida was saying that we can never understand what the words are talking about *without the words*, or without some sort of way to signify in the most general sense, which is what the word 'text' means here. You cannot sneak around the language to get to a supposedly naked reality. So 'text' is a technical term for a coded or textual system. It means that, even when you want to signify something, you make use of a system of signifiers. When you learn to speak a second language, you have widened your world, not built yourself a second prison to enclose the first.

So, I do not know what it could even mean to be locked up inside a prison house of words, but I do know that it is not what 'exorbitant' means. Beyond the orbit of reading that respects the original context (a first reading he called a 'doubling commentary'), especially the author's intentions, there is a second, more productive, more 'critical' reading (whence 'critical theory', or sometimes just 'theory'). This second reading (i.e., productive interpretation) passes outside of – or, maybe better-bends – the orbit of what the author consciously and intentionally meant to say, which corresponds to Heidegger's 'destruction' or 'hermeneutic violence'. As we recall (Chapter 1), the French word *déconstruction* first appeared as a translation of Heidegger's German word

Destruktion. The result would be an ellipsis, a reading with two centres (the first reading *and* the second), the two faces of Hermes: radical hermeneutics. The second reading seeks something at work in the text behind the author's back, something that the author did not see coming:

> The writer writes *in* a language and *in* a logic whose proper system, laws, and life his discourse by definition cannot dominate absolutely. He uses them only by letting himself after a fashion and up to a point be governed by the system. And the reading must always aim at a certain relationship, unperceived by the writer, between what he commands and what he does not command of the patterns of the language that he uses.[3]

That's what he was telling his students. In other words, to get at what Derrida is saying, ask yourself what it would mean to put things in your own words. The problem, of course, is that our words are not our own; we do not own them and cannot stipulate what they mean. We did not make them up and they are not our private property; they are the common property of the language that was already running when we first opened our mouths, the one we heard and learned by miming. When little children pick things up, we say, 'Listen to that little monkey!' So, as soon we agree to use a word, we agree to a contract whose fine print we rarely pause to read; we just click 'I accept' so we can get on with the download. As soon as we use a system of signs, we sign on to a whole string of associations and connotations of which we are not the author.

In other words (again), if I say that English is 'my'

language, that is not because it belongs to me but because I belong to it (Heidegger and Gadamer). To learn it is to begin in the middle of a language that is already up and running. It means to catch up with it, to learn how to enter it, how to get into it and to flow with ease along its currents. I have agreed to a whole take on (interpretation of) the world. That, I venture to say, is what I say happens to Derrida himself when he signs on to 'principles of reading' without signing on to 'hermeneutics'. If he had read the fine print, he would have seen the decision was not his to make. The word followed him out the door through which he made his exit.

Saying What I Do Not Mean to Say

So, in any piece of writing (or speaking or signing or signifying, etc.), there are both certain things over which my little finite Johnny-come-lately conscious 'I' exercises control, and quite a lot of things over which it does not (something bigger than us). To take up the language is to dive into the waters of a system by which I am also inundated. If I misspeak, something gets itself said that I did not mean to say. When I was studying German in Germany, I was out drinking beer one night with my German friends (which promoted fluency, of course). Having finished up a superb Pilsner Urquell and thirsting like a deer for running streams for yet 'another', I said to the bartender in my best German, '*Ein anderer, bitte.*' After the barman asked me what I wanted, my friends told me I had just asked in perfect German for *another kind* of beer, which was not what I meant to say. I should have said '*Noch einmal, bitte*', one more of the same, please. The rules of the language were running on their own, with serene indifference to me and my thirst and my tiny little *ego cogito*.

Total immersion – the best way to learn a language – also means immersion in a sea of rules. As soon as I open my mouth, I am inundated by a whole history of inherited presuppositions, a tidal wave of overt and hidden meanings, a flood of ancient genealogies of which I know nothing, ancient expressions and turns of phrase of which I am completely ignorant that have since hardened into literalisms, a sea of associations, allusions and puns, rhymes and rhythms, metaphors and metonyms, a host of accumulated connotations and denotations, and, in general, all kinds of unintended linguistic effects over which my own conscious intentions have only limited control. When Descartes took pen in hand and opened his *Meditations* by saying he was putting all of his presuppositions out of action, he was kidding himself. If he were really serious, he would also have had to put his French and Latin languages out of action and put down his pen, and then where would he be?

Derrida adds a further qualification. If 'exorbitant' means to push past beyond the author's conscious intentions, that might sound like he is interested in the author's *un*conscious, which picks up on the slips not of the tongue but of the pen. But, for Derrida, psychoanalysis represents an attempt to short-circuit reading, to pick the lock of a text, to step outside the text and pretend that the psychoanalyst holds the extra-textual key to the 'secret' hidden in it. The psychoanalyst does not read the text but treats it as a 'symptom' of something non-textual, something which, in the language of the day, was called the 'transcendental signified'. But Derrida sought a meticulous reading of the *text itself*, a reading that will be 'intrinsic and remain within the text',[4] not outside the text but outside the orbit of the author of the text, which included equally both the consciousness of the author and the author's unconscious. A psychoanalytic reading of a patient's writings may be useful to a psychoanalysis of the patient, or to an intellectual history of the author, but it is an extrinsic way to read the text. A poetic innovation, any insight of any sort, may or may not be the product of a tormented soul. It doesn't matter. What matters is how it opens up the world.

Nothing guarantees, of course, that the second reading, the exorbitant one, the deconstruction, is good news; sometimes it is bad news. The only guarantee is that it is *risky*. Real hermeneutics is always a risky business. But remember Climacus's warning about making things easy. Without this risk, we will get nowhere; we will spin our wheels on the same old familiar ice and never come up with anything new. We will protect the old instead of expecting the new. We will end up continually repeating the same.

Two Types of Repetition

The official job title Derrida had back at the ENS was *agrégé-répétiteur*, meaning Derrida was to be the coach, the one who 'rehearsed' the students for the exam (the *aggrégation concours*), where the French word for 'rehearsal' is *répétition*, as in 'once more from the top' (or *noch einmal* in German). The job title was positively prophetic – it required a whole theory of 'repetition' (or, as it is sometimes called, 'iteration' or 'iterability'). So, the young professor said, there are two kinds of repetition, the repetition of the same and the repetition of the different. There are (at least!) two kinds of hermeneutics, two interpretations of interpretation, a safety-first hermeneutics and a risky hermeneutics, as there are the two faces of Hermes. *This a central tenet of postmodern hermeneutics.*

First, there is repeating the same, repeating the original reproductively, in the mode of the respectful, doubling commentary. This kind of repetition repeats backwards; it goes back to what has already been said or done or made and repeats it. The second kind of repetition repeats forward; it is turned towards the future and is trying to produce something new.

The first serves a purpose as the model for the apprentice, who learns by imitation, by the reproduction of what has already been produced. For this kind of repetition, originality is outlawed as a mistake, at fault for straying from the original. The second kind of repetition is for the innovator who is bent on letting the new break in, break through, break out.

The first kind of repetition is like a pianist learning a piece for the first time. The second kind of repetition is that of the virtuoso. Or of a composer plunking at a piano, trying this and trying that, repeatedly attempting to find something that is not there because it does not yet exist. For the first kind of repetition, the fault is to hit the wrong note, to do something different. For the second kind of repetition, the fault is to compose the same, to do what has already been done.

The first kind of repetition tries to guard against every

possible variation or deviation. The second exposes itself to what it cannot see coming, where the beginning has no idea of the ending.

The first kind of repetition is under our control; it has a fixed model to imitate, a rule against which to measure and monitor variations, to keep watch over straying and deviation. The second is not in our control and, faced with an idiomatic situation, finds itself on its own.

The first kind of repetition is the repetition of the possible; it sticks rigidly to what it considers realistic, realizable, doable, possible. The second is the repetition of the impossible, and its idea is to do the impossible.

The first kind of repetition is eminently sane and sensible; the second kind is just a bit mad, touched as it is by a faith in what seem incredible, a hope against hope in what seems hopeless, and a love of the impossible, all of which are quite exorbitant.

The Rabbi and the Poet

In earlier works of this same period in the 1960s, Derrida came back (repeatedly) – three times, to be exact – to the two types of interpretation, which turn on the two types of repetition. In an essay on the French Jewish writer Edmond Jabès (1912–91), these two types of interpretation are personified by two figures: the rabbi and the poet; the one theological, the other atheological. Derrida was raised in a Jewish family and, while as an adult he abandoned the practice of his religion, he retained a very Jewish respect for reading, the Jews being a people of the Book. This essay is one of the few instances in which he lets himself use the word 'hermeneutics', and it is the occasion of a couple of striking formulations. In the Jewish Scriptures, the Jews are elected by a God who, after conducting a somewhat cloudy conversation with Moses on Mount Sinai, gives Moses a tablet of commandments, thereby electing the Jews – with or without their consent; they were not consulted in advance – to be a hermeneutic people, destined always to commentary and exegesis, to the interpretation of a sacred text:

> In the beginning is hermeneutics. But the *shared* necessity of exegesis, the interpretive imperative, is interpreted differently by the rabbi and the poet. The difference between the horizon of the original text and the exegetic writing makes the difference between the rabbi and the poet irreducible . . . The original opening of interpretation essentially signifies that there will always be rabbis and poets. And two interpretations of interpretation.[5]

In the beginning is hermeneutics – I love this formulation; it cannot be improved upon; well, only slightly maybe, with a little supplement: in the beginning is hermeneutics, and also in the middle and in the end. For the Jews in particular, who are summoned by an 'interpretive imperative', meaning the injunction, the command, the plea issued to the Jews – and, by proxy, to the rest of us, the Jews here standing in for all humankind – to interpret, always. Hermeneutics first, last and always, interpretation all the way down.

So, there are two different ways of responding to the imperative. The rabbi responds to the Book, which contains the Law, and so stands within the theological provenance of hermeneutics, the theology of Judaism, whose history is a history of commentaries on the Book. This interpretation is pious, humble, respectful, obliged to expound the deepest, inexhaustible treasures of the Book, which are passed on from generation to generation.

The second figure, the poet, suffers no such restriction and has no original to obey. The hermeneutics practised by the poet is freer and more open-ended, more productive than reproductive, more autonomous than heteronomous. Of course, even here, with the poet, there can be no question of pure autonomy, of absolute freedom – remember the pre-existing system called language which is already running. So, the poet's autonomy is relative only to the rabbi; it cannot be pure. These two different ways of responding to the interpretative imperative imply a deeper responsibility by which both are subjected to a deeper call.

Rousseau and Nietzsche

In a paper that he read at Johns Hopkins University in 1966, which made Derrida something of an overnight celebrity and introduced post-structuralism to the United States, the first interpretation of interpretation is described as sad and negative. The first interpretation, the rabbinic commentary, but here marked Rousseauian, is characterized by a kind of guilt, a futile attempt to return to the original. It suffers from a 'nostalgia for origins', for 'the lost or impossible presence of the absent origin' – the sad realization that the gap, the hermeneutic distance, cannot be crossed.[6] It is not even an ideal we can strive for; it is actually an illusion, as there really never was an original. When it comes to the Bible, this is in fact an astute historical point. Modern historical-critical biblical research has shown what a patch quilt the Bible is, the product of centuries of stitching together and *re*daction.

Now, the howls we hear in the background are not the ancient pedagogues but Derrida's students back at the ENS. *Mon Dieu!* they cry. What are we to do now? How are we to pass this exam and ever find a job? Are we expected to go about this dreary business knowing it is a sad and 'useless passion', to borrow a famous phrase from Jean-Paul Sartre (who was still in those days *the* philosopher in Paris)?

Derrida, ever the good coach, had different advice. They are to go about the business of reconstituting the original but to do so *without illusion*. The students should keep constant guard against anachronism, against reading the present back into the past, but they should avoid the illusion of thinking that the original really is *original*. The so-called original has not dropped from the sky; it, too, is the effect of everything that precedes it, of the systems of signification of which it was a part. There never was anything that was originally original. (There is nothing – never anything – outside or without some conditioning context or another.)

But if the first affirmation is sad and Rousseauian, with the sadness of nostalgia, dreaming of a lost state of nature, a lost origin, the second takes the form of a joyous Nietzschean affirmation, where there never was an original to lose or lament and interpretation is free and open-ended, joyful and creative:

> There are thus two interpretations of interpretation, of
> structure, of sign, of play. The one seeks to decipher,
> dreams of deciphering a truth or an origin which escapes
> play and the order of the sign, and which lives the necessity
> of interpretation as an exile. The other, which is no longer
> turned toward the origin, affirms play and tries to pass
> beyond man and humanism, the name of man being the
> name of that being who . . . has dreamed of full presence,
> the reassuring foundation, the origin and the end of play.[7]

The first interpretation (the counterpart to the rabbi) is bent
on discerning and deciphering the meaning, but the second
interpretation (the counterpart to the poet) is bent on the
invention of new meanings and even of effects that are otherwise than meaning. The first interpretation assumes a centre,
and the task assigned to interpretation is to regain the centre
and to bring the book, and indeed humankind, itself to fulfil-
ment. The second interpretation is elliptical and decentred
and marginal, and it does not lament but celebrates the
multiplicity of centres.

The first interpretation assumes an original Truth, and
the task of interpretation is to recover or discover the Truth.
The second interpretation assumes there is no Truth, capitalized and in the singular, and it affirms the multiplicity of
truths in the plural and the invention of new and coming
truths. The first interpretation wants to cling fast to the
ancient Truth, the venerability of *veritas*; the second assumes
the vulnerability of *veritas*; it wants to invent new truths,
on the assumption that the truth, like the Messiah, is always
to come.

Husserl and Joyce

Finally, in a third text from the 1960s, Derrida describes the two interpretations of interpretation as Husserlian and Joycean.[8] The first, inspired by Husserl, envisages history as the transmission of a univocal meaning from generation to generation by means of a clear and perfect reproduction of the original, unaltered by the repetition. The second interpretation is inspired by James Joyce's exploitation of every graphic, phonic and semantic link within any given language and between different languages, every association and alliteration, every pun and play on words, which promotes the production of new and unpredictable effects, famously, scandalously, engaging in a play of evocative equivocations and poetic provocations. But Derrida's point is that, left to itself, the one is as futile as the other, and both are anti-historical. To maintain oneself in the element of pure univocity, were such a thing even possible, would only paralyse or sterilize history, confining it to the repetition of the same, depriving it of the equivocity that enriches history. By the same token, without allowing some room for univocity, the work of repetition would be unintelligible. There would be nothing to repeat or innovate upon, which would make a creative repetition no less impossible.

It is Never a Question of Choosing Between Them

Now Derrida come to his real point – and nothing could be more important to understanding the distinction between the two interpretations of interpretation than this – *it is never a question of choosing between the one and the other*.[9] Interpretation is always conducted in the space between (*inter*) the two *inter*pretations of interpretation. Interpretation negotiates the price (*pretium*) between the two. Were the first interpretation to obtain without interruption, the tradition would die off, calcified, rigidified, rendered incapable of producing anything new. We would be consigned to the repetition of the same, the very spectre that haunted Nietzsche's Zarathustra, who was menaced by the thought 'All is the same, all has been.' But were there to be nothing but uninterrupted interruption, death would be no less inevitable, this time the issue of utter dissipation.

It will come as no surprise that Joyce himself coined a word – a neologism, by way of a productive repetition – for this impasse. As we would just as easily be squeezed to death by pure unbroken order (*cosmos*) as dissipated by pure unleashed *chaos*, we are enjoined by the hermeneutic imperative to embrace what Joyce called the *chaosmos*, the chaosmic, the mutual interplay and continual disturbance of one side by the other, which is the condition of possibility of producing novel effects. We can see this miscegenation of chaos and cosmos in the actual history of rabbinic interpretation itself, which, far from being reduced to the pieties of univocal reproduction and doubling commentary, produced the most prodigious and impious readings, double binds and double crosses, in which the rabbis break out into arguments not only with one another but even with the Most High, blessed be his name. In its actual history, rabbinic interpretation allows itself to be exposed to the poet. But, by the same token, nothing protects the poet from piety, from probing the divine depths where the poet, too, is visited by the mystery we call God, not only in overtly religious poets like Gerard Manley Hopkins or mystical poets like John of the Cross and Angelus Silesius, but in more subtly a/theological poets like Seamus Heaney and Emily Dickinson.

Is There a Third Interpretation of Interpretation?

Considering the porousness of the two kinds of interpretation, the inclination of one to bleed into the other, are there not grounds for speaking of a *third* interpretation of interpretation, the one that maintains that all real and genuine interpretation takes place in the distance between the first two interpretations of interpretation? I recommend against labelling this space in between them as such, lest we obscure the larger point. The being of interpretation is being-between (*inter*) the two, which means, following its historical genealogy, that an interpretation is always a negotiation. So, the difference must be irreducible. An interpretation happens in the *space between* the regular and the irregular, the commensurable and the incommensurable, the normalized and the exceptional, the centre and the margins, the same and the other, or, as Derrida will put it later on, the possible and the impossible, or the conditional and the unconditional, ideas in whose religious resonance I am interested. Interpretation happens as *intervention*; an interpretation is an *event* of inter*vention* upon the con*ventional*. It never comes *ex nihilo* – which is also Heidegger's point when he says that authenticity occurs as a modification of inauthenticity.

Furthermore, if we went on to say that there is a *third* interpretation of interpretation, we run the risk of making it seem that Derrida is reinstating the old Hegelian triad in which we split the difference between the thesis and the antithesis and raise them up, hand in hand, into a happy higher synthesis, thereby installing a peaceful reconciliation of opposites. But if you think Derrida has come to bring peace, you are mistaken; he is not calling for constant peace but for the sword, the cutting edge of interpretation, intervention, interruption, the disruption, which is, by a kind of paradoxical logic, the only way to keep a thing safe from stagnation and ossification.

The voice of deconstruction is more impious than the hermeneutic voice.[10] So, unlike Gadamer, who moves on to a *fusion* of horizons, Derrida prefers the figure of disjointedness, the crack, or fission, or *fissure*. That is why Derrida once said, with the devil in his eye, that if truth be told, 'I am a very conservative person.'[11] What he means is that the only way to protect a text is to put it at risk, to expose it to its future. The only rest Derrida seeks is ceaseless unrest. The only peace he finds is in remaining constantly vigilant about stability, unity, order, meaning, presence, essence, ruling regime – let us say *structure* – lest it prevent the intervention, the genuine interventive interpretation, to which every structure must be continuously, relentlessly exposed. Every pious interpretation must be exposed to poetic impiety, every order to creative disorder, in order to keep the future open. It is not a question of choosing between the two, nor of fusing them, but of allowing the one to *haunt* the other, to keep the other up at night by making strange noises in its house. It is not a question of reaching an ontological reconciliation, but of creating a 'hauntological' disturbance, to make use of a pun we will revisit below (Chapter 7).

Occupying the place in this crossfire requires discernment, a singular judgement cut to fit singular contexts, which is never merely a matter of the application of a rule to a case but a matter of insight into a unique situation – the hermeneutic situation – in which we find ourselves. The interpretive imperative goes all the way down. The injunction – the call or the command we are under to interpret – is inescapable. It always and already lays claim to us, so relentlessly as to constitute the very thing, if there is such a thing, that makes us who we are, we who do not know who we are, we who are defined by this very unknowing and by this very question. In hermeneutics, it is just as Augustine said, *quaestio mihi magna factus sum*, I have become a great question to myself, a matter we will also revisit below (Chapter 11).[12]

The problem of the interpretive imperative is of a piece with the question of who we are, of being 'human', and that takes us back once again to the question of humanism, and to a new critique of humanism, this time coming from the structuralists.

Structuralism, Post-structuralism and the Age of the Program

Of the three masterpieces of postmodern hermeneutics – including Heidegger's *Being and Time* and Gadamer's *Truth and Method* – Derrida's *Of Grammatology* (even if he didn't intend for it to be a postmodern hermeneutical masterpiece) proved to have the most prescient title. It might easily have been entitled *Of Programmatology*, a word with a ring to it today, in the age of the program, meaning we are up to our ears in computer programs meant to be our assistants (but which may end up running everything). At the time (the 1960s), Derrida was wading into the structuralist debate – which, to put it in contemporary terms, was a debate about whether everything can be programmed. As you might have guessed, based upon his taste for the marginal, elliptical, exorbitant and the chaosmotic, Derrida resisted that idea. That resistance came to be called 'post-structuralism', which was a fellow-traveller of the hermeneutics of play in Gadamer, who was worried about the unchecked rule of method.

The structuralists took a scientific approach to language, which is the opposite of the hermeneutic approach. Accordingly, Derrida's critique of the structuralists – the 'post-' in Derrida's post-structuralism – kept a door open for hermeneutics. As I construe it, Derrida's idea of the *un*programmable is the challenge made by a postmodern hermeneutics to the age of the program. In this chapter, we will first lay out what 'structuralism' means, in order to understand the *post*-structuralism of Derrida, which is the defining moment of a genuinely postmodern hermeneutics. That will involve swallowing a small dose of 'structural linguistics', which is where structuralism got its start.

The Word / World Problem

I was once criticized by someone who said that he was interested in thinking about the world while I, like all these hermeneutic rascals, was content to think about words. The remarkable thing to me was that, after saying this, he continued to speak. To my astonishment, he continued to use more words, a flood of them, really, and sometimes – he is a fluent speaker and an eloquent writer – with dramatic emphasis on the word 'world'. The more he assured us that he was concerned with the *world*, not words, the more loudly he kept using the *word* 'world'. The more tightly he tried to cling to the world, the more he clung to this word. That suggests to me – it never occurred to him – that the real distinction is not between thinking about the world and thinking about words, but between thinking about the world by also paying critical attention to words and, well, not. That is what the philosophers call the 'linguistic turn', what Gadamer (following Heidegger) meant by saying that being which can be understood is language, and what Derrida meant when he said there's nothing outside the textual systems we rely upon to make sense. Let's call it here the word/world problem.

Contemporary linguistics begins with a very simple point. If we look up the meaning of a word in a dictionary, we are sent on to other words. Words are defined by other words. This observation is completely innocent and devoid of revolutionary import. Yet a revolution ensued that rattled the world of letters back in the 1950s and 60s, and its aftershocks are still being felt today. It sent the cultural conservatives rushing madly to the exits, shouting, 'Fire!' They were convinced that the post-structuralism it resulted in pretty much meant that the end of the world was at hand, certainly the end of the West, definitely of marriage and the family, and at the very least the end of the core curriculum. The barbarians are at the gates. God is dead – and the conservatives were not feeling all that well themselves. Post-structuralism spelled – or, better, smelled of – relativism, and the mark of the beast is on the relativists.

Why all the panic? To say that words are defined by other words is to say that there is never any point where a word folds up its tent, or throws its arms up in frustration, and simply disappears into the world. There isn't any one Master Word that is hard-wired to the world or to reality, such that every other word is wired up to the Master Word, like someone on water skis linked on to a linguistic speedboat bent on making it to the other side. But – and buts are important in post-structural theory – that does not mean that words do not have a *reference* to the world. It just means that words do not have a reference to the world *independently* of their *difference* from one another. *No reference without difference.* This would permanently disturb the sleep of the cultural conservatives, who took this to be a sceptical denial of the real world, which consigns philosophy to relativism, reducing morality to a word game and turning the tradition into empty verbiage. They went to bed every night fearful that they would awake in the morning only to find that the post-structuralists had somehow stolen the world out from under them while they slept.

Differential Differences

Words – now let's call them 'signifiers', the scientific way of putting it – are arbitrary signs. That does not mean you can use any word, grunt or gesture you feel like making and expect to be understood. Arbitrary simply means that there is no intrinsic connection between the word 'king' and His Royal Majesty (they don't look alike, etc.). Where we say 'king', others get the same job done by saying *roi*, with no injury done to His Majesty. What matters is that for the people using a given system of signifiers (English users or French users) the difference between 'king'/ 'ring'/ 'sing' and '*roi*'/'*loi*'/'*moi*' be discernible. The signifiers are significant in virtue of their discernible difference from one another; they make or produce a meaning – now, let's say 'signify' – in virtue of the difference between the signifiers, both phonically ('ring'/ 'king'/ 'sing') and graphically (like 'bear'/ 'bare').

Let's call that a 'differential' space, which is a function of the 'play' of the signifiers. Once again, by 'play' we do not mean open marriages, free sex or public nudity. We mean the perfectly serious and sober phenomenon of how these signifiers 'play off' one another, as in contrasting colours. It is the differential space between colours which enables us to discern them, which is also the reason the same colour can look quite different against different backgrounds. Anybody who has ever bought a rug that they positively hated after they got it home can understand that. Colour theory is *relational* all the way down, but that does not imply the *relativism* so dreaded by the conservatives, which is an important distinction. Language works the same way, which is why the meaning of a given word or phrase or sentence is irreducibly *contextual*. Taken out of the (con)text, we can make anybody say pretty much anything we want. Without some context, words just don't work; they collapse under the stress. Politicians learn this the hard way, since, in our media-driven world, their every utterance is subject to being torn from its context and sent circulating around the world on Facebook or Twitter before they so much as finish their sentence. With Photoshop, we can even 'edit' pictures – a textual figure – and put someone in a scene (recontextualize) in which they never took part, which explains the 'fake news' on the internet. Editions, redactions, citations – all are a function of differential differences.

For us postmodern types, differential differences are a wonderful thing. They have a distinct advantage over the sort of difference that has received more press in philosophy and in politics – let's call that 'oppositional' difference, like right/wrong, on/off, present/absent, thesis/antithesis, living/dead, etc. These are binary differences, meaning an ordered pair, where one member of the pair is privileged and the other is defined as, well, the opposition. One very simple way to think of modernism is that it loves ordered pairs – subjective/objective, absolute/relative, rational/irrational, spirit/matter, religious/secular, public/private. Postmodernists love differential differences, which also has an ethico-political payoff: they distrust binary differences like straight/gay, male /female, native born/immigrant, preferring instead a play of differences where no one term is granted a special privilege. Differential difference is more egalitarian, more democratic, less belligerent. So, there is an important difference between differential difference and oppositional (binary) difference.

Structuralist Linguistics

Pondering this simple point (which is rich with implication) – that words are defined by other words – led to the revolution in the study of language called modern linguistics, which was started by a Swiss linguist, Ferdinand de Saussure (1857–1913).[1] Saussure's linguistics would prove to be the main competition faced by German hermeneutics (and so *post*-structuralism would keep the door open to a postmodern hermeneutics). Considered the founder of modern linguistics, Saussure was trying to put the study of language on a scientific footing, which is a very modernist goal. By that, he did not mean turning it over to mathematics and laboratory experiments but coming up with a rigorous and objective way to go about its business. This he found in treating language in *purely linguistic* terms, free of all sorts of psychological, philosophical or theological interference. In Saussure's world, no one was allowed to say, 'In the beginning was the Word, and the Word was with God and the Word was God', so that all human language is a finite and imperfect image of the Word of God. Well, of course, they were allowed to say that, if they wished, but after hours, on their own time, not while they were on the clock, not *qua* linguist. That sort of claim would provoke irresolvable extra-linguistic debates and grind everything to a halt. No Master Word (like 'God') or Master Things (like God again, this time without the scare quotes, or Matter, or Physics, or whatever) allowed.

All that has to go and, with it – here comes the revolution – the traditional and seemingly common-sense approach to language. Language is no longer treated in the classical humanist manner as the way an inner consciousness expresses itself in outer signs which signify concepts and refer to reality. Consciousness? Reality? That's just psychology, metaphysics. Do we really have to agree on all that before we can get this science off the ground? Like Heidegger, but for reasons very much their own, de Saussure and then the structuralists sought to displace the primacy of the speaking human subject and strike a blow to the 'inner self', upon which centuries of philosophers and theologians, poets and mystics, have piously pondered.

So instead of Gadamer saying 'being which can be understood is language', let's just stick to semiotics, please, to a system of signs, of signifiers and signifieds, arbitrary, differential elements combined according to valid (agreed upon) rules of combination. Instead of saying that a 'noun' is the name of an entity or substance, let's say instead that a noun is a signifier that can take a number (singular or plural);

instead of saying a verb refers to an action, let's just say it can take a tense (past, present or future). In short, let's stick to functional definitions, easy on the metaphysics and psychology, please. In linguistics, sentences – 'chains of signifiers', 'linguistic strings' – are well formed (according to the rules) or they are not, and we are excused, thank you very much, from deciding whether they are 'true', or 'correspond to reality', which is someone else's problem.

How Many Sentences are There in the English Language?

This was revolutionary stuff, at least in revolution-prone Paris, where they love everything that is avant-garde, which is a French expression, of course, meaning ahead of the pack, on the cutting edge, although structural linguistics would prove to be more than merely a French fashion. Here's where things get really interesting. As in any formal system, there are both elements (like numbers, words) and rules of combination of the elements (like the rules of addition and subtraction; grammatical rules). You can see how thinking about language like that is eventually going to give someone the idea of a 'computer'. Now ask yourself:

How many words are there in the English language?

At any given time, we might be able to make a reasonable guess (although it is changing constantly, almost by the hour).

How many rules of combination (rules of grammar) are there?

The answer would be found in a grammar book and it would depend on how specific you want to be.

How many sentences are there?

Enough with the questions! We cannot even begin to count that. There are just too many sentences out there, especially nowadays, with texting and cell phones. Answering this is impossible, not just because it would be too hard to count in practice but because it cannot be counted in principle. Not as long as we have to do with a 'living' language, where there are always speakers speaking, constantly encountering new situations. Not to mention all the new speakers being born every second of the day, and who knows how much they are going to have to say?

There is a finite set of rules that governs the combination of a finite number of elements (words) but a potentially infinite number of combinations (linguistic strings, like phrases and sentences, which are effects of the rules). How can something infinite result from two finite things? Where is the infinity coming from? The culprit here, if culprit it be – I think it is actually good news – is time. The rules are synchronic (apply all over the system at the same time), but the sentences flow across time (diachronic). So, the reason for that unlimited number of new sentences is the inextinguishable flow of time which keeps changing the *context*. We can't step in the same linguistic river twice. Even if I repeat the same thing to the same audience using the same words, at the very least the time has changed and a subtle shift has set in. That temporal shift could even make what I just said false – for instance, if you had just asked me exactly what time it is. The first time I tell you it will be the truth, but if I repeat the same phrase even ten minutes later, I'll be wrong. Sometimes we even have to change what we just said in order to say the same thing, as when answering the question, 'How old are you?' 'Last year you said you were fifty years old, this year fifty-one – make up your mind!' Each utterance is a new occurrence in a new context. That is why we keep coming up with new words which, if they are felicitous, will assume a place within the existing body of words and become standard. We keep looking for new ways to put familiar things and to invent ways to put new things.

Is There a Universal Grammar?

Time is the rub and the nub of the problem. Over and above the rules that make up the grammar of a 'natural' language (like French), the structuralists said there are rules of a pure, deeper 'universal grammar' of any possible linguistic system, a universal structure common to every language, whence the term 'structural' linguistics, or 'structuralism'.[2] An adjective always modifies a noun, whether it is put in front of the noun, as in the English 'red mill', or after it, as in the French *moulin rouge*. In the United States, Noam Chomsky (1928–) was saying something similar, but in a very *materialistic* way, when he identified this deep grammar with the way the brain is hard-wired. The alternative to Chomsky's materialism would be *idealism*, to say these rules 'hold', ideally, in any possible world, just the way '7 + 5 = 12' holds, regardless of how our brains are wired up neurophysiologically.

At this point, Saussure steps in like a good referee, blows the whistle and rules the ball out of bounds. In linguistics, the debate between materialism and idealism is immaterial. The two sides are never going to settle their differences. Regardless of whatever back-up the physicists or metaphysicians or theologians want to come up with, in scientific linguistics it suffices to say there is a set of formal rules, which Saussure calls *langue*, language in the formal sense – let's say linguistic form. The actual utterances made by real flesh-and-blood living speakers he called *parole* – let's say speech acts – 'events' of actual speakers speaking in conformity with the rules. Individual speakers formally qualify as speakers – remember, he is not talking about the *psychology* of language acquisition – by making well-formed utterances in accord with the rules (and disqualified if they do not). The number of elements and rules is finite, but the number of actual utterances is potentially infinite. We cannot foresee who is going to say what under what circumstances, but we do know the *form* to which these utterances will conform when they do say something.

A Machine for Making Meanings

So, in structuralism we have a nice neat (binary) scientific distinction: the linguistic forms are universal, necessary and atemporal (synchronic); the actual utterances (events) are particular, contingent and temporal (diachronic). Meaning, on this account, is an effect of the deployment of signifiers in rule-governed ways. This differential play is not 'somebody', not God, not Being or the World Spirit, not the inner self. It is an *impersonal formal system*, a bit like a *writing machine*, a *technology* of meaning-making, a machine that makes meaning by producing differential effects. (Pay attention to this technological point – it is going to become important as we advance into the 'information' age.) So, in linguistics, there is a technology behind the living word, like a machine producing animated effects on a screen. This is not a noisy, smelly, clunky machine, typical of the old technologies, but quite a fine and delicate, slick, slightly invisible informational system. We could even say that behind the living word is a dead (impersonal) structure, but that would be rather dramatic for Saussure, who was Genevan and not given to Parisian melodrama. But you can see that the old distinction between the living and the technical looks a bit less sharp – less binary and oppositional – than it did before we started. For as long as human beings have been speaking, they have been engaged in a technological operation. Aristotle defined a human being as a 'rational animal', a living thing (*zoon*) equipped with *logos*, which meant reason but also language. In Saussure's terms, Aristotle was describing animals whose minds are meaning-making machines.

Speakers are not inner selves but nodes on the grid, instances where the system gets 'instantiated', points where the rules are being deployed in a particular time and place. In this understanding, books are redescribed as 'texts'; historical situations as 'contexts'. Concrete historical human life is invaded by an ahistorical formalism reminding us more of the mindset of the Enlightenment and miming the methods of the sciences.

There is an interesting implication here. We could, in principle, have an uninterpreted formal system, in which the elements would be purely arbitrary marks. That helps us understand something that happens in contemporary quantum physics, when the physicists follow the mathematics into spheres that they cannot imagine. They can do the maths, but they do not know what they are talking about.[3] That is, they do not know what the world the mathematics is calculating would mean, what it would 'look like', how it can be visualized or experienced.

You can see the humanists looking around nervously. They smell trouble. The technological, the 'post-human' (a term we will be returning to later) – for the humanists, *that* is the mark of the beast. It's downright spooky. You see where I am going.

Postmodernism or Post-structuralism?

While the French structuralists (1950–60s), who had taken up the work of Saussure, created a sensation, a sweeping movement that affected everything – literature, anthropology, Marxism (*pace* Sartre), psychoanalysis – we need to recall that this is Paris, where the intellectual scenery can change rapidly. Accordingly, the structuralists were soon enough challenged and ultimately overtaken by the post-structuralists. Predictably, today, everybody is vying for the spot of what comes after post-structuralism. The post-structuralists were also known as philosophy's 68ers (*les soixante-huitards*), as in the 1968ers, the year of open revolution in France and of terrible turmoil in the United States and, as I said, the year of the unofficial roll-out of postmodernism, which is the more popular term for post-structuralism. If modernism means method, uniformity and laws of geometric clarity – like Bauhaus architecture – the postmodernists prefer amalgamations and irregularities, like post-Bauhaus architecture, which was the historical context in which the word 'postmodern' was first coined.

There were several equally brilliant, distinctive and innovative theorists of the day, foremost among them Michel Foucault, Gilles Deleuze, Jean-François Lyotard and Derrida. While I continue to use the word 'postmodernism' here, I concede it is an overused, much abused term mostly meaning contemporary culture at large. Philosophically, the word 'post-structuralism' is more precise, although the postmodernists all reject that word as well.[4] Nothing new here. The existentialists did pretty much the same thing. That is a useful reminder that these thinkers have important differences and take different approaches. Still, it does not negate the fact that these words are useful ways of identifying currents of thought, whether those swimming in that stream like it or not.

Preferring the Dead Letter to Living Speech

Of all the post-structuralists, Derrida is the most pertinent to our purposes because he was coming from Heidegger and Husserl[5] (the sources of postmodern hermeneutics) and he took on Saussure frontally. Derrida made two criticisms of Saussure.

1. The first criticism, far from criticizing Saussure's formalism, pushed it even further. Derrida objected that even the great man, Saussure himself, betrays a psychological prejudice, a human, all-too-human, preference for speech over writing.[6] The 'pure form' of the signifier is of itself

neither phonic nor graphic; it is simply an arbitrary and differential mark or trace. The pure form of difference is indifferent to these material embodiments, just the way the rules of chess are indifferent to the substances of which the pieces are made. The use of hand signs, smoke signals or Morse code meets this requirement (of discernible differences) every bit as much as speech. From a strictly formal point of view, Saussure betrays a lingering metaphysical and psychological prejudice (that is, his presuppositions conflict with his position). Speaking, we might say, is just writing with air. Speaking is not a pure, transparent medium in which the self is immediately present to itself, not a 'pure spirit' (*pneuma*). Pneumatology is just an airy grammatology. Spoken words may be invisible, not inscribed in stone or papyrus, but their differential play mediates the world; it is still the crucial mediator even when we conduct an inner monologue with ourselves, which always takes place in our native language. So, Saussure fell for an old prejudice of privileging the 'living' word and the seemingly self-present speaker over the 'dead letter'.

This first criticism of Saussure, as Derrida himself points out, had already been effectively made by a man named Louis Hjelmslev (1899–1965), a Copenhagen linguist.[7] Hjelmslev had argued that pure linguistic form neutralizes the psychological distinction between phonic (speaking) and graphic (writing) substance, or indeed any other material substance (hand-language, etc.). These linguists were not saying that writing precedes speech historically, or that it is more important psychologically, but that, from the point of view of pure linguistic form, each is equally an arbitrary differential play. Derrida made this point famous by coining a neologism, *différance*, which was not only a strategic misspelling but a homophone in French with *différence* (the correct spelling), the upshot of which was to say that linguistic difference is equally phonic or graphic, spatial or temporal.

A Political Aside

Derrida is also alluding to the old – and lethal – debate between the living spirit with which Christianity associates itself and the dead letter of which the Jews are accused. This binarity, Christian/Jew, has a murderous history that stretches from the Gospels to *The Merchant of Venice* to the Holocaust. If the privileging of speech is a psychological, metaphysical and even a theological prejudice, a lethal religious and political issue also lingers in its background. Indeed, Derrida would go on to show that this privileging of speech over writing is complicit with a much wider and deeper system of metaphysical binarities, going all the way back to Plato and Aristotle – between body and soul, matter and spirit, time and eternity, death and life, and, in the widest sense of all, presence and absence.

There is no little irony in observing that Derrida's 'deconstruction' of anti-Semitism relies upon the strategy of 'destruction' he found in Heidegger, who was a Nazi (Chapter 1). His alliance with Heidegger was a dicey and strictly philosophical business – the two never met – and a source of constant trouble for him. Derrida was a French-speaking Algerian Jew, whose childhood life and education in colonial Algeria during the Second World War were disrupted by the

Pétain government in Algiers, a puppet of the Vichy government in Paris. Heidegger was an erstwhile Catholic from southern Germany who became an anti-Semite. This was further complicated by the revelation in 1988 that Derrida's friend Paul de Man (1919–83), a Belgian literary theorist who had become the leader of the Yale University school of deconstruction, had held obvious anti-Semitic opinions in his youth. Every time Derrida tried to show that the theoretical work of these two controversial figures could not be simply reduced to National Socialism, all hell descended upon him.

Post-structuralism and the Unprogrammable

2. So, what does this have to do with hermeneutics? The characteristic feature of postmodern hermeneutics is its affirmation of unforeseeable openings, surprising 'events', unprogrammable effects. This can be seen in Derrida's second criticism of Saussure, which applied to both Saussure and Hjelmslev, which is that there is no finite, atemporal set of rules that could contain or anticipate the infinity of possible utterances, written or spoken in time.[8] This is because, in time, we cannot see what is coming, not fully or perfectly. So, the 'event' has more teeth in it than the structuralists are prepared to admit. The event is not just an *instance of a rule*; it is idiosyncratic and unanticipatable; not lower than the universal, but higher (Kierkegaard).

In other words, it is not just the content that changes while the form remains eternally the same, but that linguistic form itself is reformable and transformable. The forms – the rules – are just another set of effects of the system, just as time-bound. Any set of rules that could be formulated would be itself a subset of the formal system at that time. The rules do not absolutely regulate the system because they do not exist outside or above the system, they are produced *by* the system; they are not essences governing the system but temporal effects of it, like a freeze-frame.[9]

Language may be a formal system, but it is an *open-ended system*, not a closed one. It is not, in principle, entirely programmable or formalizable, and if it were, it would be undermined. There is always something unruly about a linguistic rule, always something unpredictable about the system (the structural mutates into the post-structural). Language is an ever-rushing stream in which we cannot step twice. Linguistic rules are not truly atemporal but merely temporary status reports subject to future revision. That is what Derrida meant when he said that they are not transcendental (strong, closed systems) but 'quasi-transcendental' (weak, open systems), an expression that might otherwise be a bit mystifying. Time cuts deeper than structure. Even the current laws of physics did not hold at an earlier time in the history of the universe.

An Example

Let's take a concrete example of what Derrida means, the creation of a metaphor, which requires that the system has rules and that the rules have just the right flex. Metaphors are a function of bending the rule in an optimal way. Too much bending and the metaphor is ridiculous and does not catch on. But too little bending and the metaphor is just flat, stale, nothing new. If I say, 'That leaves me cold', we all understand what that means, but I am not going to win any literary prize for coming up with the metaphor 'cold', which is familiar to the point of being (almost) literal. A metaphor requires an optimal irregularity or novelty, a 'catchy', eye-opening, insightful innovation, but one with roots in current usage. I was trying to be metaphoric above when I said the 'rules' are like a freeze-frame or that we cannot step into the same linguistic river twice. When it comes to metaphors, it is sink or swim in this river: too little movement or too much thrashing about and you will drown.

Parisian Atheists, not Pietist Theologians

The mark of Hermes the prankster is on the post-structuralists, who contribute to the hermeneutics of play (of traditions, art-works, scientific theories, whatever) but, unlike the more humanistic hermeneutics of Gadamer, they are happy to embrace the writing-machine, dead letters, technologies of writing and other non-human phenomena. They are of a different mindset. Nowadays, in the information age, too many of us speak of hardware and software, programming and processing, databases, input and output – to describe *ourselves*, our 'souls'. The humanists, on the other hand, have a salutary fear of turning over thinking – or imagining, loving: everything we prize – to formal systems and their *programmability*, making everything we do a function of the rules we are obeying.

Derrida and the generation of the 68ers approached it all unafraid of the encroaching information age. Derrida himself even boasted of the 'end of the book'![10] They welcomed it with eyes wide open, worlds removed from the old academic culture. They were the first generation of jet-set philosophers, frequently lecturing in the United States, avant-garde in their artistic and literary tastes, more flamboyant in their personal lifestyles, and very leftish in their politics – whereas Kierkegaard was a royalist, Nietzsche a flaming elitist and Heidegger actually a Nazi, and all three heartily despised modern communications media. While Heidegger spoke with contempt of typewriters (although I received a short letter from him that is typewritten), Michel Foucault was in the vanguard of theoreticians contesting the normalization of sexuality by the 'family values' set, whose hair he set on fire not only with his work but by being openly gay and living a fairly wild life. In short, the post-structuralists were Parisian atheists, not pietist theologians – the grandparents of classical hermeneutics. If this was hermeneutics, it was an eccentric, exorbitant, outsider hermeneutics. If this was interpretation, it was interpretation from the margins.

A Plea for Contamination

So, Derrida plays Hermes the rogue to argue for the non-human and even technological element in human language. He displaces the classical humanistic distinction between the living word and the non-living script, natural life and the artificial, by way of a contamination of categories that is central to his theoretical project. He exposes binary oppositions – beginning with speech and writing – as historical constructions subject to *de*construction. *Of Grammatology* sets out to undo the rigour (as in *rigor mortis*) of the opposition between nature and culture, to contaminate the soul with technology, and to blur the distinction between the material and the immaterial, the living and non-living, the human and the inhuman, the natural and the artificial, the native and the foreign, the natural sciences and the human ones.

These binaries, Derrida argues, are complicit with an entire system of political oppression: colonialism (European reason versus the 'savages' of the new world); patriarchy (the father contains the seed and the mother merely supplies the matter); human exceptionalism (animals are for food and amusement; natural resources are for our convenience). The post-structuralists distrusted all-encompassing systems wherever they are to be found – from totalitarian politics to dogmatic religion to the computerized society where the big Other is Big Data. Politically, the 68ers were reeling from the devastation wrought by totalitarianisms of the left and the right, from what they called 'totalization', by which they meant the reduction of the multiple play of differences to a single overarching Big Story.[11]

A God with a Thousand Faces

This taste for commingling and contamination is the mark of Hermes, who had many faces, not just the two we're exploring here, one of which was as a boundary-breaker. Originally, the statues of Hermes were used as markers to warn people away – the huge penis was not a Freudian thing but a symbol of a warrior whom you did not want to annoy. Eventually, the strangers who had come to engage in trade, not warfare, agreed to meet outside the town limits at these markers, which were eventually relocated to town centres. That is why Hermes became the god of the *agora*, of trade and commerce, of communication and commingling. Hermes is a god with a thousand faces and so the hermeneutics of Hermes is a highly polymorphic, polyvocal, pluralistic undertaking. Derrida worshipped at this altar (so to speak).

A Humanism to Which We Cannot be Opposed

Instead of reacting against the technological, Derrida insists upon the way it insinuates itself into and decentres everything that calls itself human, living, spiritual. He was not spooked by technology, but he was worried by a totalizing or *reductionistic* technologism, by the attempt to use the new information systems to close things down and to turn everything over to the program, to the rules, to the police of language, culture and life. Derrida's work had an avant-garde, postmodern, politically subversive cutting edge. He didn't argue against techno-systems; he loved his Mac, on which he did all his work. But he argued against *closed* systems – whether technological, political or theological.

As one of the vanguard postmodern feminists, Donna Haraway, said, there is a humanism which we *cannot* not desire,[12] not the old humanism of the 'inner self' but a new post-humanist humanism, which would turn on a non-programmable programmability that was intent on keeping the future *open* to the coming of what we cannot see coming, which of course is very risky hermeneutic business. The new form that totalization takes today is not Soviet or Nazi totalitarianism, or nineteenth-century mechanistic determinism, but *programmability*. That really would spell the end of the play, and hence of hermeneutics, of Hermes the trickster, and of deconstruction, too. Derrida was calling for something risky, which he later on called 'auto-immunity'. That is, a living organism breaks down its own immunities to the technological, but not in such a way that it simply succumbs to the machine, simply becomes a machine. The programs do not go all the way down.

Everything that Derrida would do after 1967, everything that would later on come to be called 'deconstruction' and that I am calling postmodern hermeneutics, would depend upon this analysis. He never departed from it; he never stopped using it. Even as the topics to which he turned over the years would shift – from mostly literary analyses through the middle 1980s to ethical, political and religious questions in the last two decades of his life – this analysis informs everything. Every technological calculation belongs to a calculus of the incalculable, which provides for the open-endedness of the human situation, its unforeseeability, which gives life its salt, fills life with promise while exposing us to risk, since nothing happens if we are not ready to assume a risk.

How to Program for the Unprogrammable?

The questions asked by postmodern hermeneutics in the emerging post-human world abound. Are the information systems in which we are immersed completely rule-governed? Are our bodies completely governed by genetic codes? Or is there room for novelty, invention, the surprise, the unforeseeable, the fortuitous, in the strong Derridean sense of the 'event', which is the characteristic concern of the postmodern. The central issue in contemporary AI work, and in particular in robotology, comes down to this. We know how to build machines today, sleek and shiny, minia-turized, even hand-held machines, dazzling, digitalized information-machines that can perform amazing feats at breathtaking speed that are slowly beginning to make human beings look bad. We know how to build machines that follow rules – but we are at a loss to build machines that do not. We do not know how to build machines that are smarter than rules, higher than the universal, as Kierkegaard said, machines that know how to exercise judgement in idiosyn-cratic situations on the basis of a preconceptual grasp of a body of implicit knowledge and know-how. We can program machines to do the programmable. But how do you program a machine to do the *un*programmable, that is, to *interpret*? Humans do not sort through every possible mathematical combination of a complex series of os and 1s until they finally hit the right one. They interpret.

In such situations, the robots are stupid, but the people

working in the AI industry are not stupid. They know all this and they are working on it. Maybe they will never succeed but, if they do, I am saying it will be because they figured out how to build something that can figure things out by itself – and then maybe the computers will start building their own computers . . . They will then have succeeded in building something that can interpret situations it has never run into before, that will correct its mistakes, that will mime the fluid, plastic, neural networking needed to complete the totally fantastic feat of walking across a room full of objects without bumping into everything and tipping over and lying there helpless until somebody picks it up, or without being stopped dead in its tracks by one simple flaw in its program instead of adjusting for it and moving on, the way any two-year-old can.

Will Watson Replace Hermes?

If the AI people do all this, they will not have reduced us to a machine, they will have created a hermeneutical being like us, not a machine. The unnerving thing is that they know this and are working on it. Are we are heading for Hal, from Stanley Kubrick's 2001: A Space Odyssey, for a world in which the computers start acting on their own initiative, start talking back to us, or talking to one another in a language we cannot understand? Or, to bring us up to date, is our future found in Watson, the IBM computer that is supplementing everything we do with computer-assistance programs so powerful that we worry they will supplant us altogether?[13] Suppose the robots acquire hermeneutic skills? Does Hermes have a dark side? A 'messenger' in Greek is an *angelos*, but angels come both good and bad.

I will come back to this question at the end of the book under the figure of the post-human (Chapter 9).

The Roguish Hermeneutics of Vattimo and Rorty

What Gadamer had to say was put in a sober and elegant prose, and no one ever accused him of being a radical. But what he said could have radical and explosive consequences, and that shows up in two very postmodern, positively roguish figures who enjoyed playing the role of Hermes the prankster to their respective Apollos. I refer to the Italian philosopher Gianni Vattimo (1936–) and the American Richard Rorty (1931–2007). They linked up Gadamer's rendering of conversation and the ubiquity of interpretation with some unlikely characters – American pragmatism (John Dewey) and Nietzsche's acerbic critique of the Western Christian tradition. The result might be thought of as two distinctively postmodern versions of Gadamer's *Truth and Method*, each much more sceptical, more ironic, about *both* truth *and* method.

Vattimo: Hermeneutics as Weak Thought

For Vattimo, who studied with Gadamer in Heidelberg, hermeneutics takes the form of what he calls 'weak thought' (*pensiero debole*),[1] an idea he draws from a reading of the 'history of nihilism' in Nietzsche and Heidegger. Vattimo says that hermeneutics is *nihilism* and, alarming as that may sound, whenever we go astray in the postmodern world it is because we fail to be nihilistic enough. So, clearly, everything depends upon what he means by 'nihilism'.

Nietzsche and the History of Nihilism

Vattimo's notion of interpretation is influenced by Nietzsche, who struck the most extreme position that has ever been taken about interpretation when he claimed that there are no facts, only interpretation, and – before you ask – admitted that this, too, is an interpretation.[2] Each of us has an interpretation, a perspective on life, Nietzsche said, but these perspectives are judged not by their truth but solely by their value for life. Perspectives are not true or false, but weak or strong, life-affirming or life-denying, and that goes for his own perspective, which Nietzsche thought was the healthiest and strongest of all. Nihilism for Nietzsche meant a decline in life-force. Our values – in which our vitality is writ large – have become nothing. That, for him, was a good thing which he encouraged under the name of 'active' nihilism. He meant that our Christian-Platonic values, where the worth of life is ultimately placed in the afterlife, and the meaning of virtue is found in slavish meekness before the demands of life, are life-denying. In Christian Europe in the second half of the nineteenth century, we have begun to realize this inner rot. Well, Nietzsche realizes it, but he is ahead of his time in bearing this message, though gradually, in the next century, everyone will see it, too.

God is Dead

The history of nihilism is summarized in the most famous thing Nietzsche ever wrote, 'God is dead . . . And we have killed him.'[3] Notice that he does not say, 'God does not exist', or 'There is no God.' Nietzsche disavows making metaphysical statements about the nature of ultimate reality. He is saying that God is a fictitious perspective. But you can't hold that against God. So is everything else. What matters is that this fiction, which once served the purposes of the aristocracy in keeping the masses in line, has become the enemy of life because the masses are now getting out of line. The Platonic-Christian tradition is a decayed and corrupt will to power, a longing for escape from the turmoil of space and time. The death of God refers to the cultural-historical life of Europe, which he thinks is moribund – a society of superficial 'mass man', of comfort-loving bourgeoisie – exactly the same diagnosis Kierkegaard made under the name of 'Christendom'. Kierkegaard and Nietzsche agree: when Christian Europe calls itself Christian, that rings hollow. Europeans seek a comfortable existence, evading the need to act or think in a decisive way. They proposed the same solution, reinvigorating the passion of life, but this they located in decidedly different places. Kierkegaard wanted to restore the passionate faith of the early martyrs, of primitive Christianity. Nietzsche, on the other hand, saw the antidote in paganism, in the tragic spirit of the early (pre-Socratic) Greek experience of life, which looked the human condition in the eye, gritted its teeth, and said yes to life, warts and all, in all its tragic fury. What does not kill me makes me stronger (he also wrote that).

Weak Thought

Vattimo gives another twist to the history of nihilism, one that is closer to Heidegger than to Nietzsche, and closer still to Gadamer. The history of nihilism is hailed as our emancipation from the violence of metaphysics.[4] This Vattimo takes from Heidegger's critique of the history of metaphysics as the history of the manhandling of Being, of subjecting Being to the wilful constructions of human thinking. This leads Vattimo to describe metaphysics as *strong* thinking, whose concepts grasp (from the Latin *con* + *capere*) the ultimate nature of reality and lay claim to objective truth. That poses a mortal threat to anyone who disagrees. Absolute Truth tends to discourage debate. Once you conclude that the ideas that you have inside your head come from God or Nature or Pure Reason, once you think you are hard-wired to Absolute Truth so that your views do not simply represent your perspective, then the rest of us are in trouble. Vattimo's signature concept, his way to describe nihilism, is to call it the history of the *weakening* of these structures, of their becoming-nothing, their becoming unbelievable, which, for him, is an emancipatory development.

The name of this weakening is hermeneutics, that is, the displacement of objective-absolutizing thinking by interpretation.[5] For Vattimo, the postmodern age is the 'age of interpretation',[6] and hermeneutics is the post-metaphysical, post-modern philosophy par excellence. Vattimo does not try to prove his position directly for two reasons. First, because, as Lyotard says, in the postmodern era metaphysics has become unbelievable and we have become 'incredulous' towards its 'big stories'. Vattimo does not have to defeat the opposition; the opposition is just making itself unbelievable, which leaves hermeneutics as the last man standing. Second, as Nietzsche said, this assertion about the ubiquity of inter-pretation does not claim to be the objective truth, and does not pass itself off as another entry in the competition for the Big Story. It, too, is an interpretation. But Vattimo thinks it is the *best* interpretation – not because of its biological vital-ity (Nietzsche) or attunement to early Greek poetic thinking (Heidegger), but because it is the most *democratic* and ultim-ately the most non-violent, the most Christian, the most *loving* thing one can say. In hermeneutics, we do not out-argue, we out-narrate; we tell a better story.

Four Forms of Weakening

The weakening of metaphysics (strong thinking) into her-meneutics (weak thinking) occurs on four levels. First, as we have been saying, the strong claim to know the ultimate nature of reality (ontology, metaphysics) weakens into interpretations. Second, strong thinking claims to provide a 'theory of knowledge' (epistemology), which sets forth the 'method of attaining truth', which can ensure the certitude and clarity of our knowledge (think of Descartes). Post-modernists greet such extravagant claims with a yawn and are much more sensitive to the messy ways in which knowledge is actually acquired. Today, epistemology has weakened into (Gadamerian) conversation in which the partners to a dialogue bring their several perspectives to the table in the hopes of hammering something out, by hook or by crook. So, Vattimo unmoors conversation from metaphysics – it was the instrument of Platonic 'recollection' – and gives it a completely hermeneutical meaning.

Third, metaphysics comes equipped with ethical principles which provide us with a guide to conduct. In ethics, good and evil are black and white; principles are universal and unchanging; and anyone who disagrees is branded an ethical relativist. More postmodern yawns. In a time of advanced communication and transportation systems, we have a sharper appreciation of local differences and of a radical plurality of ways to be human. So, we are of a more radically Aristotelian frame of mind and hence suspicious of the arrogance of principles. For postmodernists, principles must be weakened into a more pliable, plastic practical wisdom, making judgements cut to fit the idiosyncrasies of the particular situation.

Fourth, classical metaphysics is prone to announce powerful political principles which are meant to organize society and to bend history to their purposes – like the classless society or the glory of the *Volk* – which usually end up spilling a great deal of blood. To this, hermeneutics offers the messy processes of democracy, in which the assumption is made that nobody knows the Big Story but everybody has a perspective. Nobody holds the power by divine right or right of birth, everybody has a say, and the power is to be divided up as widely as possible. If hermeneutics was tied in with National Socialism in Heidegger, it here turns up as democracy.

Seeing their strong metaphysical principles weaken into contextual hermeneutic judgements, the more conservative among us look up to heaven for help. Is this not the road to relativism? they ask. No, it is the age of interpretation. True, that is a risky business – like trapeze artists performing without a net – but it is not nearly as dangerous as the alternative. After all, when religions persecute heretics, when Hitler, Stalin, Mao and other 'strong men' murdered millions of people, when nationalism and racism, homophobia and sexism rage, the problem is not that these people are relativists. The problem is absolutism. The problem is the confusion of an interpretation with a truth that has been handed down from on high. Hermeneutics is a risky business, but it has the best chance to keep us safe.

After Christianity

For Vattimo, hermeneutics is the best alternative because it is the most loving. Just or democratic we can understand; that is how philosophers usually talk. But shouldn't he leave love to the theologians? Vattimo thinks that hermeneutics, interpretation, weak thought, is ultimately the issue of the Christian God of love and Jesus's gospel of loving our neighbour. Of course, God is dead and Christianity has become unbelievable – as a *strong theology*, a Big Story, as the One True Holy Catholic and Apostolic Church. Vattimo grew up as a daily communicant (daily Mass and Holy Communion) Italian Catholic. But a gay one. So, he suffered deeply from the Church's reactionary attitude to same-sex relationships and to sexual matters generally. That interpretation of

Christianity – as an absolute truth delivered to us by God, where the Church is the earthly vicar of a God-man – is dead, a victim of the history of nihilism, and good riddance. Thank God I am an atheist, Vattimo likes to say.[7]

After that Christianity comes another, postmodern Christianity, not as dogmatic truth but as a *message*, as a story, like a great novel or poem.[8] Christianity withers away as a powerful institution with fixed doctrines (and even once with an army to enforce it against the infidels). It weakens *into* the secular institutions of the modern democracies, which respect the dignity of the individual. Democratic institutions are the secularized residue of the Christian doctrine of the people of God, of the friends of God, the brothers and sisters of Christ. The process of weakening shows up in St Paul's *kenosis* (Phil. 2:7), where God 'empties' out or weakens into the world. Secularization is the incarnation or consolidation of Christianity into the world. The transcendent God and his Church are dead, but they have acquired new life in the secular European order. The secularization of Christianity is not the destruction of Christianity but its *deconstruction*, its reinvention, or re-actualization, in the world, in the age of interpretation. Modern democratic institutions – Vattimo was twice elected to the European Parliament – are the political enactment of the gospel of love, what has become of God, what God has become, today.

At this point, Vattimo sounds like Hegel on the Absolute Spirit (*Geist*), in which the transcendent God of the Jews abdicates his transcendence and comes down to earth as the Christian Spirit-in-the-world. But, for Vattimo, the Absolute Spirit has hit the earth with an even greater thud, since

Hegel's Spirit is still a very strong metaphysical concept. In Vattimo, the Spirit has become a Gadamerian conversation. Heidegger's Being weakens into language, which weakens into conversation. But this is a conversation not of an exotic Graeco-German poet-thinker communing with Being but of actual concrete human beings in democratic society. People bring their own perspective, are willing to put their presuppositions into question, with the hope of learning something from one another. In the beginning was the Logos, but in the end, the Logos has become human dialogue.

Rorty's Yankee Hermeneutics

Meanwhile, back in the United States, the Absolute Spirit of Hegel was busy becoming 'the conversation of mankind', which is the way it is described in the major work of Richard Rorty, whom I take as the most interesting American philosopher of the second half of the twentieth century.[9] Rorty plays Hermes the prankster to the Apollo of analytic philosophy, the establishment Anglo-American discourse which looks upon Nietzsche, Heidegger and Derrida as an unholy trinity of witch doctors and dangerous relativists. Rorty held a prestigious chair at Princeton, a citadel of analytic philosophy, and in his early years appeared to be perfectly at home there. I invited him to speak at Villanova University back in the 1970s and afterwards at dinner remarked, half in jest, that his critique of metaphysics sounded to me like Heidegger – to which he replied that that is where he got it. We all laughed, but that proved to be quite true, not just a bit of dinner-time banter, as I thought at the time. It earned him such disapproval among the college of analytic philosopher-cardinals – similar to Vattimo, Rorty had a powerful Church to deal with – that he eventually moved on to Stanford as a professor of humanities (read: *not* the philosophy department).

IDEAS ARE NOT THE MIRROR OF NATURE

Rorty's heresies were twofold. Not only was he dabbling in the black magic of continental philosophy, but he also went back to the classic American philosophy of pragmatism embodied in the work of William James (Harvard) and especially John Dewey (Columbia), a native New England American philosophical movement which was all but wiped out by the imported British (old England) analytic movement. Dewey and James were well-known, influential public intellectuals but, under the influence of the analysts, American philosophy had been shrunk down to a body of technical article-length studies completely unreadable by, and of no interest to, a wider public.[10]

Rorty had a deep-down suspicion of anything high-blown. He thought the history of philosophy was full of extravagant vocabularies that admitted of simpler explanations, which he would render with a dead-pan humour and a dead-on ear for the idioms and cadence of American English. When I once criticized his interpretation of Heidegger as selective, as neglecting what Heidegger was really saying about the History of Being, he replied by thanking me – not the usual way philosophers of any flavour react to criticism – for pointing out what was 'upbeat' (the part he could use) and what was 'downbeat' in Heidegger, namely, the extravagant utterances about Being, the part he couldn't use.

He saw an affinity between Nietzsche's claim that the idea of truth should be replaced with usefulness for life, and American pragmatism, where, for Rorty, it is replaced with the notion of successful speech acts. We say a belief is true if it is getting the job done, and by calling it true we aren't adding anything to that, except a compliment. 'True' is the praise we heap upon a belief that is paying its own way, a belief that works, but 'true' doesn't do any work itself. We don't have to get worked up about a successful belief and go on to say uncalled-for things like declaring it objectively true, or insisting that it represents reality or mirrors what is 'out there'. All that is unnecessary rhetorical baggage, clutter that gets nothing accomplished other than to antagonize other people who might have other views.

Non-foundationalism

So, Rorty's position is resolutely 'anti-essentialist' or 'anti-realist'; he does not think our nouns are picking out essences in the real world, which he regards as completely unnecessary hype. Our nouns are successful acts of naming, not mirror reflections of True Being, in just the way that knowing someone's proper name facilitates conversation and interaction but does not expose their soul to public view. To say a statement represents a fact just means that holding that belief *works*. Rorty's views are non-foundationalist, that is, he thinks our ordinary, natural, everyday life can conduct its own affairs, thank you very much, and it does not require special intervention from on high by the philosophers to supply some transcendental or metaphysical back-up and to declare it grounded. Nor is philosophy a higher tribunal to which the particular disciplines appeal when disputes break out among them. In science, as in life, he thinks we go with what works until it doesn't, and then we fix it.

Philosophy is a Form of Writing

Philosophy, then, is just a form of writing. It is not a special Method, which provides the way to attain the Truth and separate it from mere Opinion. A lot of philosophy is really just describing what we like to do when we are off the clock, in the privacy of our homes, after hours and at weekends. There, we should be free to redescribe ourselves as 'poor existing individuals', or 'being-in-the-world', or as getting in touch with the ground of being – or whatever gives us a sense of personal satisfaction. So, good philosophy is just as often found in literature and other works of art. Philosophers themselves are geniuses of imagination, people who invent highly creative vocabularies to redescribe the various ways to live our lives. That also goes for religion. The only limit here is to keep this stuff out of the public sphere, that is, not to treat our private self-descriptions as normative for anyone else. Unlike most postmodernists, Rorty has a strong (modernist) public/private distinction. So, a lot of good philosophy consists in making fun of philosophy when it becomes pretentious, as it does in metaphysics, which is why he greatly admires the wicked wit of Kierkegaard, Nietzsche and Derrida.

A belief is enhanced by consensus, when everyone agrees about its success, and that comes by way of a conversation conducted within circles of people who share enough in common to reach agreement and to understand why and where there is room for disagreement. So, instead of declaring Truth or Objectivity, let's just speak of conversation in which we have reached inter-subjective agreement and let it go at that. Like Vattimo, Rorty avoids valourizing the idea of the 'other' – this is one of their common disagreements with Derrida and French postmodernists – and favours widening the circle of the same to include as many different points of view as possible. Eventually, what looks alien and other ends up in the circle of the same, of what we all have in common.

Contingency, Irony and Solidarity

The title of one of his most important books, *Contingency, Irony and Solidarity*, condenses a very great deal of Rorty's thought.[11] The beliefs we hold are contingent upon an accident of birth, which puts a particular language on our tongue, certain ideas in our head and particular books in the libraries we visit. Appreciating the contingency of our birth and beliefs implies holding them with a certain irony, with just enough diffidence and distance to keep them revisable while also treating them as the tools we have been given. We hope for solidarity, sharpening the sense that we are all in this together, which should, accordingly, imply treating each other with compassion. Solidarity and compassion are not based on a divine command or an argument of pure reason; indeed, it reflects poorly on you if you need such back-ups in order to be motivated to be compassionate. But there is room for persuasion. We can use conversation to make being cruel and merciless look bad and being compassionate look good. We would all profit if we knew more about one another, could see what was compassionate and what was cruel in others, and could each learn from each other.

The Collaboration of Vattimo and Rorty

Setting up a framework in which contingent and ironically held beliefs and differences of opinion get hammered out by conversation, comparisons and persuasion, not by violence, is pretty much what we mean by democracy. Democracy is not an Eternal Truth, capitalized and in the singular, but the least bad idea anybody has come up with so far. Rorty is a classic, paradigmatic American liberal, who was, in particular, worried about the declining American labour movement. In November 2016, two weeks after the American presidential election, a remark Rorty made in a 1998 book hit the internet.[12] In the book, he complains about the growing gap between the working class and leftist intellectuals too preoccupied with identity politics, and he predicts the election of a right-wing 'strongman' – enter Donald Trump – who will be elected by neglected blue-collar workers sick of having their manners corrected by postmodern professors and will undo all the gains made by the left in the past forty years. The remark went viral and the book had sold out by the end of the day. When Rorty came upon Gadamer,[13] and later on Vattimo, he was struck by the resonances. A lot of what he was saying as a pragmatist was also to be found in what Heidegger and Gadamer called hermeneutics, and what

Heidegger and Derrida called deconstruction of the metaphysics of presence. Their vocabularies were extremely odd, he thought, but the point was pretty much the same, that is, each seems to be saying that beliefs are successful interpretations. This ultimately led to a collaboration between Vattimo and Rorty in the latter part of their lives. In 1989, at a centennial celebration of Heidegger's birth, Hubert Dreyfus invited them both to be speakers, as was I, and I still remember seeing them huddled together at lunch, having a conversation none of us would dare interrupt.

This collaboration issued in a little book entitled *The Future of Religion*, in which Rorty, a lifelong atheist and secularist, was brought around to saying nice things about religion – provided that, by religion, you mean what Vattimo meant. He never came round to believing in God, but he did conclude that atheism is a far too metaphysical and dogmatic (strong) position to hold. So, he redescribed himself as anticlerical, that is, opposed to the efforts of those who attempt to make their private religious beliefs into public policy for the rest of us. Religion, too, is not an essence but a vocabulary, and, if it is explained the way Vattimo explains it, as having weakened into compassionate secular institutions, it can provide a useful vocabulary for a democratic society. Rorty still prefers the vocabulary of the Enlightenment and the American founders, which is all right with Vattimo, because Vattimo thinks that, too, is the offspring of Christianity.

In sum, in Vattimo and Rorty, hermeneutics means a call for conversation, to sit down and talk, to work things out, in a spirit of democratic exchange, of give and take, putting our own presuppositions into question, while putting in our own two hermeneutic cents, all within the framework of a pluralistic postmodern life.

At this point, we have a good sampling of the constellation of the radical thinkers who have forged the main lines of postmodern hermeneutics. From here on in, our time will be better spent watching contemporary hermeneutics at work, catching it in the act of interpretation, right in the midst of postmodern life. As Rorty would say, hermeneutics describes the way we make our way successfully around the world. So, in the chapters that follow, I will pick several success stories, several work-worlds, several forms of life – the law, the hospital, the university, the information age, religion – in order to see the workings of hermeneutics in the concrete.

The Call of Justice and the Short Arm of the Law

In 1989, Drucilla Cornell, one of the leading political and legal theorists and feminist philosophers in the United States, convened a conference at Cardozo Law School, where she was then professor of law.[1] Unlike many law schools, which train their students to defend the rich against the poor, Cardozo is a magnet for radical legal theory and its students are more likely to become public defenders of the poor against the upper 1 per cent, a radical idea first put forward by the Jewish prophets (profits versus prophets). Cardozo, the law school attached to Yeshiva University, is located in the Greenwich Village section of New York City, adjacent to the New School of Social Research, which was founded back in the 1930s by Jewish intellectuals in flight from Nazi Germany. The New School numbered Hannah Arendt, Theodor Adorno and Max Horkheimer among its faculty, and Derrida had an appointment there in the 1980s and 90s as a visiting professor. He loved coming to New York every autumn, and Drucilla Cornell was a good friend and supporter. The topic of the conference Cornell announced was 'Deconstruction and the Possibility of Justice'. Over the years, Derrida had acquired a reputation – quite unjustly, if I may say so – as a literary theorist and aesthete who enjoyed playing with alternate readings of arcane texts while the real world was going up in flames all around him. So, the idea was to bring Jacques Derrida before the faculty and law students at Cardozo, where the cause of social justice is uppermost in everyone's mind, to respond to the question, 'What does deconstruction have to do with justice?'

New Directions

The lecture Derrida gave was a shocker. It was a threshold statement marking off the new direction Derrida's work would take in the last two decades of his life. If you think I am about to say this is all like the radical shift in the 'later' Heidegger's work announced in his *Letter on Humanism*, think again. Contrary to Heidegger, Derrida's underlying assumptions had not changed at all. The most fundamental concern of Derrida is with the distinction between the programmable, the foreseeable effect, the predictable result, which confines our beliefs and practices within parameters set in advance, which normalizes and regulates; and the non-programmable, the unforeseeable, the marginal, the outsider, which allows for the eruption of something new, of the surprise, the fortuitous, the coming of what we did not see coming. For him, that distinction remained a constant.

But the lecture does signal a new emphasis on Derrida's part on the practical matters of ethics, politics and religion; matters which, as he points out, had interested him all his life and had been addressed in various ways in the past.[2] We saw the political significance he attached to the classical distinction between the living spirit (Christians) and the dead letter (Jews). *Of Grammatology* is itself a deconstruction of Rousseau's dreamy distinction between a supposedly pure nature (natural law) and a corrupting culture (positive law). But Cornell had shifted the perspective. She was asking, 'What does the deconstruction of the law mean relative not to nature but to *justice*?' From here on in, Derrida was going to give such matters more sustained attention in his seminars in Paris and his lectures around the world.

Is There Something Undeconstructible?

It was here, in his discussion of the law, which is deconstructible, that he said – to a very surprised audience – that justice is 'undeconstructible'. We were all convinced that there is no such thing as the undeconstructible, which sounded like some God or the eternal Platonic Idea, some imperishable being or substance, which would be very foreign to Derrida's thought. Whatever has come to be has been constructed, and whatever has been constructed is deconstructible. The undeconstructible does not exist, we all nodded in solemn agreement. If we were a Vatican consistory, we would have recommended that the Pope declare that an infallible teaching. We were that sure.

True, there is nothing undeconstructible, but – here is what we did not see coming, what we did not expect Derrida to say – that does not mean there is nothing to it. The undeconstructible does not exist. Of course it does not exist! So what? This nothing is telling us something. The undeconstructible does not have the power, prestige and presence of reality. So what? It has instead the power of a weak force, like the power of a ghost. Ask Scrooge or Hamlet if they think that their ghosts amounted to nothing at all. The ghost is a felicitous figure of the interpretive imperative – not an Imperious Voice but a spectre we are not even sure is there – which Derrida used at greater length a few years later in *Specters of Marx* to spook, to spoof the Reaganite–Thatcherite euphoria following the collapse of the old USSR in which Marxism was declared dead as a doornail.[3]

So, Derrida would address the question of the law, and address this audience of serious, action-oriented law professors and students, people with the harsh reality of injustice on their minds, by speaking of justice as the ghost of something undeconstructible. Justice does not exist. Justice is always coming, always promised, but it never quite arrives, not as such. What does exist is the law, and the fearsome assembly of institutions – courts, police, jails – which enforces the law. These existing things are more or less just, which also means they are more or less unjust, but justice *as such*, justice in itself, if there is such a thing (*s'il y en a*) – and how could there be? – does not exist. This was spooky talk.

Like a Messiah Who Never Shows Up

Justice, he would explain, is not a matter of a bricks-and-mortar courthouse but of a more immaterial call. Justice is a hermeneutic call for action, not a Categorical Imperative but a softer sigh, a gentler lilt, like the quiet whisper of 'perhaps'.

Justice is not a Graeco-German Call of Being, not a Supreme Being (God) or a Pure Form (Plato) demanding things with the roar of a king. Justice is a kind of may-being (*peut-être*), which disturbs us night and day, like the ghost of a hope, like a promise that keeps the future open, or like the memory of the dead. To the real and sometimes bloody force of law, Derrida opposes the spectre of a justice to come, the promise of a coming justice.

It had been some time since Derrida had 'practised' his religion. Still, this all sounds so messianic, like the Jewish religion of his childhood coming back to haunt him, like a ghost, a *revenant*, like something 'come back' from the grave. But justice is also an *arrivant*, something coming, like a messiah who is coming but never shows up. This would have had a familiar ring to the Jewish traditions of Yeshiva and the New School – but the more secular deconstructors in the audience were starting to squirm in their seats. The whole idea seemed too theological, too Platonic, too Idealist, almost other-worldly, and nothing like what we had come to expect from him. We were used to hearing him explain how deconstructible, how contingent, how revisable and repealable things are; we had never heard him speak of something that could resist deconstruction. Was he succumbing in his later years to his own version of Absolute Truth?

Hauntological Hermeneutics

I was once invited to give a workshop introducing the faculty of a small college to deconstruction. When I began by saying that I had chosen this lecture by Derrida for them to read in advance because of its clarity, the whole room instantly erupted in laughter. They evidently did not find Derrida's avant-garde style to be all that clear. Maybe I should have just said it contains some of his best lines. In any case, the innovation of the lecture, the undeconstructible, leads straight to the most helpful formulation of what Derrida is up to – a kind of deconstructive, or postmodern, hermeneutics – to be found anywhere in his work.

But this is here described as a spectral operation, as a hauntological hermeneutics, an imperative that pays a visit on us like a ghost in the night, and what requires more interpretive skill, what demands more of our powers of discernment, than communicating with a ghost? What demands more *subtilitas* than a conversation with the subtle substance of a spectre? How much trouble does Hamlet have trying to discern what the ghost of his father is asking of him? How difficult is it to read between the lines of the real to find the insinuations of the unreal? In that sense, hermeneutics is always and necessarily hauntological, and never ontological; it is always hearing ghosts, while the ontologists, the ontologicians, are content to explore the stable substance of the real.

Now, in the interests of full disclosure, I have to confess that there is no mention whatsoever of the word 'hermeneutics' in Derrida's lecture, not one. So what? We are not bound by the author's intentions. And we have just seen that the fact something does not exist is no objection to its insinuating hyper-reality. The word does not appear, but the whole lecture is haunted by hermeneutic apparitions. That is what hermeneutics does, unearthing what is hidden, making clear what is obscure, explicating what is implicit, interpreting what has hitherto merely been described.

Justice is (the) Impossible

Derrida does, however, several times mention the word 'interpretation'. The question is how to interpret the law in the light, or under the call, of justice. Derrida never ceases to *practise* hermeneutics, and never more clearly than when he addresses what he called in this lecture the 'aporias' of the law, which we will examine below. An aporia literally means 'no way to go' (*a* + *poras*) – no entrance and no exit, no way forward and no way back. The aporia provides an exquisite model for Derrida, and a deliciously paradoxical imperative or double bind: go where it is impossible to go! *The thing that makes the practice of the law possible is that it is impossible.*

No doubt the lawyers drew little consolation from this point, but the man was famous so they heard him out. The point is general: the condition that makes it *impossible* to move – to act or to think, to make or to imagine, to do theory or to practise – is just what makes it *possible* to be really on the move, to make our best moves in art or science or every-day life. Anything short of that is just running on automatic pilot, letting the collision-avoidance system take over the wheel of the car, just drifting, our oars in the boat. Anything short of the possibility of the impossible represents a kind of commonplace possibility, the stuff of a safety-first hermen-eutics and a tepid, non-alcoholic deconstruction, a kind of deconstruction lite. It sticks to the safe side of Hermes deliv-ering the post, and takes flight from the prankster. So, if

Drucilla Cornell asks Derrida about the possibility of justice, Derrida replies that justice is possible just when the situation for justice is impossible.

What gives interpretation a cutting edge, the thing that triggers hermeneutical intervention, is the *undeconstructible*, which is *the impossible*.[4]

It is *the* impossible that sets the tensions of the hermeneutic situation to their greatest intensity. The hermeneutic situation par excellence is the double bind in which we find ourselves; our ultimate possibility (*posse*) and power (*potens*) are a function of being in an impossible situation.

One might object that this is all going nowhere. So far it sounds like this:

THE LAWYERS: Let's be practical.

DERRIDA: That's what I am doing.

THE LAWYERS: What difference does all this make when it comes to the real world, to the injustice outside the law-school doors?

DERRIDA: Everything.

THE LAWYERS: But what are we supposed to do?

DERRIDA: Do the impossible.

So, there is more work to do. The lawyers are not smiling.

Abraham and Isaac: Paradox or Paradigm?

At the risk of making things even worse, Derrida introduces a famous example of doing the impossible: the command God gave to Abraham to sacrifice his son Isaac to God, to make the impossible choice between a command from God on high and the love of his son Isaac, in one of the foundational stories of Western religion, the double bind in the 'binding of Isaac' (Genesis 22:1–19). This story was a paradigm for Kierkegaard's idea of the leap of faith, and it was through Kierkegaard's interpretation that it made its way to contemporary continental thought.[5] (Jewish interpreters like Emmanuel Levinas have a different interpretation, almost perfectly contrary to Kierkegaard's.) Abraham was asked to make an existential decision, one with a very sharp cutting edge, a word which literally means to 'cut off' – from *de* + *cidere* in Latin – the other alternatives. When Abraham was about to execute his decision, he was stopped by the angel of the Lord (the state-of-the-art instant-message system available to the Most High in those days).

But it seems ill advised in the extreme to bring up this story to a bunch of lawyers as a model for understanding the law, especially ones dedicated to protecting the weak against the strong. The sacrifice of an innocent child by a highly uncommunicative father who has been hearing voices? Even if he did not actually go through with it, the lawyers are all thinking, surely the man is guilty of attempted murder, or at the very least of reckless endangerment – unless, of course, he is *non compos mentis*. Was Abraham mad? Kant, who was a Knight not of Faith but of Pure Reason, concluded that Abraham should have asked a few more questions before proceeding up the mountain intending to violate the law.

So, here we are, interpreting Derrida's interpretation of Kierkegaard's interpretation (of Luther's interpretation of Paul's interpretation) of Abraham's interpretation of his voices in Genesis 22. A multistrata hermeneutical complex, stacked four storeys high – this is what Gadamer calls the 'history of effects', seeing something through the lens of a long history of which we ourselves are a part. To this, the biblical historians add still another stratum: did this episode even occur? Or is it a piece of religious-literary imagination? Suppose Abraham never existed? So what? Lots of things do not exist, but that doesn't mean there's nothing to them.

How was Abraham to choose between his pure duty to God and his love of his son? Or between his love of God and his love of his son? Or between his love of God and his duty to his son? Or between his duty to God and his duty to his son? How are we to interpret the difference between duty and love, between a command and love? Can love be commanded?

The Paradox is a Paradigm

For Derrida, this famous Kierkegaardian paradox is the paradigm of what makes a real decision possible – as opposed to simply following the instructions on the label. That is exactly the problem that the law poses for us, according to Derrida. Although the lawyers must think this is an exceptional situation, and exceptions make for bad laws, Derrida thinks it is the universal condition under which justice is to be done. First there is a *law*, like the law that prohibits murder, doubly so in the case of your own child, and then there is the *slack* in the law – suppose someone, God, for example, steps in and suspends the law? What, then? So, Derrida interprets God, Abraham and Isaac as three *place-holders*: Isaac is the universal law: thou shalt not kill; God is the slack in the law, the exceptional circumstance, since the law never quite fits every situation; and Abraham, well, that is us, in the hot seat, called upon to decide, in the accusative. Justice occurs in the triangulation, which feels like a strangulation. Justice springs up in the slack in the law, and interpretation is called upon to deal with that slack, to inhabit the space which the law leaves open. The light of justice breaks through the cracks in the law. Because the law never quite fits, or only very loosely, or sometimes not at all. Life is lived not in the law but in the slack. Whatever their differences, Gadamer and Derrida were never closer than in these pages.

Deconstruction is Justice

But the lawyers, arms folded, brows wrinkled, are still not convinced. They need reassuring. Derrida begins, only half in jest, as if he were being ambushed, as if this were an inquisition, a torment.[6] Of course, it was not. He was among friends and admirers and Cornell was trying to provide a forum for him to refute a bad rap. But still, the question itself had the sound of a personal challenge. It was as if Cornell were asking, with a tone of scepticism or even sarcasm (which is believable if you have ever met Drucilla), *What can deconstruction possibly have to do with justice?* Is it not irresponsible to talk about the deconstruction of the law, when there is so much violence and suffering and injustice in the world?

Derrida's response was shocking: deconstruction *is* justice, he said. In French, this was a play on words: *est* and *et* are homonyms. So, he had taken the theme of the conference, *déconstruction et justice* (deconstruction and justice), and made it read *déconstruction est justice* (deconstruction is justice). This was scandalous, and Derrida knew it. As Derrida said, it shocks 'not only the determined adversaries of said deconstruction or of what they imagine under this name' – they think deconstruction is anarchy, not justice – 'but also the very people who pass for or take themselves to be its partisans or its practitioners'.[7] To the latter, this sounded much too much like the soaring idealism of Plato's *Republic* or, worse still, maybe even downright religious. They did not know what to think. The Derrida they knew did not talk like this.

Should versus Must

Derrida's immediate point of departure is a saying of Pascale in the *Pensées*:

> Justice, Force – It is right (*juste*) that what is just should be followed; it is necessary that what is strongest should be followed.[8]

We *should* be just; we *should* do what is right. But we *must* do, we are compelled to do, what is stronger than us. Taken in and of themselves, justice and force belong to two different orders. The law belongs to the order of force; it compels us under threat of punishment. The law has police, guns, courts, jails, execution chambers, whether it is just or not. But justice of itself, which is but a call, lacks all of that, is of another order; it is without real force. Of course, we want to keep justice and the law joined together, because the law without justice is a tyrant and justice without force is impotent. Justice has (is) an appeal, but the law has force. 'And thus,' Pascale concludes, 'being unable to make what is just strong, we have to make what is strong just.' We cannot make justice strong, because justice is an appeal, not a being; a should, not a must; an ought-to-be, not an is. It is an imperative, a solicitation, like the voice of conscience, not a thing, with mass and weight. It is like a ghost. So, the only alternative is to make what is strong just, to take what is real, the law, and to make the whole institutional apparatus that supports and enforces it just. We can make just laws, even as we cannot make justice into a being that compels us to do what is right.

Mystical Authority

The law is a historical construction, which may or may not be just. In fact, to a great extent, the force of law is the result of the fact that it has been constructed. The law has force because it exists, because it happens to be the law and has been for as long as we can remember; in other words, because of custom. The force of law is the force of custom. That gives it what Pascale (following Montaigne) calls a 'mystical authority', where 'mystical' means something like 'magical', like a cartoon character who walks off a cliff but does not fall until he looks down and notices that nothing is holding him up. The law can be like that. The law holds up as long as we don't look down and don't ask what holds it up, which might be nothing more than the fact that it is and has been the law. The *origin* of the law might be just that, that someone seizes the moment and asserts authority and others fall in line. Someone, in the beginning, declares, this is the law. (Or: we are independent of the mad king back in old England.) The origin of the law, the instituting, founding moment, is by definition beyond the opposition of legal and illegal, since in the act of founding the law there was no pre-existing law to obey or break. (Abraham, by the way, if there was one, lived long before the establishment of the Torah.) Its origin is an 'interpretive violence',[9] that is, a hermeneutic violence which acquires a real violence, in which the law is proclaimed *as* the law. We credit the law with authority, like money without a gold or silver standard to back it up. The force of law, like the value of money, is sustained by the common consent to accept its value, to 'believe' (*credere*) in its value, like giving the currency *credit*. What if, for whatever reason, everyone stopped believing in the value of a currency, or in the laws of the land?

The Undeconstructibility of Justice

To get to the crux of Derrida's point: the law, inasmuch as it has been constructed, historically founded and instituted, is always and in principle deconstructible. But that is not bad news, because that is the very basis for the reform of the law. Whatever has been constructed can be *de*constructed and *re*constructed – which does not, however, go for 'justice in itself'. We deconstruct the law in the name of justice, which calls for just laws, even as no law is ever up to what justice calls for. Together, the deconstructibility of the law and the undeconstructibility of justice go hand in hand to make up deconstruction:

It is this deconstructible structure of the law or, if you prefer, of justice as the law, that also ensures the possibility of deconstruction. Justice in itself, if such a thing exists, outside or beyond law, is not deconstructible . . . *Deconstruction is justice.*[10]

The imperative of justice puts pressure on the laws, and the consequence of this is decisive:

Deconstruction takes place in the interval that separates the undeconstructibility of justice from the deconstructibility of law. Deconstruction is possible as an experience of the impossible, there where, even if it does not exist, if it is not *present*, not yet or never, there is (*il y a*) *justice.*[11]

Deconstruction takes place in the slack, in the distance between the two. Indeed, we live our daily lives in the distance between the two. We do what is possible in the light of the impossible, of which we are dreaming. We try to construct laws in the light of justice even as the white light of justice makes it plain that no law can ensure that justice will be done. Justice in itself, if there is such a thing – and there is not – is what is being called for. The deconstructibility of the laws arises from below, by being historically constructed, and from above, by yielding to the unrelenting pressure of justice, which does not exist but is always being called for, always coming. Justice does not exist, but 'there is' (*il y a*) justice, justice happens, not as a thing that is or exists, but as a call.

The Experience of the Impossible

So we may take it as a general feature of experience that:

(1) Whenever and wherever there is a construction – and when is there not? – there is deconstructibility.

(2) And whenever there is deconstructibility – and when is there not? – it is in virtue of what is *un*deconstructible, what is being called for, in that order.

The deconstructible and the undeconstructible go together. So, the call for justice, Derrida thinks, reveals a general feature of experience, of genuine experience. The multiple possibilities of life are laced with desires and dreams and demands – of the impossible. Everything important in life depends upon the possibility of the impossible, upon the paradoxical 'experience of the impossible'. On the one hand, to experience something is to traverse it, to cross over it, like taking a holiday in a foreign city; on the other hand, the impossible is precisely what we cannot traverse. Yet we must – because justice demands it. 'Justice is an experience of the impossible: a will, a desire, a demand for justice.'[12] And as with justice as an impossible thing that is always coming but never arrives, so with any X, be it a work of art, or a work of science, ethics or religion, whatever experience we undergo.

Incalculable, Unprogrammable

Furthermore, the law belongs to the order of calculation, while justice is an incalculable imperative. This means that the law is something like a machine that is meant to process cases – the law is like a program – but justice must be infinitely sensitive to the peculiarities and the idiosyncrasies of the singular situation, that is, it must be sought by means of the *subtilitas applicandi*, the right touch for the peculiarity of the case before it. So 'justice demands that one calculates with the incalculable', which means that 'the *decision* between just and unjust is never ensured by a rule'.[13] I am never assured of being just because I have followed a rule; the opposite might be the case. In the United States, the big corporations have influenced lawmakers to make the tax and financial laws favour their interests, with the terribly unjust result of excluding millions of middle-class and poor people from their just share of the wealth. But it is all perfectly legal.

In the language of *Of Grammatology*, there is no programming of justice, no more than there is a programming of language (structuralism). Justice, like language, is not a closed, calculable, programmable system but an open-ended call. But neither is justice (no more than language) an anarchic, antinomian, lawless anti-system. Just acts, like speech acts, take place in the distance between the calculable and the incalculable. It is never a matter of choosing between the rabbinic and the poetic, the Husserlian and the Joycean, the reproductive and the productive, but of inhabiting the space between them. Everything takes place in the interval between the two interpretations of interpretation.

Avoiding Responsibility

Now, the adversaries of deconstruction think that this is all a sophisticated attempt to evade responsibility. What better way to avoid our responsibility than to say that the rules are slack and that we must play it all by our hermeneutic ear? But, in fact, the opposite is the case. What better way to evade responsibility than to say, 'I am only following the rules'? 'I only work here. I do not make the rules.' That excuse is lame, even lethal, the one that was regularly invoked at Nuremberg. We cannot simply be responsible *to* a law, Derrida says, we must assume responsibility *for* it, be responsible for our responsibility. When we pound on the table and say, 'This is the law', we must confess that we are pounding in our interpretation. But we must take responsibility for our interpretation. Justice demands it. Justice asks that we ask where the law has come from, on what ground it stands, for we know – and justice demands that we know – the law is deconstructible. This requires a knowledge of the history of the law, of where it came from, under what circumstances, how it has evolved. That does not diminish but intensifies responsibility.[14]

The Three Aporias

So, after so many detours, Derrida says, let us directly address, 'without the least detour'[15] – he had been speaking for about an hour by then – three aporias (conundrums, double binds), which are really just three forms of the same aporia: the in/calculability of justice. He is joking around again, but again quite seriously. Derrida is here *doing* what he is *saying* – that justice cannot be addressed simply and directly, that it is difficult to discern, not as simple as following a rule. (The three aporias that follow could have been penned by Gadamer, they are that close here.)

1. THE EPOCHE OF THE RULE

Because a law ensures only legality, not justice, the judge and jury require *subtilitas*; they cannot simply, ham-fistedly, apply the law to the case. Indeed, they must treat it not as a case, as an instance of a universal, but as a unique and singular event, acting as if the law does not exist, suspending the application of the law – just long enough to make a fresh judgement:

> Each case is other, each decision is different and requires an absolutely unique interpretation.[16]

To suspend the law is to hold it in suspended animation, to leave it in temporary abeyance, so as to see this situation *as* it is in its *singularity*, not *as* a particular under a universal.

The aporia then is to treat the situation as both regulated and unregulated; the judge and jury do not abolish the rule, but they are not restricted to repeating the rule in a literal or univocal way. If they were, then we would not need them. All we would need is a kiosk, and the lawyers could key in the appropriate data, like passengers at the airport getting their boarding pass, and let the computer program process the case. We can never say that a law is just, and much less that a person is just, since justice always takes place in ever-changing and shifting circumstances of the singular situation. At best, we hope that justice has happened in a given act and can happen again – in the next case, which we cannot see coming. (While Derrida is speaking to American lawyers, he comes from France, where the Napoleonic Code is in effect, there is no rule of precedent and the judge has a lot more discretion.)

2. THE HAUNTING OF THE UNDECIDABLE

A decision is made in the impossible situation of the oscillation of conflicting demands (the double bind). This 'amounts to learning, reading, understanding, *interpreting* the rule'.[17] Undecidability means the oscillation between two rules – the rule of God (sacrifice your first-born son) versus the rule of law (the prohibition against murder). Or better, the oscillation between the calculable rule as such (the law) and the incalculable demand of justice, which exceeds the law as such. Every just decision must pass through this *ordeal*, the word Kierkegaard used to describe the test to which God submitted Abraham. Anything less, Derrida says, would not be free; 'it would be only the programmable application or the continuous unfolding of a calculable process. It might perhaps be legal; but it would not be just.' But the ordeal is never passed, over and done with; even after a decision is made, we are not sure if it was just. Time will tell; over the course of time, we may regret our decision. Good laws can go sour with the passage of time; they can even become a monster. A decision is always haunted by the spectre of undecidability, before, during and after; it can never be chased away. It always comes back, like a ghost.[18]

The idea of justice, Derrida adds, is 'infinite', which is not a reference to God, but to the unrelenting demands of justice, which are never met. I am always left partially guilty, having failed to give everything that is demanded of me, just the way I cannot feed everyone who is hungry.[19]

3. URGENCY

If we insist that the future is always open, that justice is always coming and hence always deferred, does that not suggest a kind of lassitude, simply waiting for a Messiah who never shows up? Or, even worse, a despair, lacking any hope that justice will take place? That is a common criticism of Derrida. Justice deferred is justice denied. When DNA evidence proves the innocence of a person imprisoned for the past twenty-five years, that is twenty-five years of ruined time; it cannot be repaired. Justice does not – cannot – wait for the Messiah or for advances in science. But far from contradicting Derrida's point, that is Derrida's point, his third point – the urgency of justice. Justice cannot wait. Derrida is not saying that we need to defer action until these aporias are resolved. He is pointing to the necessity to act under the constraints of the aporia, the necessity to bring deliberation to a halt and to act. There will always be more to deliberate, but the call of justice does not wait. We are not provided with 'infinite information and the unlimited knowledge of conditions, rules, or hypothetical imperatives that could justify' a decision.[20] There are times when we have all the information we need and we just have to decide.

'The moment of decision is a madness, says Kierkegaard.'[21] Justice is rendered like a gift given without reason, without there being anything in it for us. Justice is the madness of someone who puts its interests before their own. Deconstruction is that madness. It deploys that madness everywhere – in ethics, in the law, in politics, in hospitals and schools and counselling. So, if we demand that deconstruction be *practical*, its answer is to say that the most practical thing of all is mad, a madness for justice, for the impossible, for the undeconstructible.

So, we must act without guarantees, 'in the night of non-knowledge and nonrule, although we try to know as much as we can'.[22] Justice demands that, at some point, the urgency of the decision overrides any inclination to defer. This decision is not, however, pure 'decisionism', acting for the sake of acting regardless of the content of the decision. The moment of the decision is not only active but also passive or submissive, because I respond to the pressure of the other-in-me, to the call of justice that presses in upon me.

Promises, Promises

We might at this point be tempted to conclude that justice is an infinite *ideal* which can be only asymptotically realized in practice, but that is not quite right either. Justice is not an ideal essence but an imperative, an open-ended *call* to be brought to bear in particular and ever-shifting and unpredictable circumstances. There is no form or essence that we can foresee, no definition that we can hold up like a template, no idea or ideal which we can empirically approximate.[23] Remember that in hermeneutics things do not have an essence but a history. Justice means not just its actual history thus far because 'justice' is a word of elemental promise, of the unforeseeable future of what it is calling for.

In the first edition of this lecture, the version he read at Cardozo, Derrida said he hesitated therefore to call it a messianic promise, for fear that would tie it down to some determinate ideal which would constrain its open-endedness. In the later, revised version he did call it a messianic promise, but with some hesitation, which is that we do not restrict this promise to the Jewish Messiah, or the Christian one, or some philosophical equivalent like the Hegelian idea of the Spirit in history or Marx's dream of the classless society. In each case, we would be claiming to know what justice means and to know where the future must go. But we do not know what justice means, its definition or essence, because we do not know the future and do not know what it will come to mean, what it will have meant. To say that justice is a call is to describe the open-ended demand that the law remain flexible, plastic, pliable, reinventible, exposed to whatever is coming.

Perhaps

Derrida is distinguishing between two senses of the future. The first he calls the future present (using the French *futur*), the reasonably foreseeable future, without which, make no mistake, life would be pure chaos. This is to be distinguished from the 'absolute future', using the other French word for the future, *avenir*, the unforeseeable future, the 'to-come' (*à venir*). This 'absolute future' is something contained *in* politics and law that is not contained *by* politics and law, something which gives them their future and allows them to be continually reinvented and transformed. This interpretive excess means that 'perhaps' is built into the very idea of justice and of the interpretation of justice, and of any X that may be substituted for justice. The interpretive imperative comes in the gentlest of forms, not as an intimidating voice like the one that filled Abraham with fear and trembling but as the softest whisper of a perhaps. Perhaps belongs not to an ontology or onto-theology of being but to a hauntology of may-being (*peut-être*):

> 'Perhaps' – one must [*il faut*] always say *perhaps* for justice. There is an *avenir* for justice and there is no justice except to the degree that some event is possible which, as event, exceeds calculation, rules, programs, anticipations and so forth. Justice, as the experience of absolute alterity, is unpresentable, but it is the chance of the event and the condition of history. No doubt an unrecognizable history, of course, for those who believe they know what they are talking about when they use this word, whether it's a matter of social, ideological, political, juridical or some other history.[24]

This is risky business, of course, because we are exposed by this excess to the unforeseeable. We take what has proved itself in the past and put it at risk. So, we have to calculate. The unpredictability of what is coming is not meant to provide an alibi for not calculating the possible outcome. We have to 'negotiate the relation between the calculable and the incalculable'. We have to *interpret*, which means to negotiate the price (*inter* + *pretium*) between the two, but without the benefit of an algorithm that would guide us. This means that the familiar zones of 'morality, politics, or law', the 'national and the international, public and private' will likewise be exposed to continual reinvention. Every advance in freedom takes this form. He concludes with a list of issues which is as timely now as it was then – including abortion, euthanasia, organ transplant, extra-uterine conception, drugs, the military uses of science, homelessness and the treatment of animals. In the last two years of his teaching, the seminar topic was capital punishment.

So, let's get practical. The interpretive imperative is a call for action.

Gadamerian Nurses

'I Love Institutions'

In 1993, at the inaugural celebration of the new Ph.D. programme in philosophy at Villanova University, we held a round-table discussion with Derrida, the guest of honour for the occasion. I started by asking him whether this was not a strange thing for him to do, celebrating a new institutional programme. Is not deconstruction the enemy of institutions and programmes? Of course, I knew better, but I was, like Drucilla Cornell, giving him an opportunity to beat a bum rap. After a recitation of his life-long involvement in many institutional initiatives, creating new and innovative institutions in Paris, he added that, far from being an enemy of institutions, deconstruction is a philosophy *of* institutions, intent on keeping institutions open to the future. In this regard, he said, a roguish twinkle in his eye, a bit like Hermes, that he was a 'very conservative person', and we, like Apollo and Zeus, could only laugh, while knowing he was also being serious.[1]

An institution is truly conserved not by being conservative but by sustaining the tension between its memory of the past and an attempt to do something new. That is a risky business and liable to fail, like some of the initiatives in which Derrida was involved. A living institution attempts to devise programmes that produce new objects, that propose new projects, that think concepts hitherto unthought. A living institution programmes for the unprogrammable; it crosses borders and examines things that have no legitimacy in terms of the received standards of the day. 'I love institutions,' he added – especially ones that give him honorary degrees, he once quipped – and then he went on to say that the only thing that is dismantled in the deconstruction of institutions is the obstacles that they throw up against their own future, which is not a bad way to characterize the deconstruction of anything.[2]

There is Nothing Outside an Institution

The point here is that interpretation is not a free-floating, immaterial spirit. It is stubbornly stuck in the glue of institutional life, where its role is to agitate like an itchy Socrates or a devilish divinity. Institutions interpret, and institutions need to interpret themselves (their 'mission'). Interpretation is all about how to keep institutions open – hospitals, schools and universities, churches and museums, courts and political bodies – not just open for business but open to the future. Events do not take place in mid-air; they happen in institutional settings. There is almost nothing outside institutional contexts. Successful revolutions are simply an early stage in the formation of a new institution. So, everything depends upon how institutions interpret themselves and how institutions themselves interpret.

Events happen – as interventions on institutional conven-

tions, as disturbances of institutional inertia. Events happen –
in the law, in ethics and politics, in the market, in the classroom, in the hospital, among pastors and social workers,
whenever and wherever we are in William James's buzzing,
confusing world.

Gadamerian Nurses

A few years ago, I received an invitation to speak from the
Canadian Institute of Hermeneutics. While the name of the
association suggested another assembly of philosophers, my
comfort zone, it turned out that it was made up of nurses, both
practitioners and professors of nursing, as well as people working in the faculties of education, social work and psychology.
An institute of people teaching and working in the practising
professions all interested in hermeneutics? Hermeneutical
nurses, teachers, counsellors and social workers? Not my comfort zone. But what could be more obvious? Right from the
start, going back to the Pietist theologians who got it going,
hermeneutics has been considered practical knowledge. Old
Rambach, again, *subtilitas applicandi*, having the right touch, the
light touch of applying. The expression 'applied hermeneutics',
like 'biology of life', while useful to emphasize a point, is actually redundant – that's what biology *is*, no need to add 'life'.
That's what the art of interpretation *is* – application, practical
knowledge, concrete know-how. Academics are used to hearing
the complaint, 'That sounds good in theory, but how does it
work in practice?' But when it comes to hermeneutics, that is
upside down. The right question is, 'These are good practices,
but how do they work in theory?'

Gadamer wrote a book entitled *The Enigma of Health*.[3] He had lived into his one hundred and second year and evidently knew a thing or two about health as well as hermeneutics. So, my expectation was that I was going to hear a lot about that book from these nurses. But not so much. For one thing, Gadamer's book was more about health and less about the health-care professions, but for another, it made more mention of physicians than of nurses. As it turned out, these nurses were actually far more interested in *Truth and Method*, and I very quickly discovered they knew their Gadamer very well.

Illness Which is Understood is Language

The more I heard, the more it made perfect sense. Nurses occupy a delicate niche in the hierarchy of power in the health-care professions. They are the troops on the ground. The physicians make the big calls about the course of treatment; the nurses stay the course. They administer the pills, check the vitals, keep a daily, hourly vigil and take the time to talk to the patients. This last point is as vital as any vital sign. Conversation allows the patients to bring their experience of illness into words, to reach an understanding of what is going on, and so to make decisions about their own care. Illness which is understood is language, to adapt one of Gadamer's most famous sayings. Patients spend a good deal more time talking to their nurses than to their physicians and surgeons. The 'talking cure' is not restricted to psychoanalysis; every illness requires it. But this is conversation between human beings – not Heidegger's back and forth between poets and Being, and not a Freudian detective trying to detect clues of the unconscious in the crevices and corners of the discourse of the patient on the couch.

To give you an extreme example, one nurse told me a horror story about a physician who stopped by to inform a patient that the results of her tests were back. The tests revealed that her condition was terminal and he said he would have a member of his team come to see her later in the day to discuss palliative care. Then he left in a bit of a hurry. Busy man, busy day. The patient, shocked and hysterical, rushed out of the room in tears, shouting for her husband. But the nurses don't get to leave the patients to their demons. They are asked to 'nurse' (same root as 'nourish') the patients back to health, or, if they are not going to get better, to nurse them all the more in a hospice. Obviously, when health care is working well, the physicians have a great deal of nursing skill, even as the nurses have a considerable knowledge of medical science. But things do not always go well. That occasions 'difficult conversations', like the one they were going to have with this patient.

The Three Aporias of the Nurse

The nurses are situated *in medias res*, in the middle of things; less literally, in the soup. They occupy that most delicate of junctures, the hospital bedside, where a multitude of rules and regulations converges – the hospital's rules, medical insurance rules, the physician's instructions, federal laws concerning patients' rights and their own code of professional conduct. Talk about the force of law! The analogy is perfect: the relation of the well-being of the patient to these rules and regulations is like the relation of justice to the law. In fact, it is not merely *like* it – the patient's well-being *is* a call of the justice owed the patient. That transforms the job of nurse into a *vocation*, a calling, driven by a call of mercy, care, love. As one of them writes, 'pediatric oncology chose me'.[4]

That Derrida and Gadamer are on the same page here is clear from how perfectly Derrida's three aporias of the law are in play.

1. The suspension of the rule: 'Each case is other, each decision is different and requires an absolutely unique *interpretation* [my italics].'[5] That line from Derrida should be posted on the top of the chart of every patient in every hospital. The rule has to be lifted, held in mid-air, not abolished, for then there would be chaos, but given some slack, just long enough to see the singularity of this case. Every case requires a 'fresh judgement' of the situation of this patient, with this personal story, with this disease, not as if that disease were simply one thing which always meant the same thing.

2. The undecidable: the rules can easily conflict with each other, and a decision must be made about which rule to follow; add to that the deeper incommensurability of any calculable rule with the ruleless incalculability of this patient's life. In any given case, simply conforming to that rule would ensure a correct action, but not the care that is required. Obeying the rule would protect the nurse from the wrath of the attending physician, or protect both the nurse and the hospital from legal action. But the best way to do justice to

the patient might expose the nurse to the recriminations of the physician or the hospital or the law. Then the irresponsible thing to do is follow the rule and not assume responsibility *for* the rule we are following.

3. Urgency: the situation calls for action now. Care delayed is care denied. After all, hospitals are a place where an entire room is prepared in advance for emergency cases, which is pretty much what Derrida calls being prepared to be unprepared. What else is triage except emergency hermeneutics? What else is an emergency than an event?

The Hermeneutics of the Next Case

There is an interesting expression that recurs in *Conducting Hermeneutic Research*, a collection of studies by these professors and practitioners, in which the authors refer to the hermeneutics of the 'next case' – or the 'next patient' or the 'next practice' (the 'best practice' is the 'next practice').[6] A great deal of hermeneutics is condensed into this expression, and it is worth taking a closer look at it.

First, the *next*: medical practices are gradually accumulated skills acquired by experience, which Aristotle called 'habits', literally, what we 'have' (have acquired or picked up). Experience here means a complex of expectations that are sometimes confirmed and sometimes frustrated by the actual course experience takes. That requires what Aristotle called 'practical wisdom' (*phronesis*). Like the ability to ride a bike, *phronesis* can be acquired only by practice. It means knowing what is to be done in the concrete situation. It is a know-how not precisely calculable; asking a patient to give a number from 1 to 10 to score their pain pales in comparison with hearing an unsolicited 'Ow' or 'reading' the pain on their face.[7]

Experiential know-how is acutely sensitive to its own contingency. It requires what Keats called a 'negative capability', the ability to sustain uncertainty. Experience is a relatively stable knowledge – otherwise, we would have to reinvent the coffee maker every morning – but also a relatively unstable one, vulnerable and exposed to what is coming *next*. It keeps itself ready to be corrected by the future – by the patient in the *next* room, the *next* patient to occupy this bed. The 'next case' packs the punch of the event, of the coming of what we cannot see coming.

Cases

The word 'case' comes from *cadere*, to fall, to befall, and has an instructive undecidability, oscillating between two different senses, one that abuses hermeneutics and one that hermeneutics uses. In the first sense, it means a particular instance of a universal, a specimen of a species, something that 'falls under' the universal. In that sense, postmodern writers reject the word 'case' and prefer the word 'singularity', meaning something singularly itself, an unrepeatable situation or a unique individual, which rises higher than the universal and is not a case of what, or something that falls under a rule. 'Casuistry' is the science of cases, of pruning a singularity down to a case which submits to principles. Judging then would be reduced to plugging a case into a principle, which completely determines – or *programmes* – judgement. Once again, a good computer would do as well or better. In hermeneutics, we do not apply principles to cases. Rather, we apply what Gadamer calls 'the fecundity of the individual case' to the principles, which always stand to be corrected. Principles are temporary and artificial harmonies constructed from the incessant noise of the world.

In a second, more suggestive sense, one that postmodern writers can make use of, a case is what has befallen someone. In this sense, case is not related to 'casuistry' but to 'casualty' or 'accident' (*ad + cadere*), a matter usually requiring medical attention. The case in this sense is what the principles do *not* see coming. So, there is a Gadamerian dialogue between our acquired (habitual) horizon of expectation and the contingent, unexpected in-comings which each new case brings in, what Derrida calls the event. As the accident befalls the patient, the accidental also befalls the physicians and the nurses, whose interpretive know-how is each time tested, reshaped and transformed (deconstructed) by their experience.

Once again, at points like this, Gadamer – upon whom these authors primarily rely – and Derrida are hard to tell apart.

Only as Hermeneutics is Oncology Possible

'Yes, that makes sense to me. Isn't all of oncology hermeneutic?' Those are the words of an oncology department head after hearing a lecture analysing Gadamer's expression, 'the fecundity of the individual case'.[8] The speaker had in mind in particular the life and work of Robert Buckman, an esteemed oncologist at the University of Toronto and the author of sixteen books on communicating to patients the 'difficult knowledge' of a cancer diagnosis, who had himself recently died of cancer at the age of sixty-three. Buckman proposed wearing one's medical experience lightly, with humility, a readiness for the unexpected and a sense of vulnerability.[9] 'Cancer' is not one thing but a shorthand for a number of related pathologies; even when a particular form of cancer is diagnosed, the object of the treatment is ultimately the individual (singularity) not just the disease.

That's also why it makes no sense to demonize technology. Genomic testing these days supports the practical wisdom of the physician and the nurse by fashioning a course of treatment tailored to the individual. Even so, there is no magic formula for the course of treatment. To cite a line from Thomas Aquinas, 'whatever is received is received according to the mode of the receiver'. Each person who receives the news of this diagnosis will receive it in their own way, one patient calmly, the other with terror, and neither they nor the physician know how the treatment will unfold. Cases are not applications of rules; they productively determine and develop the rules. Cases do not simply obey the rules – they talk back to them.[10]

The individual case is 'fecund', an infinite density, not a sum total of transparent universals. Science is of the universal, Aristotle said, but individuals are the only things that exist. Science is a system of shorthand notations for the prolificacy of what exists; it simplifies complexity, reducing the racket of the world to harmony. Hermeneutic judgement inhabits the distance between the universal and the individual, negotiating the difference. The nursing station is strategically positioned at that point, in between the calculable and the incalculable. As one theorist said, it is a matter 'of choosing well, to paraphrase Aristotle – to do the right thing, at the right time, in the right way, and for the right amount, and for the right reason'.[11]

Teaching Hermeneutics a Lesson

Hermeneutics has something to learn from the nurses. Postmodern theorists usually assume a situation where the powers that be have lined up to prevent the unexpected event. But the people working on the ground in hospitals (and social workers, or teachers, especially in impoverished and underfunded schools) have exactly the opposite problem. Like soldiers on a battlefield, they lead lives of *overexposure to the event*, of constant visitation by emergencies, catastrophes, life-changing injuries, death both expected and unexpected, both natural and untimely. The problem they face is not to overcome the tendency to prevent the event; it is to prevent being burned out by too many events, or worse, as a survival technique, anaesthetizing themselves and adopting an attitude of disinterest, of serene Stoic *apatheia* (unfeeling).

A number of the nurses I met work in paediatric oncology. The very words send a chill down the spine. The Rotary Flames House they established served families of local children suffering from a progressive, life-threatening or terminal condition. The RFH gives parents charged with around-the-clock care a chance to entrust their children to trained health-care professionals in order to have some time together, say, a weekend, to regroup, refresh, re-create, before reassuming their unrelenting duties on Monday morning. Here is a programme that affords *protection* from the event and gives the parents a shot at some normality. Here, the way to keep the future open is to *prevent the event*.

Why Do Children Die?

The question 'Why do children die?' is one of the most important medical science can raise, and to any well-formed scientific question, there is in principle a scientific answer. But taken as a human tragedy, the loss of a child is one of those questions where seeking an explanation, like theologians serving up old saws like 'God writes straight with crooked lines', does not cut it. Speaking of the Holocaust, Lyotard said it is an obscenity even to *look for* a justification of that sort, like Hegelians who propose treating it as a 'negative moment' in the progress of the Spirit in history.[12] Of course, parents who have lost a child to cancer might dedicate the rest of their lives to raising funds for cancer research, and that is surely to cause a great good to come from their tragedy. But it does not remove, explain or justify the tragedy, and it is nothing that they would have agreed to in advance to further the cause of cancer research. The pain of that loss is precisely that it is in itself a humanly senseless and irremediable loss. It is like the irreparable harm done by being unjustly imprisoned for the best years of one's life. Parents can have another child, but they cannot replace the lost child. They cannot make this senseless loss make sense. What they can do is give the rest of their life thereafter a sense instead of letting it be destroyed by the loss. We cannot change the past, but we can change the meaning of the past, the meaning it will have for us in the future.

These nurses willingly insert themselves in this world of unbearable grief in order to help these children and their parents have a future. Speaking as a philosopher with a special interest in religion, I would say these nurses are dealing daily with the mystery of our lives, with matters that in a generic sense are profoundly religious, whether or not one is personally involved with any confessional or institutional religion. Perhaps it was part of their professional protocol to keep religion a private matter but, once I raised the question with them, it turned out that they often had occasion to talk with patients about matters of faith and of ultimate meaning. It makes sense. In the past, nurses were sisters, and the profession has been intimately connected with orders of religious women from the beginning. Nursing, pastoral counselling and clinical psychology bleed into each other.

So, while the question 'Why do children die?' does not have an answer, it does have responses, and some responses are better than others. The situation is impossible in the hermeneutic sense of the word: it shatters the horizons of expectation of the parents. It happens to others, not to us. But sometimes the impossible happens, and what is possible then, and necessary, is to deal with it, to do the impossible, to go where one cannot go, to think the unthinkable. It is necessary for the parents to go on, just when it is impossible to go on, and for the nurses and physicians to work with people to whom the impossible has happened. To put this in the language that Gadamer gives them, there is no *method* for dealing with a *truth* as elementally punishing as this.

Difficult Conversations

There is not a lot one can say *to* these parents, but there is everything to be gained from speaking *with* them. There is no magic formula to pass along. Conversations with the parents are less a matter of communicating objective information and more of a deeply personal, affective and healing contact. Here I am reminded of Levinas's brilliant analysis of a commonplace greeting, 'hello', given to a perfect stranger we pass on the street. It has next to no semantic content but it serves to acknowledge the infinity which has just passed by us, the inexhaustible depths of the other person, which is why we do not salute fire hydrants or lamp posts. The salutation is salutary, healing, wholesome. Of course, experienced nurses can pass along helpful information to the parents, but what is really effective here is their very being there *with* the other, being there *for* them, talking with them and holding their hand through their nightmare, allowing the parents to bring their grief to words. Grief which is understood is language. Unspeakable grief which is understood to be unspeakable is also language. The language does not explain, but it helps heal; it does not justify, it helps makes whole; it does not change the past, it changes the meaning of the past. While avoiding a magic formula of any sort, theological, ontological or oncological, we must not dismiss the real magic of healing talk, of the Gadamerian conversation, which lets an event of grace take place. Not grace of some supernatural sort, but the human grace of being there for the other, where the event of grace emerges in response to the event of grief.

That is why the Gadamerian hermeneutics of the conversation is so important for their work. Having been trained by mountains of manuals and buried in technical information – all of which is necessary, make no mistake, I want nothing to do with an assault on science and technology here – they *also* require *another interpretation* of language, a non-objectifying language. Language cannot be shrunk down to a body of concepts, propositions and arguments. Language is what lets the world be the world that it is, in all its majesty and misery, letting things be laid out so that they can be experienced *as* the things that they are (Heidegger). Such language does not make things transparent. Instead, what language releases, what language lets be seen, is the mystery of what cannot be seen, in which we are all caught up – this innocent child, these grief-stricken parents and the nurses and physicians keeping vigil over death until death parts us all. 'It is the blight man was born for, / It is Margaret you mourn for,' Gerard Manley Hopkins writes.[13]

Learning through Suffering

Hermeneutics describes the experiential world that is running all the time, beneath the radar of rules, algorithms and objectifying knowledge – from the micro-adjustments we make at the steering wheel of our car all the way up, or rather, down, to this point of contact with the mystery, where scientific discourse gives way. Hermeneutic truth is drawn from the depths of this experience. Nancy Moules, a central figure in this group, invokes the pathos, the specific passivity of hermeneutic knowledge, the *pathei mathos* of Aeschylus, learning through suffering, described by Gadamer. The most instructive experience is negative experience, Gadamer says, when we suffer a blow from which we learn a thing or two about the uncertain ways of the world. Moules is referring here to learning from suffering shared with the parents, the literal meaning of 'com-passion', suffering-with.[14] In the caring professions, this is surely the first of the virtues. What is possible in this impossible situation is to respond with compassion, to be the companion of the passion and the tragedy, to divide the grief of the parents by sharing it.

Impossible Mourning: An Interview

Ultimately, the only people who can 'understand' what these parents are going through is other parents who have also been there, have also visited this terrible place. Moules provides a telling transcript of an interview she conducted with parents who had lost a child to cancer and who, in the interest of helping other parents, were willing to share their experience – willing to speak about their unspeakable pain, to revisit a nightmare from which they were trying to learn to move on.[15] These parents are in a position of what Derrida describes as 'impossible mourning', going back to Freud's distinction between mourning and melancholy. If their mourning is successful, they have absorbed the blow and moved on and in that sense forgotten the child; the alternative is failure, to be defeated by the blow, unable to move on (melancholy). So, Derrida says, this impossibility of succeeding, this faithful infidelity, is the only possible success in mourning, keeping the wound open without being immobilized.[16]

Free from any hint of aggressive interrogation, the style of Moules's interview allows a space for the event of language – the event of understanding – to take place, to *let* it happen, not *make* it happen. There are not a lot of full-blown, grammatically polished propositions here, mostly half-starts, sentences broken off, occasional tears and even laughter, sometimes discreetly circling around, sometimes nudging obliquely, haltingly and painfully towards a centre of unbearable pain. In one of the most telling moments, the parents report the shattering effect of someone who one day gave these parents the statistics on the high divorce rate among couples who suffer the loss of a child. At that point, the purely destructive force of objectification came crashing into a site of the utmost hermeneutic delicacy (*subtilitas*). To say this was inept, impolitic, a lack of social skills, is to trivialize its destructiveness, which took all the parents' courage to overcome. Arriving like a messenger of a dark, cold death, of an inexorable fate, this person was saying the future is closed to you, what lies ahead is more destruction, embrace your terrible fate, despair all who enter here. Statistics hold for large numbers, and they are important, but in life, each case is singularly itself.

CONDUCTING HERMENEUTICS RESEARCH

This interview – as distinct from the statistical study – is an integral part of the research these Gadamerian nurses do as professors of nursing. They do not engage in objectifying, quantitative research, not because this is not also important, but because it is not everything, not totalizing, as the post-structuralist philosophers put it. What they call 'hermeneutic research' is focused on the non-formalizable, the non-programmable, non-objectifying side of the healing arts. This is not an added bit of ornamentation, a supplement put in an appendix to the main body of the scientific manual where the really important statistical stuff is found. It is intrinsically constitutive of the hermeneutical-clinical situation taken holistically. No healing happens without it, or, if it does, it happens in spite of its absence. The hermeneutical whole is a complex of factors that are both subjective and objective, to use the distortive categories of modernity which make it almost impossible to understand experience.

The hermeneutic scene is the point of contact between the self and the world, and that world has features that are both mathematical and non-mathematical, quantitative and qualitative, and things work best when these two can find a way to negotiate their differences. The great breakthrough of the modern world – and it was hermeneutic all the way down – was the discovery of a new way of *reading* the world *as* a book *written* in the language of mathematics. That discovery, which goes all the way back to Pythagoras and Plato, where it was mixed with what we call mysticism, shaped the modern world. But everything depends upon preventing this mode of understanding-*as* from becoming a monstrous, monocular monovision which treats *everything as* measurable, quantifiable, programmable.

Rigour versus Exactness

While we are all for the 'exact' knowledge mathematical science provides, there is a 'rigour' – to invoke a distinction Husserl made[17] – of another sort that consists of a sensitivity to the plurivocal, polymorphic make-up of the world in which we actually live, a plurivocity we have put under the protection of a prankster god. The task of hermeneutic research, then, is to show the unique *rigour* of another, non-quantitative, *non-exact* discourse. Consider the rigour, the extraordinary discipline, the astonishing economy of a poem, like the one I cited a few pages back, in which the poet manages to evoke the mystery of our mortality in fifteen short lines of verse. Hopkins was a Jesuit priest, but he was not peddling any theological solutions there; he was not trying to dissipate mortality with a big story about salvation but to *sustain it as a mystery*. We cannot have an exact definition or proof for everything, and to demand such a thing, Aristotle said, betrays one's lack of *paideia* (culture, cultivation, education). Hermeneutic research is a difficult discipline, an exacting art, like the delicate touch or tact, the *subtilitas*, we see in Moules's interview. Such interviews are conducted by not conducting anything but by allowing oneself to be conducted by the impulse of the *logos* which drives the dia-*logue*, as Gadamer says, which means, as Derrida says, to let the event of healing happen and come to words in this conversation.

A Pedagogy of the Event

It should not go unremarked that the hermeneutic *subtilitas* on display here can be found in many other places – in counselling, pastoral and social work. When teachers raise genuine questions with their students, no one is conducting, everyone is in a state of genuine searching ignorance. They do not know where they are going – but they do know that much, which is what the mystical theologian Nicholas of Cusa (1401–64) called 'learned ignorance'. The outcome is not programmable, and certainly not measurable or calculable. Attempting to evaluate education by its strictly measurable outcomes, as in 'outcomes based' education, which involves incessant and distracting testing, a very prevalent practice in the US, is a distortion of the event, a disaster for education and a failure to appreciate the rigour of the educational scene.

When the event happens in education, it may be that no one knows it. How many teachers hear from students many years later who tell them they have never forgotten something the teacher said one day – which the teacher has forgotten. One day, a teacher asked a question, or made a remark that caught the student's attention, which set off a slow chain reaction that did not surface there and then but only much later. By then the teacher has completely forgotten the remark, and maybe even the student has, too. It is only years later that this restlessness and suspicion, whose source the student can no longer identify, comes to fruition. The student's life has been transformed. An event has happened and nobody can say how. Maybe the very best teachers are ones who set off quiet and unobserved revolutions that no one noticed at the time and no one can remember later.

How can we measure that? How can we observe outcomes that are long and obscure in the coming and of which no one has retained a clear recollection? How can we truly evaluate a teacher – or a student? How can we calculate the incalculable? How can we measure the invisible, inaudible imperative which has called the teacher and the students together, in the same room, closed the door and given them an hour together in order to let the event happen? To be sure, it is never a matter of choosing between the two. I am not saying there are no standards and that we cannot evaluate bad teachers. I am just saying evaluating teaching is a delicate hermeneutic art, which requires rigour but does not submit to exact measurement.

Programmes That Do Not Programme

A conservative pedagogy attempts to transmit the tradition univocally. A pedagogy of the event transmits the tradition as a construction that has been constituted from below, as an interpretation that we have forgotten is an interpretation, not as a god that has dropped from the sky. To teach is to give the tradition a future. To teach is to take a risk – even sometimes a life-threatening one, like teaching young girls in cultures that forbid it. The educator 'leads' (*ducere*) by providing the occasion for students to lead themselves out of the secure spaces afforded by the received interpretation into the great outdoors of the possibility of understanding otherwise. In the process, of course, the instructors are in turn instructed by the students. To be sure, teachers must prepare students for the future we can all see coming, like their careers, just like the young professor Derrida was doing back at the ENS. But more important still – and it is never a question of choosing between them – they must prepare them for the future for which they cannot be prepared, for the in-breaking, unforeseeable one.

Teachers must educate students into *freedom*. They must therefore devise programmes which do not programme, carefully calculating curricula which leave room for the incalculable. They must assume we are all – teachers and students alike – in the *un*truth, and that the truth is still to come, and that there is no Teacher, capitalized and in the singular, who has the Answer. This requires the heart, the courage, the passion to say, 'Let's see what comes!' to the coming of what we cannot see coming. Of course, there must be norms and standards for teachers, systems of formation, apprenticeships in the discipline. But this must be undertaken with a strategic depreciation of method and an appreciation of the event, with respect for a rigour that eludes exactness.

Who is the Author of These Words?

Everything hermeneutics has to offer to the professions is on full display in another difficult conversation that Moules recounts, with a mother whose six-year-old daughter, Aaron, was dying of cancer. The mother kept a vigil at the bedside of the child while whispering, 'Keep fighting; hold on', and the family insisted that the child be kept on 'full code'. That required that when the child went into cardiac arrest, a special team would arrive and the family would be asked to leave the room. The result would be not only the prolongation of the suffering of the child but also that the mother, at the end of this long vigil, would be deprived of the most important moment of all, being there to hold her daughter and allow her to die peacefully in her arms.

As the family's support nurse, Moules was asked to talk to the mother. What Moules did *not* do was present a clearly reasoned argument to the mother, assuming the position as the person with experience and authority in situations like this. Moules did not ask the mother to trust her professional judgement, as if she were in the know. She did the opposite. She started from the assumption that this was the mother's decision, that the mother was the authority on her pain and suffering, and Moules told the mother that she trusted her to know best. After all, it is the mother, not the nurse, who knows what it is like to watch her child die. So Moules did not offer direction or the benefit of her experience but a question. 'I do wonder,' Moules said, 'if you believed that Aaron was continuing to fight for you, would she ever need to hear your permission to stop?'[18] So, Moules simply suggested to the mother that the child might be continuing to fight an unwinnable battle and so prolonging her pain until the mother herself gave the child leave to die.

The nursing staff were frustrated that Moules was not

more aggressive, but an hour later Aaron's parents put her on 'no code', and within a few hours the child died in her mother's arms. Afterwards, the mother said:

> Suddenly it just dawned on me, that I could create the right scene for Aaron's death and that she needed my permission to let go. So we took her off full code and I started telling her that if she was tired, it was all right to quit fighting, that it was okay to go. And then she died. I held her.

The mother had in fact made her own the possibility that Moules held out before her. Moules had completely rejected the standard clinical framework according to which the mother is 'in denial', 'resistant', and that her 'job' was to break down that resistance. Instead, she approached the scene with what Gadamer calls 'tact',[19] and in the process she gives us a striking example of what Kierkegaard called 'indirect communication' – whereas the staff wanted a direct one.

'Did I teach this mother something, or was I taught?' Moules asks.[20] We are witness here to a conversation 'born out of the willingness to suffer together', not simply passively, but actively offering words of compassion, which here take the form of the subtlest, gentlest and most non-interrogatory of suggestions. 'Whose words were they?' she asks of what the mother said. Who is their author? Of course, the answer is that they are the words of both the nurse and the mother, or better still, of both and neither, and there is no authorial authority here. That is precisely the structure of what Derrida calls 'undecidability' (both/and and neither/

nor) and of what Gadamer calls the play of conversation, because both she and the mother were carried along by the momentum of the event. As Moules says, their words 'existed in the space we created between us' and the 'conversation "belongs" to no one'.[21]

The Spectre of the Post-human

HAVE WE EVER BEEN HUMAN?

A New Game in Town

Between 1870 and 1970, the world was utterly changed by five new technologies – electricity, chemicals and pharmaceuticals, automobiles, communications (telephone, radio and television) and urban sanitation. If we woke up in a home in 1860, it would feel like another world and the public streets would be repulsive. A home in 1940, however, would feel just a bit clunky to us – I've been put up in European hotels like that – but we could make our way around and the public streets would be fine. That, according to economist Robert J. Gordon, in *The Rise and Fall of American Growth*.[1] Since 1940, we have vastly improved upon these innovations, but we have not produced anything *fundamentally* new. As Lyotard would say, we've made new moves in old games, but we have not invented a new game. And that, Gordon maintains, explains why this was a period of economic growth that we can no longer expect to continue.

Far be it for me to tell the economists how to measure economic growth, but I beg to disagree on one basic point – I think there's a new game in town. I see a sea change in our self-understanding, a paradigm shift, a mutation in our deepest presuppositions about ourselves and our world: in short, an alteration of our basic hermeneutical framework. While the period between 1870 and 1970 introduced unheard-of new conveniences into our lives, it left our understanding of our place in the order of things pretty much intact. We had a better understanding of how these mostly mechanical technologies worked, and we treated them, with some confidence, as tools made for our convenience. We loved our radios and refrigerators but nobody worried we *were* a radio or a refrigerator. They did not shock our confidence in our own importance as a species. We still entertained the comforting illusion that there is an unbridgeable distance between the human and the non-human, the natural and the artificial, human life and the machines we use to wash our clothes or drive to work.

Nowadays, we are not so sure. We are squirming in our humanistic seats. There are forces afoot that are rattling our hermeneutical timbers, effecting a shift in what the theorists call our 'imaginary', the implicit background image we have of our world and of our place in the world. An eerie new imaginary is taking shape – not only postmodern, post-industrial and post-religious (Chapter 10) but even, spookiest of all, *post-human*. Our imaginary is now being shaped not by religion, art and philosophy, as it had been in the past, but by the new technologies.

Welcome to the Post-human Imaginary

Thanks to the relative ease with which we can travel around the world – 'we' meaning those of us who can afford the airline fares and 'relative' meaning if you put up with long

security lines and miserably cramped seats – and to new electronic communication systems, we have a sharpened appreciation of the plurality of cultures, of the many ways to be,
the multiple mutations and *interpretations* of which being-
human is susceptible. Indeed, more than ever before, we
realize that any given culture *is* an interpretation, not an
eternal form of being. Having an acute sense that being-
human can mean being many different things, we are less
likely to stick our neck out with universalist claims. We are
asked not merely to tolerate differences, which is condescending, but to affirm them (we're still working on that).

But beyond globetrotting, we have ventured off the very
surface of the globe. We have escaped the gravitational pull
of the earth (it was not so long ago that we needed someone
to discover that there was such a force) and have launched
extra-planetary travel – astronauts on the moon, exploratory
vehicles to other planets. One of these vehicles, bearing the
iconic name of *Galileo*, actually escaped the gravitational
field of the solar system (although Galileo himself did not
escape the clutches of the Pope for saying the system was
solar). With that, humankind entered endless interstellar
space. It is getting hard to hold our heads up when we are
told that we are but latecomers on a little rock rotating
around a nondescript star, which is but a single speck of dust
in an incomprehensibly vast universe. Now add in that the
odds are greater than ever that there are, have been and will
be countless other forms of intelligent life in the universe.
We are not alone.

In the unlikely event that there is any residual anthropo-
centrism still stirring in our mortal bones, it gets worse. Our

bones, our bodies, our very being, are being invaded by new body-snatchers – the information technologies. Occasionally, in the past, when the sceptics sneered that we are nothing but machines, they meant those smelly, smoky, noisy, clunky assemblage of gears, wires and metal of the industrial age. But today the clean cut between the human and the non-human has disappeared into thin air, almost literally: into the cloud of digitalization. We started out anthropomorphizing the technology – when a computer does not connect with an attached device, we say the computer cannot 'see' it; when the computer is processing data, we say it is 'thinking' – but we end up with the technology techno-morphizing us: when we think, we say our brains are 'processing' information or suffering from an 'information overload'. Which one is the metaphor?

The old debate between materialism and idealism is obsolete. We are in fact neither a machine nor a ghost-in-a-machine, neither a pure spirit nor a clunky set of gears but a *tertium quid*, a third thing that no one ever thought of before – bits of information. Complex, delicately tuned bio-technological information-processing systems. Cyborgs, Donna Haraway called us, thirty years ago.[2] That's post-human, and that's really spooky. Who are we? Or *what* are we?

How to Make Plato and Aristotle Howl with Pain

So, nowadays, we find ourselves wondering, have we ever been human?

If you identify the human with the pure soul, as Plato

does, or with pure thinking, as Descartes does, with any sort of body-free or immaterial stuff, then the answer is clearly *no*. Never. As we saw in more detail in Chapter 5, if we identify the human with the 'rational animal', as Aristotle does (he coined the phrase), along comes Saussure, who says that what Aristotle calls *logos* (*ratio*, reason, language) comes down to a faceless meaning-making system. Language is not the outer expression of a person's inner thoughts, as we thought in classical humanist philosophy, but an *impersonal* structure, an anonymous, non-human system of signifiers – 'ring'/'king'/'sing' – which produces meaning by the discernible differences among them. In the beginning was the *logos*. Maybe, but look inside the *logos*, and there, lying at the heart of human understanding and making it possible, is not a speaking subject but a CPU, a semiotic system. So, the very thing that seems to make the purely human possible *also* makes it impossible to be purely human – that's a 'deconstructive' move, by the way – which strikes another blow at our pride.

While Plato would gloat with I-told-you-so pride at the mathematical side of contemporary physics, he would hate the way we flirt with virtual reality. Confusing the virtual and the real, the representation and the original presence, is the cardinal sin in Platonism. But think about it. Human intelligence owes everything to the power of *representational* systems, to the rule-governed, coded use of signifiers or place-holders. The amazing thing about signifiers – they're like magic – is that they work in the *absence* of the real thing. That is exactly what makes memory and imagination possible, without which we would be dumb as a post. The ability to call to mind things that are *not present*, things removed from us in space and time, by means of substitutes, simulacra, icons and images – the very realm of copy and imitation that was censored by Plato – that's the whole trick! That is the very *mark* of intelligence, not a wound in its side. To speak of something when it is right in front of our nose is impressive; but it is even more amazing when it is *not*. Our trafficking in virtual reality has extended intelligence beyond our wildest dreams, not blunted it. Language is the most ancient system of virtual reality we have devised, and modern information systems are the continuation.

If we think about it that way, we have to ask, is not *all* intelligence *art*ificial? Does not everything depend upon the artful use of artefacts, of signs, stand-ins, surrogates and representations? From the very first moment, some unknown clan of higher anthropoids somewhere started making barely articulate gestures to one another to indicate, say, that this situation looks a little sketchy and should be avoided, or that this morsel of vegetation is edible and that one is not. Meaning and truth are not *clouded over* by these systems of signs; they are *constituted* by them. Signs and copies do not land us at a further remove from reality, as Plato argued, they give us access to reality in the first place. Meanings (*signi*fications) are their very *effects*. Presence is produced by the differential deployment of representations.

We have *never* been human, not in the classical humanist sense.

Matter Does Not Matter

We recall (Chapter 5) that Saussure said that the material substrate or substance of a signifier is arbitrary. All that matters are the identifiable differences among the signifiers, in just the way that the rules of chess are indifferent to whether the chess pieces are made of plastic or pixels, wood or ivory. Speech makes use of invisible air and flows in time; writing makes use of a visible palpable substrate and is spread out in space. As mentioned earlier, Derrida caused a stir – in the best spirit of Hermes, he did it on purpose – when he chose 'writing' as the metonym or shorthand for *any differential coded system* of any sort, written or spoken, linguistic or non-linguistic. This was a poke at the humanists, at the psychological and humanistic primacy that was given to speech in Western thought and culture. But in order to avoid outright confusion – which resulted anyway – he distinguished writing in the everyday sense from 'archi-writing', the general structure of the 'trace', of the coded system of differences of any sort. His choice of words turned out to be prophetic, as we will shortly see.

The idea of a formal system, of a machine for making (*facere*) meaning with signs (signification), has proven to be a windfall for the field of AI. Simulating these systems on computer programs has transformed our lives – to the point that we find ourselves wondering if we are one of them. Is that what thinking really *is*? A scary thought.

Now, ask yourself: if, in fact, human understanding is a complex neuroplastic information-processing system, what is to stop us from lifting off these purely formal operations of human consciousness and transferring them from one substrate to another, from nucleic acids to silicon or to some other still more subtle substance to come? What is to stop us from one day effectively taking the data of our conscious life and 'uploading' it on to a computer where it can then be downloaded into a shiny new android, a robotic body guaranteed to outlast those miserable mortal coils in which we shuffle about now? Along the way, of course, we should make sure to store a back-up copy in case of an accident, like the resurrection ship in *Battlestar Galactica*. 'Oh, death, where is thy sting?' St Paul asked (1 Cor. 15:55). Today, a new wave of highly robotological neo-Paulinians – Hans Moravec and Ray Kurzweil chief among them[3] – are working on the same question. (Or maybe we should call them neo-Cartesians, since this is a techno-version of Descartes' pure *cogito*.) In the meantime, while we are waiting for the coming of this techno-rapture, in which our flesh and bones will be left behind, what is to stop us from grafting computer programs – foreign languages, global positioning systems: whatever you need – on to the human body and thereby vastly improving human intelligence with various computer-assisted skills?

Matter Matters

What is to stop us? Well, quite a lot, according to another interpretation of human intelligence. Let us give Moravec and Kurzweil the benefit of the doubt. Let us assume that we could at some point in the distant future develop the technology to peel away, layer by layer, the conscious life of the brain and relocate it in a robot. What we would end up with is a highly truncated cognitive being, a spooky monster whose life would be restricted to its explicitly cognitive conscious functions, a being that would make Mr Spock look positively effusive. What would be left behind, on this interpretation, is everything else which makes humans human, which would be quite a lot – all the pre-cognitive and non-cognitive, pre-conscious and subconscious life, the vast amount of human intelligence that is not explicitly conceptual, linguistic, representational; everything body-bound, everything affective, emotional and corporeal, everything that remains implicit and *embedded in the bodies* that will have been left behind.[4]

For example, we do not learn to type by first memorizing a keyboard and then putting this prior mental representation into practice. Typing is what Heidegger called a mode of being-in-the-world, which, as Maurice Merleau-Ponty – who fleshed out Heidegger's insight – showed in *The Phenomenology of Perception* (1945) is a matter of being bodily engaged in and with the world, so intimately, in fact, that the keyboard feels like an extension of our hands.[5] In other words, it *is* a matter of matter, of the so-called material substrate. The knowing, which is not a knowing-that but a knowing-how, is embedded in the fingers, in the eye-to-monitor coordination. If someone asks you, in the abstract, where the letter 'c' is located, you consult your fingers, not a theoretical picture of the keyboard in your head. So, too, with playing a piano, or swimming.

In fact, of what is this *not* true? Indeed, even the so-called purely linguistic operations are not purely formal cognitive systems. Speaking is a way of forcing air through your lungs and manipulating your tongue, and it is orchestrated with a full ensemble of bodily gestures, facial expressions, regional accents cum upstairs/downstairs sociopolitical class distinctions. The verbal floats in a sea of non-verbals which we learn to 'read'. That is why we learn a lot more from a face-to-face conversation with someone, where we get a chance to read their body language, than from reading a transcript – or an email, tweet or text – all so many attempts to leave our body behind. Each language, as Merleau-Ponty said, is a way to sing the world. If you plan to study Italian, you must learn to inflect your words melodically in the Italian way (not to mention learning how to use your hands). British English requires another body, as if releasing your words is causing you some pain. A communication is never a pure disincarnate message but something embedded and embodied in the material medium – the medium saturates the message. If a friend loses a loved one, sending your condolences by email, a telephone call or by paying them a personal visit send very different messages.

Two Post-human Spooks

So, it turns out that there are (at least) two interpretations of human intelligence and two different versions of the *post*-human spectre – one disembodied, the other embodied.

In the disembodied version, the AI version, human intelligence is interpreted as a complex formal system transferrable to other material substrates. The human is not opposed to the technological; the human has always been technological. This is an oddly immaterialist, neo-Cartesian dualist option, which treats the human body not as the external container of the spiritual soul but as the replaceable substrate of a formal system.

The embodied version is materialist and biological and recognizes how much of being-human is non-formalizable and non-programmable. So, *this is a much more hermeneutics-friendly milieu*, which is why Derrida wrote a book on the animals that we all are.[6] It shows up today in the environmentalist and animal-rights movements, which point out how much harm human exceptionalism causes the environment and what Haraway calls our 'companion species'.[7] The materialists insist that human animals are animals, that the proper distinction is not between humans and 'animals' but between human animals and non-human animals. They take enormous satisfaction in pointing out the unnerving likeness between humans and their fellow primates – they have 'faces', they look at us. Derrida's book starts with his cat staring at him as he steps out of the shower, stark naked and exposed to the cat's view – what is the cat thinking?[8]

Just so, humans exhibit a great deal of unnervingly animal behaviour. The search for the human difference – we speak, we laugh, we know that we die and we bury our dead, as opposed to the 'dumb animals', etc. – is a fool's errand. Instead of thumping our chest and proclaiming ourselves just a little less than the angels, entitled to lord it over everything else (Ps. 8:5), we should instead see a graded continuum of analogous behaviours, visible both in the stages of the history of evolution and in the series of transformations from embryo to the mature adult. The human is not opposed to the animal. The human is a particular inflection of the animal, a complex twist taken by certain animals, as when Nietzsche savaged the Christian idea of sin as the product of animals intent on making themselves sick.

It is Not a Question of Choosing between Them

Having made a distinction between these two forms of the post-human, embodied and disembodied, let us now deconstruct it. As Derrida likes to say, it is never a matter of choosing between the two interpretations of interpretation. So, just as Derrida predicts, this distinction, between the technological-disembodied and the biological-embodied, does not quite hold up. They are not as much at odds as it seems. Whoever, or whatever, we are is some sort of techno-bio-system, or quasi-system.

Modern genetics demonstrates that the ubiquity of the (archi-)writing defended by Derrida is not just a metaphor. It is a metonym of extraordinary depth, range and importance, so you can now see why I remarked above upon the prescient character of the young Derrida's singling out writing. The genetic code is written into the very core of our bodily life. This puts Derrida's critics in an extremely ironic, even amusing, position. They crowned themselves the lord protectors of the real world, anointed themselves knights sworn to defend material bodies against the frivolous partisans of texts and taunted Derrida's textualism. When Derrida wrote, 'There is nothing outside the text', they looked up to heaven for relief, with anxious and unctuous eyes. Their objection is best met today with a condescending smile. What is going on in contemporary genetics and brain science is not opposed to the model of textuality; it is based upon it.

The Myth of the Invention of Writing

In Plato's rendering of the myth of the invention of writing (*Phaedrus* 274c–275b), King Thamus worries that writing would not *aid* the soul, or *remedy* its forgetfulness, as claimed by its inventor, Theuth – the Egyptian name for no other than Hermes. The king feared it would weaken memory by making it dependent on something external and corrode the inner purity of the soul. As Derrida points out, *pharmakon*, the Greek word for aid or remedy that Plato used, meant both remedy and poison, an ambiguity that is alive and well today in the English 'drug'.[9] Are contemporary informational systems going to cure us or kill us? Are we being cured or dying of an overdose? Are we being helped or becoming drug-dependent? I doubt anyone anywhere ever condensed the dilemma posed by modern technology more effectively than Plato.

It is not a question of choosing between writing-systems and bio-systems. Indeed, it was the biologically oriented Aristotle who said that the soul starts life as a blank tablet which is written upon by subsequent experience. But bio-systems are not just *like* a writing tablet, they *are* a writing tablet, whose information is stored in nucleic acids; and they are not blank at all but come pre-loaded with a complex system of genetic coding. DNA is such a remarkably powerful system of storing information that 'DNA molecules can be the basis for an archival storage system potentially capable of storing all of the world's digital information in roughly nine litres of solution, about the amount of liquid in a case of wine.'[10] On this point, the very mathematically oriented Plato was, oddly, nearer to the mark. He held that the soul comes into the world with memory-traces of the pure Forms acquired in its previous life in the upper world, obscured in this life by the body, which are recollected on the occasion of experience.

So, just as the brain's neural network is a perfectly good example of what Derrida means by *différance*, even so, DNA (our genetic alphabet) and RNA (our genetic word-builder) are perfect examples of what he means by archi-writing. Organic life, both body and mind, is coded from the start, which is why Derrida was comfortable writing about *both* formal systems and animals.

There is thus a genetic counterpart to the hermeneutic circle. Our lives are played out in the circle between what we bring with us to the world and what the world brings to us, in the interplay between the genetic make-up *with* which we are born and the world (the hermeneutic situation) *into* which we are born. These are the terms in which the old nature/nurture debate is reinscribed today.

Pharmacological Effects

King Thamus's worries were not without foundation. When I was writing my doctoral dissertation back in the 1960s, I laboriously copied quotations on to index cards and recopied them into my handwritten text. So, I greeted word-processing as a gift from the gods. But of course, copying and pasting digitalized texts into a computer document, instead of writing them out, word for word, relieved them pretty much of the need to pass through my head and hand, where they tended to stick.

That is what we might call the pharmacological effect, the ambiguity of technology, the poison/cure, the promise/threat, that Derrida identifies in his interpretation of this myth, and it is widespread. Watson, we might say, is emerging everywhere, and we have embraced his advance with unchecked enthusiasm. It's Plato's nightmare: as virtual reality waxes, contact with reality wanes. As virtual communities, internet websites, texting, videos and Facebook friends wax, real friends and real communities wane; as distance learning waxes, real classrooms wane.[11] People are more in touch with other people around the globe, but without touching, without personal interaction. We have very little real contact with our electronic contacts.

Automobile drivers love their GPS, but as one scholar, named Julia Frankenstein – I presume this is not an assumed name – at the University of Freiburg (where Husserl and Heidegger taught), points out, the result is that we ignore the landmarks, do not absorb the environment, and allow our lived sense of the landscape to erode.[12]

The ubiquity of websites and blogs, which has enhanced communication, has also served to degrade it. It promotes an archipelago of the like-minded sharing posts which reinforce what they all believe to begin with. Cable-television networks cater to their own target audience and demonize people with a different opinion, the perfect opposite of a Gadamerian conversation. We have a proliferation of information and of 'fake news',[13] which threatens the work of a free press and hence of democracy itself.

Computers promise to be of invaluable help in medical science, storing enormous amounts of medical literature and diagnosing symptoms which stump the best of physicians. Physicians and their patients spend many months of trial and error coming up with a diagnosis of symptoms that a computer program would diagnose almost instantly.[14] Such computer-assisted work can be found almost anywhere – teachers, lawyers, aeroplane pilots – everyone upon whose experience, whose savvy, we count on in real-life situations, threatening to reduce them to utter dependence on computers. Casualty-avoidance systems in automobiles can save lives, but completely self-driven automobiles, like the Googlemobile, risk leaving the human driver unable to take over the controls when needed. We want the computer to supplement our skills, but in each case the blessing is mixed; the supplement is dangerous; the cure may turn out to be toxic.

The Latest Human Edition

The notion that every patient is different (Chapter 8) acquires an even sharper edge when we can tailor the course of treatment to fit the specific genetic map of the patient. If every patient is different, DNA testing can identify those differences.[15] We can start formulating algorithms of singularity, algorithms that prescribe personal diets, personal courses of medication, cancer treatments, exercise programmes, and on and on. Of course, there is no one-to-one correspondence between gene and genome. It takes a 'chorus of genes acting in concert'[16] to get anything done, and there is wide variation in the effects produced by but a single gene. It takes a great deal of mathematics and a capacity for dauntingly difficult experimental work to get to understand the textuality, the interwoven, interactive, differential effects that prevail in contemporary genetics.

By learning to read the genetic code, we can understand the how and the why of birth defects, of inherited diseases, of genetic predispositions to develop diseases later on in life. That will eventually give us a grip on how to prevent or correct them. Recent genetic research has brought us to a critical point. With the development of the CRISPR-Cas9 technique in 2015, genetic intervention has become an actual, practical possibility. We can envisage a point where we can edit *out* genetic defects that result in terrible birth defects and life-long suffering. By the same token, we can envisage someday editing *in* all sorts of very desirable genetic traits – presumably producing a whole new generation of people who are taller, smarter, stronger, faster, better looking, with better memories, longer-lived – whatever we want. We are now talking about altering the genetic codes in ways that will be passed on to subsequent generations. We envisage getting to the point where we can redesign the human race.

But with what long-term consequences? Talk about the coming of what we cannot see coming! When we alter such a complex network, how can we know what else we will have altered? How will altered genetic codes affect the genetic pool and get passed along to future generations? The post-human spectre hovers over this research, of which the monster created by Dr Frankenstein is the literary emblem. Mary Shelley's novel is more relevant than ever.

Designer babies give family planning a whole new meaning, children cut to fit the needs of – well, whom? The parents? The state? The military? The corporations? The computer industry? For God's sake, maybe even genes that promote religious belief? The Book of Genesis meets Genetics?[17] King Thamus was right to say that there is a need for civilian review. Somebody must exercise judgement. *Hermeneutic* judgement.

Lacking a King Thamus to put his royal foot down, the Royal Society of London, in conjunction with both the American and Chinese national academies of science, stepped in and played the royal role, calling in December 2015 for a moratorium on editing the human genome in any way that will affect the gene pool. Until when? Until science can have a better sense about the unforeseen consequences, and 'we' can agree about how to proceed. We who? A 'broad societal consensus', meaning an untidy democratic process of back and forth, a messy stew of conflicting views – of scientists and political leaders and popular opinion in the international community.[18] An effective editorial board engaged in hermeneutics, deliberative, interpretive communication. In short, we hermeneuts would say, we need *phronesis*, inter-*pret*ative insight which ap*prec*iates what is at stake.

Mortals, Gods and Robots

The rule of thumb that obtains in AI research and robotology is that what is hard for humans is easy for the machines, and what is easy for humans is hard for the machines. Watson can calculate at blazing speeds and solve problems in seconds that it would take centuries for a single human being to solve, but a two-year-old is better than a robot at walking across a room without falling over and being rendered useless until help arrives.

In the present state of the art, computers can *calculate* strictly *cognitive* problems, but they run up against a wall, sometimes literally, when they hit hermeneutics. They reach their limits when they are required to *interpret*, that is, to do things that cannot be solved by calculation but only by negotiation. They are stumped when they encounter a novel situation where, unprepared by any rule, what is required is a fresh judgement. Robots are matchless in performing routinizable operations, whereas simple but unprogrammable things, like turning a doorknob, are just too tricky for them. As someone quipped, if you want to protect yourself against the Terminator, just close your door.[19]

In Gadamer's terms, the robots are great at following a *method*, but they get stuck when it comes to the *play*, to the spontaneous and non-methodic. That is the challenge to computer designers, who are not unaware of these objections. They hear what we are saying and are designing computers to do spooky things – to proceed by insight, not by simply running through every mathematical possibility; to correct their mistakes, to learn by experience and to be creative. In short, programmed to do the unprogrammable.[20] We may reach a point where the computers will design the computers and maybe even start to communicate among themselves in a way we cannot understand. Eerie stuff!

The challenge to the philosophers is to wade into these debates without demonizing science, without reducing science to reductionism. The post-human imaginary, shaped by the view of the universe opening up in contemporary theoretical physics, makes a much better case for the mystery of Being than most of what we hear from the philosophers and theologians today. If philosophy begins in wonder, the speculative physicists have stolen its wonder. They are theorizing multiple universes, multiple dimensions, time travel and quantum paradoxes that would be laughed out of the lecture hall were they coming from the philosophy or theology departments. What we require is a certain measure of hermeneutic teamwork between philosophers and speculative physicists, each literate about the other's work, in order to explore the emerging mysteries of the universe, because today what we have called philosophy and physics in the past are beginning to converge. When physicists say that in the Big Bang, something comes from nothing, we need a scientifically literate philosopher in the room to say you cannot actually say that, but there is something profoundly mysterious going on here and we have to find some way to say what it is.

The Hermeneutics of Plasticity

In point of fact, the brain scientists are explaining to us better than any philosopher that the brain is *not* a machine with gears and pulleys and it does not run with the mechanical rote of a clock. The brain is a network of complex neural interconnections, which is marked by its plasticity, its flexibility and transformability, its ability to absorb new information, to respond to its environment. The brain is a holistic network, so that if one part of the brain is injured another part attempts to take up the slack. It is a whole but not a closed system; it is a totality but not totalitarian; it is a network but an open-ended one. It is, in short, a certain set of potentialities which greet the rush of unexpected experience in unpredictable and different ways.

The most hermeneutic philosopher of the day, in this regard, is Catherine Malabou (1959–), whose signature concept, 'plasticity', is intentionally borrowed from brain science. The category of plasticity makes for a comfortable fit with the *subtilitas* that has defined hermeneutics ever since Rambach. Malabou moves back and forth between the greats of continental philosophy (Kant and Hegel, Heidegger and Derrida), on the one hand, and brain science on the other, without the least expectation that there would or should be a war between them. Plasticity displaces the old wars between materialism and idealism, or freedom and necessity.

Malabou argues for the *inclusion* of brain science in any sensible philosophical explanation of human intelligence and the *exclusion* of biological reductionism that explains it away. In good brain science, the brain is not a machine but a being of plasticity, of reinventability, holistic and auto-transforming. In a recent book, *Before Tomorrow*, she adopts the model of 'epigenesis', which is a process of development characteristic of embryos.[21] Epigenesis does not start with a homunculus, an exceptionally tiny human being that grows larger while retaining the same form – like those old paintings of children that make them look like little adults. It describes a progressively differentiating process, passing through successively different forms, each of which has its own gestalt, until it reaches mature form. Not one form growing larger but a series of linked transformations, from conception to maturity. Epigenesis is neither pure innatism – the same inborn form getting bigger and necessarily becoming a larger version of its smaller self – nor is it a purely accidental succession of chance occurrences. It is a coherent series of *trans*formations (foetus, infant, toddler, teenager, adult) which occur in coordination with environmental input, a cellular differentiation from simple to complex in a coordinated sequence which takes place in the body as a whole.

In good brain science, the brain is, as Derrida likes to say, open to the future, able to respond to and welcome the coming of what it cannot see coming. That re*spon*siveness is spontaneous, and that spontaneity is *re*sponsive.

The Big Other is Big Data

The concern of postmodern hermeneutics is not to demonize technology but to release its creative-productive powers, to preserve the undecidability of the *pharmakon*. Technology is not neutral; it has a tendency to take over. But it has no stable essence,[22] only several different deployments, for *good or for ill*, sometimes curative and sometimes toxic. We have no way to guarantee the outcome in advance – no Providence, no Program, no Method, no Algorithm, which can see-ahead for us and show us the way.

Far from attacking technologies, substitutions, signifying systems, place-holders, signs, imitations, representations, the so-called virtual sphere, we insist upon them. We do not merely reluctantly agree to their necessity as a necessary evil, we affirm them, seeking to keep them in play. Instead of seeking to be immunized against the toxic effect of the virtual world of appearances, images and copies, we defend an auto-immunity, in which the body breaks down its resistance to foreign invaders, willingly allows itself to be contaminated by signs and substitutes, without which nothing will get done; assuming such risk is our only hope, the only way to keep the future open.

The concern is not with the technologies of writing as such but with the attempt to stop their undecidability – by claiming to be hard-wired to the absolute truth. One big menace we face today is the Program, the myth of the Big Algorithm. Our big Other is Big Data. The main task is to preserve the play that is built into systems, because, as dangerous as this play is, it is there that the promise is lodged, and nothing is as dangerous as shutting down the play.

The Postmodern Pharmacy

Plato, one of philosophy's most brilliant writers, once famously reprimanded the world of images with (what else?) a brilliant set of images – the famous 'allegory of the cave' and the 'divided line' (*Republic*, Book VII).[23] Here, he illustrated the abyss separating the really real world from (what we call) the virtual world by dividing the sunny world of true realities and real truth above from the fleeting shadows in the cave below. So, I propose a postmodern counter-image or anti-allegory of our own – one where there is no Philosopher-King who, having dwelled for a while in the upper world, comes down below to sort things out for the rest of us.

Our life is to be compared not with prisoners in a cave but with customers entering a pharmacy – a rather unusual pharmacy. All its wares are on full display, and there is a sign on the door reading 'HELP YOURSELF', but the bottles are not labelled, and there is no one on duty to help us out, no clerks, no cashiers, no pharmacist to tell us which are the medicines and which are the poisons. But the situation is urgent, a matter of life and death. We need pharmaceutical help! Where are we to turn? In Plato's allegory, there is the Philosopher-King, an Absolute Pharmacologist, who sorts things out, supplies the Final Word, closes down the – possibly deadly – play of interpretation. Here, there is no one on hand to assist, and no signs on the bottles that we ourselves can read and try to understand.

This allegory of the pharmacy – an unnerving, dystopic counter-myth to Plato's more reassuring one – is not meant to produce panic and mayhem but to point out the need not for a Philosopher-King but for interpretation. There is of course no actual pharmacy as mad as that. The world is not a Kafkaesque nightmare. It is enough, as with every myth, to see its point, which is to wean ourselves off the idea of Absolute Truth and to insist on the messier hit and miss of interpretation, of searching for clues, putting the pieces together carefully, consulting with others, testing, comparing, in order to sort out the better interpretation. Imagine Plato's allegory, where there is no upper world and all we have to go on are the images, shadows, substitutes and stand-ins. That is not far from the truth – even the physicists tell us that only 5 per cent of the universe is visible – and the rest is made of 'dark' (invisible) matter and energy about which we know little or nothing.[24] Our postmodern myth seeks to protect the irreducible undecidability in the system, the fluctuation and instability in things. Our theory of recollection is to remember that our interpretations are just that: interpretations. Against Plato's realm of Pure Truth, we posit the inescapability of reading the signs, staying in play with the ambiguous play of things in space and time. These things are not pale images of the Eternal Truth but effects of the anonymous systems that are running in the background that have generated our ideas and ideals in the lower case.

Instead of drawing a line decisively dividing real and virtual, we advocate divining differences. We insist that no actual decision can be kept safe from this spectral pharmaceutical scene. We are not saying that everything is terrible.

We are saying everything is risky. We say yes to life, while insisting that life is a messy matter of reading signs and interpreting, and that in the end taking the risk of interpretation is our only hope. Hermeneutics is at bottom a hermeneutics of hope in the face of the promise/threat.

In the past, faced with such fateful pharmacological ambiguity, we looked to religion to cure what ails our souls, trusting that God alone can save us. But today religion, too, is just another poison/cure. Religion is in crisis and, far from being in a position to help out hermeneutics, religion itself needs hermeneutic help. So, it is fitting, at the end, to turn to religion, which is where modern hermeneutics got started.

Postmodern, Post-secular, Post-religious

My particular interest as a philosopher, my academic field of specialization, is the state of religion in the postmodern world, a state that I am inclined to say – it depends upon what day you ask me – is sorry and getting sorrier. Violence, science denial and primitive superstition, on the one side, and sneering dismissal by the intellectuals on the other side, a polarization that in the United States contributed mightily to the rise of Donald Trump. The mainline churches are emptying, young evangelicals are appalled by the bigotry of their elders towards women, people of colour, gays and immigrants, all in the name of God, and the professoriate treats religion like the Ebola virus. Religion is making itself unbelievable and, more often than not, deserves the low regard in which it is held.

My diagnosis? More fruit from the poisoned tree of modernity, and one more reason to turn to postmodern hermeneutics for help. So, in taking up religion, my idea is not to turn to religion for salvation, but to save religion from itself, to show that hermeneutics is the last best hope religion has for salvation. Why bother? Because religion, despite itself, is touching on something deep within us, lacking which we will lead superficial lives. That may sound like a bit of *hybris*, of too much huffing and puffing on my part, but I have spent a certain amount of time thinking about these things and I think I can make it stick.

I BELIEVE THAT I BELIEVE

Once, when Gianni Vattimo, who as we have seen was born and raised a Catholic and became a famous postmodern philosopher, was asked if he still believed, he answered, 'I believe that I believe.'[1] That is, with all his doubts and suspicions, he had a certain faith in faith, in a certain faith, or rather an uncertain one, a faith in something – just not in the old men in the Vatican. A lot of people in the postmodern condition can say that. They could also make the same point in the negative. That is, they could just as easily say they do not believe that they do not believe, that they are unbelievers but not entirely unbelievers, that while they do not believe in demons or an Omniscient Superbeing that does not mean there is no remnant of belief left in them.

They believe and they don't believe; they disbelieve and they don't disbelieve. That is an exquisitely postmodern disposition, an undecidability that cannot be reduced to a simple indecision or confusion: it is picking up on something *out there*, in the world, something that demands interpretation.

That is not unlike the position taken by Derrida – who was raised in a Jewish home and continued to have a religious faith into his early years as a young student of philosophy (Chapter 4), until he finally abandoned it in his mature years. But in a fascinating riff on Augustine's *Confessions* called 'Circumfession', he wrote, in a text I love to quote, that he 'quite rightly passes for an atheist'.[2] Once – actually, quite a few times, whenever I had the chance – I asked him, why do you not just say, '*Je suis*', '*C'est moi*', 'I am' an atheist? To which he replied, because he just doesn't know. That is what others say about him, and maybe they're right, but he himself is not so sure. There are several voices inside of me, he said, making for a veritable conflict of interpretations, and they give each other no rest. He does have a religion, he added, but one that no one so far has noticed, with the result that he is consistently misread.

At this point, modernism, ever sure of its footing, strides forth to say we recognize all this as a third possibility, we have a category for that, a box in which to put it, labelled 'agnosticism' – for the fence-sitters, the undecided, the cautious, who suspend judgement, who refuse to make a bid.

We can count on modernism to get it wrong. Theism, atheism and agnosticism all belong to the same modernist schema. The three all share the same presuppositions – and differ only by striking different positions within these presuppositions: the *pro* position, the *contra* position and the neutral (*ne uter*, neither/nor) position. But they are all about finding the true *proposition* to make about the classical God and classical theism. They all take place in the sphere of propositional belief – for, against and undecided. So, the last thing – the very last thing – I mean by citing Vattimo and Derrida as we come to the end of this book about postmodern hermeneutics is to land up in a position of neutral, disinterested, immunized, undecided fence-sitting like agnosticism. God forbid! If there is anything to be learned from contemporary hermeneutics, it is about the illusion of a position of disinterested neutrality.

Are We Out of Choices?

Still, have we not run out of choices? Neither theism nor atheism nor agnosticism? What's left? The impasse is due to the vocabulary we are using, which is worn out and badly in need of replacement. Not a lot of work gets done by words like 'theism' and 'atheism' any more. These words are the offspring of the modern debate over the religious and the secular, and they have proven to be more trouble than they are worth. Before modernity, everybody was a theist so there was not much call for the word. The word 'atheism' is a creature of modernity and, I concede, once served a critical purpose. Given the amount of harm that religion does to minds – and bodies, if it seizes political power – atheism was a worthy exercise, a good intellectual diet, like laying off the hard stuff. It allowed a lot of people, who are sick of the ignorance, intolerance and superstitious mumbo-jumbo that characterizes so much religion, to let off a lot of steam. Amusingly, that is still going on today among the terribly tiring new atheists, who are anything but new.[3] After all, we have already had one nineteenth century. If you feel the need for another one, go to the movies or watch a costume drama. But atheism has largely run its course and, like the old religion, now does more harm than good. And by this, I mean hardball atheism, I mean 'There is no God. Period. End of discussion.'

The characteristically postmodern idea is a bit subtler. This divide does not hold up, the line drawn between the sides is fuzzy, the walls are porous and there is no clean-cut decision to make between them. A certain undecidability and auto-immunity besets the whole scene. The 'post' in 'post-modern' does not mean 'against the modern' but having passed 'through' the modern and coming out the other end in a new and innovative form. So, my idea is not to subject religion to a modern knock-down critique but to give it a postmodern *re*-reading (repetition or deconstruction). What I am after is to deconstruct the modernist divide between religious and secular.

Post-religious, Post-secular

What shows up in contemporary hermeneutics is a post-modern phenomenon that is both post-religious and post-secular. Secularism is modernity all over again, assuming a pure divide between the religious and the secular, faith and reason, private and public, fact and value, etc. Secularism is just the old idea that hermeneutics has been battling for centuries – the illusion that there is just *one* normative, hash-settling discourse. In the Middle Ages, that was theology; today, it is science. Either way, we are knee-deep in one dogmatism or the other. Secularism is what results when you try to drive religion off the premises, ban it from the public square, exorcize all the demons and, in general, thoroughly *neutralize* or, as Derrida would say, *immunize* public space. I reject the very idea of neutralized space, presuppositionless beginnings, disinterested onlooking. That is a modernist fiction, every bit as mythological in its own way as angels and demons.

The Crisis of Religion

The postmodern point is that there is something about the religious that is worth saving, something, however elusive, that resists the secularist assault, which we see in the opening remarks of Vattimo and Derrida. The religious puts up a fight against contemporary secularism, which unfortunately often drives it to an exaggerated or distorted defence of faith as opposed to reason, of feeling against thinking. Something important is getting itself done and said *in* religion, which is why, despite all the forecasts to the contrary, it is still around today and, in some places, positively flourishing. But the problem is to figure out just what is so important – without falling into superstition and supernaturalism, on the one hand, or just dismissing religion altogether, which is the other hand – and which would only leave its own worst tendencies unchecked.

The problem is hermeneutical. The *interpretive ground* on which religion has stood for several millennia has shifted underneath its feet. That has resulted in a serious crisis. The great biblical narratives originated in an ancient imaginary and they now find themselves in a strange new postmodern one. That leaves pastors scratching their heads about how to preach and a lot of other people (sometimes including the pastors) scratching their heads about why they bother. Religious belief is fast becoming unbelievable. Religion looks ridiculous and, too often, makes itself look ridiculous. It is in serious trouble, and its condition may be terminal. My diagnosis is that it is has suffered a lapse in hermeneutical judgement.

Looking up to Heaven

Let me begin with a very simple example of the problem. When someone prays, why do they look *up*? The answer is a tip-off to the hermeneutic shift, the transformation of the ultimate framework of interpretation, which, to put it in a word, is a shift from heaven to the heavens. We are accustomed to opposing science to religion, as if religion originated in a non-scientific world and is today being challenged by science, which assumes that back in the day science did not exist. That is not exactly right. There is an ancient scientific world-view and it is built right into the Jewish and Christian Scriptures, so the true conflict is not between science and religion but between the ancient science the Scriptures presuppose and the modern science in which religion is forced to make its way today.

In the *ancient* scientific view, everybody, including God, held a flat-earth, geocentric view in which the world was divided into three regions: the heavens above, where God and the gods were to be found, the fiery cauldrons below, and earth in the middle. Some of the ancients thought that the stars were little openings in the sky through which the aroma of our burnt offerings could reach the divine nostrils and thus appease God's anger. In the airy space between earth and heaven the angels and demons did combat over the fate of the people down below. So, when Jesus was resurrected, there was nowhere for him to go but up, to 'ascend' into 'heaven', where God, his 'heavenly father', lived. Today, that would mean he is in orbit somewhere around the earth. One of the ancient fathers of the Church said that, on the way up, Jesus cleared the air of the demons, which made safe passage for the rest of us, who would follow in his airy wake. Hopefully; if you behaved yourself here on earth. Because there was, alas, another direction, another possible destination, in which case you would be dispatched down below. So, even today, when we know better, when we pray, we look up, which means that the faithful on the opposite side of the earth are looking in exactly the opposite direction. It's an old habit, hard to break, the way we all say the sun rises and sets, which is a very geocentric thing to say.

Demythologizing Religion

This ancient world-view affects everything we read in the Scriptures. It is a basic presupposition in those texts. Rudolph Bultmann, one of the greatest New Testament scholars of the twentieth century, described the ancient world-view as mythological, and it clearly deserves some sort of admonitory name like that.[4] Still, we should not forget that, when Ptolemy systematized the best of the ancient view a couple of centuries later, it was based on a considerable amount of observation and held up for over a thousand years (although he did not find any use for the divine-nostrils bit). Bultmann was making a crucial hermeneutical point. We have to appreciate how profoundly the horizon of ancient physics and astronomy is built into and presupposed by these texts, and for two reasons. First, just in order to understand them; they won't make a lot of sense otherwise. Second, in order to discount the old science – that is what he called 'demythologizing' – and this in order to understand how the Scriptures *still* have something to say, something that can be *re*-imagined and is not entirely waylaid by the ancient imaginary.

That is the hermeneutical problem par excellence for biblical religion. Clearly, the tripartite structure of the world has to go. And most people are willing to let go of demons and replace them with psychiatric disorders, but many are very reluctant to let go of their angels. In the United States, angels continue to do well in the polls, right after God and the Bible, and way better than Democrats and Republicans, which is not saying very much. We all know heaven and hell are mythological places – unless you happen to live far from the madding crowd (way too far) and nowhere near a library. There are even flat earthers and young earthers on the loose.

Secularization versus Secularism

The general name for the hermeneutical problem besetting religion is 'secular*ism*'. Secular*ization* is a political structure meaning the separation of Church and state. That is good news (irony intended) and, in the West at least, nearly everyone endorses it. The opposite of secularization is some sort of theocracy. But 'secular*ism*' is a *normative* claim that religion is an illusion. So, it cuts much deeper. It refers to a growing discrediting of religion, first launched in modernist critiques and continued by a postmodern incredulity. Statistically, secular*ism* shows up in the shrinking number of nuns and growing number of 'nones', meaning people who check off 'none' in a census asking for religious affiliation.[5]

Some of these people are second- and third-generation nones, having been raised in non-religious families; they say they don't have a religious bone in their body. Some are 'recovering' evangelicals or Catholics, people who were raised in religious families but who found the whole thing ridiculous as they reached maturity, a common problem for religion today. In the 1990s, when the Celtic tiger took hold in Ireland – for centuries, a profoundly Catholic country – the general population became prosperous and educated. Result? The churches emptied. But the Church's numbers are solid in South America and Africa. Religion flourishes in the soil of ignorance and poverty. But some of the nones resonate with the undecidability that is being picked up by Vattimo and Derrida.

Secularism

So, what is going on? Why is religion on the run? Why is secular*ism* prospering, and why is religion looking more and more unbelievable? Canadian philosopher Charles Taylor wrote a nine-hundred-page book explaining the phenomenon of secularism, so suffice it to say that what follows is making a long story short.[6]

First, it is hard to get past Bultmann's first step. Once you start *demythologizing* the Scriptures, it's hard to get off the stuff. Once you learn that beings born of woman and fathered by a god were a dime a dozen in antiquity, as were healers and exorcists and even people raised from the dead, you tend to see the Incarnation in a new (hermeneutic) light. Once you see that the New Testament Gospels were composed by

Greek-speaking gentiles who never laid eyes on Jesus, or on anybody who ever met Jesus, four decades after his death, who did not know a word of Aramaic, who were antagonistic to the Jewishness of Jesus, who were recording oral traditions meant to sing the praises of Jesus (good news) but are more like folk songs about a legendary hero than historical records – I could go on – you get to see that there is a very wide gulf between an Aramaic-speaking Jewish exorcist and healer from Nazareth named Yeshua and the Christ of Christianity, a word unknown to the authors of the New Testament, not to mention to Yeshua.[7] So modern 'historical consciousness' – the thing Gadamer was criticizing, don't forget – tends to undermine the claims that religious people make about the Bible.

Second, the acute sense of *pluralism* we have cultivated in postmodernity makes it clear that a particular religious tradition is in no small part an accident of birth. I was lecturing in the Middle East a few years ago and, afterwards, a Muslim theologian came up to me and said, look, the simple truth is that the reason I was a Christian and he a Muslim is that I was born in Philadelphia and he was born and raised in the Middle East. True story. Everybody has their own language, culture, tradition and religious narratives. It's a package deal. Having a religion is like having a language, and asking which one is the true religion is lot like asking which one is the true language. It's a category mistake; it does not make any sense. It's a hermeneutical mistake – religious narratives are not journalistic accounts of historical events or scientific accounts of the origin of the universe, and one is not true at the expense of the others. They are a very different kind of hermeneutical fish.

Finally, religious discourse is deeply undermined by the postmodern and post-human imaginary. The need for a Superbeing to create the universe out of nothing, to provide the Meaning of Life to special beings (us) who are the apple of the Divine Eye by redeeming us from sin, is just starting to look really bad, and we are increasingly incredulous. The modernists thought they could positively refute it, but the postmodernists simply treat it with a yawn – you can believe it if you like, but please don't bother the rest of us with your fantasies. Today, we have much more credible alternatives, science based but also drawn from literature and art, which together are filling the vacuum left by religion. But – and this 'but' is crucial – this science is *not* the old modernist, mechanistic reductionism. As I said in the previous chapter, the account of the universe that is opening up for us in contemporary physics is nothing less than majestic, and it is *not* lacking in mystery, beauty, awe and poetry. Contemporary astrophysics and quantum physics are not your great-great-grandfather's Newtonianism. Every imaginary includes an unimaginable, a place of surpassing mystery. The God of classical theism is turning out to be a place-holder for the infinite and incomprehensible, a place that today is being taken over by a universe beyond all imagination.[8]

Who's Trapped?

Some religious people like to pat themselves on the back with the thought that, if you don't have the classical God, you are trapped inside a confining sphere of immanence, which is, to be kind, an amusing thing to say. Trapped? A universe with multi-dimensions, not two, not even three, but possibly eleven? The universe that is unfolding today is deeply mysterious and, unlike the old religious narratives, whose authors were following their heart, the scientists are following the maths. The best way to deal with this bit of religious condescension towards what amounts to an infinite universe (meaning we'll never get to the end of it) is with a counter-condescending amusement. If your reaction to this vast, mysterious and incomprehensible universe is to ask, 'Is this all there is?', if the universe we are exploring today, in all its length and breadth and depth, seems flat, if you feel trapped by that, you just need to get out more. We should take up a collection and buy these people a subscription to *Scientific American*.

Tillich's Theological Atheism

So, the postmodern, indeed post-human, imaginary turns on an incredulity about the old theism and installs a new kind of atheism, one that is not simply at odds with religion, with a certain kind of religion, as we saw in Vattimo and Derrida. Interestingly enough, there is another atheism that has always been important to religion and performed an important theological service. I am thinking of the 'purifying atheism' of which Simone Weil speaks,[9] or the mystical atheism of Meister Eckhart's saying, 'I pray God to rid me of God.'[10] I know of no way that deconstruction can improve on Eckhart's formula. It should be inscribed on the front door of every seminary, to protect the seminarians from idolatry.

But there is still another variation on atheism, one that is not antagonistic to theology but is the basis of another kind of post-theistic theology. In this new kind of theology, classical theism is a mistake, mythological, even a tad blasphemous. The atheism of the new theology is theology's own way of bidding adieu to God (*à Dieu*). Not an atheism in the door-slamming and dogmatic manner of the common-or-garden variety atheists but an atheism that opens up the door for something neither theistic nor atheistic, neither religious nor secular, an atheism that is not the end of theology but the beginning.

That is the singular service provided by Paul Tillich, who said something of striking importance for religion and theology, thereby providing the hermeneutic clue to what I am calling the post-religious:

> God is no object for us as subjects. He [it was 1946 – give him a break] is always that which precedes this division. But, on the other hand, we speak about him and we act upon him, and we cannot avoid it, because everything which becomes real to us enters the subject–object correlation. Out of this paradoxical situation the half-blasphemous and mythological concept of the 'existence of God' has arisen. And so have the abortive attempts to prove the existence of this 'object'. To such a concept and to such attempts atheism is the right religious and theological reply.[11]

If ever I start up a school of divinity, God forbid, that would be my charter statement to which all prospective donors to the endowment of my institution would have to subscribe. It is on my shortlist of adroit and insightful theological utterances made in the last two centuries, and it points the way out of the modernist dead-end. No one has got us off to a better start in coming up with an alternative vocabulary to the theist/atheist impasse than Tillich; no one has offered a better way out of religion's hermeneutical crisis.

Half-blasphemous and Mythological

Tillich's language is very strong: the God under discussion in the classical debates between theism and atheism (and agnosticism) is half-blasphemous and mythological. Let's take each term in turn.

By *mythological*, he means treating God as a Big Somebody with personal characteristics, a doer of various deeds, a speaker (quite a multilingual one) with whom we can have a conversation, very respectfully, of course, asking for things, thanking him, etc. That's a classic mythological gesture – we see it everywhere, in Greek and Roman religion, in literature – to personify the impersonal, to make the sun, the sea, thunder, or justice or truth into a Superperson with whom we can converse and negotiate. Even our own beloved Hermes is such a creature. It makes things easier, so long as you don't examine your language too carefully.

Tillich himself is actually snagged by this problem in this very text when he refers to God in the masculine, which had been the gender of choice for the divinity right up to the time in which Tillich was writing. Mary Daly (1928–2010), one of the first and most ferocious feminists of the day – she wouldn't let men attend her classes – was willing to look past that, and she got a lot out of reading Tillich, but he would never have got away with it today. But you see his problem. His choices were limited. A lot of feminists today say 'She', but that is mostly a (well-earned) poke at patriarchy (the theorists call it a 'strategic reversal').

Truth to tell, the biblical God does not really have genitalia and so God is neither masculine nor feminine, and it seems a little insulting to call God 'it', the only remaining choice. Tillich is tolerant of this abuse because it is an inevitability of grammar. When we say 'it is raining' we don't mean some particular 'it' is doing something to get us wet. As he says, it is next to impossible for us *not* to speak like subjects speaking about objects. The main thing is to be mindful of that and to remember that God is no such thing – a particular object circumscribed by a thinking subject – even if we are forced to talk like that. When we do, we are like astronomers saying that the sun rises. Nowadays, we stand on our grammatical head to avoid saying God is a 'he', but the philosophical point to remember is this. God is not masculine or feminine or *merely* neutral, because God belongs to a different order altogether. It is a 'category mistake' to talk like that. You might as well ask what colour God is or what toothpaste God prefers.

That brings us to the next point: *half-blasphemous*. Blasphemy means to say something unbecoming about God, to make God less than God is, to treat the infinite being of God as if God were a finite being, like a particular person who says or does things, or leaves us quite perplexed by *not* doing them just when we think 'he' should (everything from preventing natural disasters to helping out the local football team). God is not a being, not even a really terrific one, not even the Supreme Being, at the top of the list of beings. No matter how many supers and superlatives you tack on, the highest being, the smartest, the most real, even if you adorn God with every omni-attribute you can think of, that still reduces God to a de-finite being, albeit the first in his class, *maxima cum laude*.

For Tillich, God is not a Superbeing but the 'ground of being', the deepest source and foundation of all beings. While individual beings come to be (from out of the ground) and pass away (back into the ground), the ground itself is everlasting and inexhaustible. God is not a thing or a super-thing – masculine, feminine or neutral – but that from which and into which things come and go. In Tillich, 'being itself' replaces the 'supreme being' and relieves it of its divine duties.

The Unconditional

If that all sounds like too much philosophical theology for our postmodern ears, Tillich offers us another, *existential* vocabulary – Tillich loved Kierkegaard and knew Heidegger personally – which plugs right into experience: the *unconditional*.

Let's start with an example. Once, when I was lecturing in Belfast, my wife and I walked by a sign advertising the *Titanic* museum, which we decided to visit. On the walk over, we recalled the great scene in the movie of the string quartet which continued to play even as the ship went under. I suspected that was Hollywood's contribution, but sure enough, there were pictures of the quartet at the museum and testi-monials to the bravery of the musicians. I found myself think-ing, if they wanted to be altruistic and brave, why not put down their instruments and help get the women and children on the life boats? Tillich's answer would be that this was more than moral bravery; it was something deeper, something he called in a really famous book 'the courage to be'.[12]

On this interpretation, these musicians were saying, 'This is what life will have been about, *merci, adieu*.' This was their unconditional affirmation of life, of the beauty of life as embodied in their art. There wasn't anything in it for them – they were not going to get a raise from their employer for their next engagement and they had no idea they would become famous. They were not doing this on the condition that they would get something in return. It was done, as Meister Eckhart would say, 'without why', unconditionally.

Or think of physicians who leave prosperous practices behind to join Doctors Without Borders and put themselves in harm's way to fight the Ebola virus in West Africa. Or sci-entists who spend themselves in pursuit of a cure for a deadly disease. Or to crack one of the mysteries of the uni-verse. Or people who spend their time and efforts on behalf of the homeless, or to protect the environment, or to fight cruelty to animals.

Or 'whatever' – so long as they do *not* do what they do because they think a Superbeing somewhere is promising eternal rewards if they do and eternal punishment if they don't. There are very few ideas that do genuine religion more damage than that one – and that idea is all over the Scrip-tures, not just Alabama.

A Matter of Ultimate Concern

Genuine religion, Tillich says, is a matter of ultimate concern, of being seized by something of ultimate or unconditional worth.[13] Period. What I like about this definition is that there is no mention of clergy, candles, inerrant books, demons, damnation, dogmas or threats of excommunication. Where is the unconditional found? Anywhere and everywhere that people affirm something that matters unconditionally, who are seized by the depth of life, of reality. Religion is the depth dimension in *all* experience, not a specific *region* of experience. It can't be confined to quarters, as it is in modernism. Tillich's religion is a religion of the unconditional, his theology a theology of the unconditional.

Not only is there no mention of churches or temples, the very existence of a demarcated sacred space is testimony to our modernist alienation. So, just as there are no temples in the heavenly Jerusalem – you won't have to get up on Sunday morning to go to church, since, presumably, God would be all in all – there is also no need of them in Tillich's religion. The important thing is that you can get the same thing done, getting in touch with the depth of things, in an artistic life or a scientific laboratory, as a teacher or a nurse, as a parent or a spouse. *Whatever* you do.

Tillich's notion of the unconditional cuts through the binary opposition of the religious and the secular – and all the *other* categories that are canonized in modernity as well, like subject and object – like a hot knife through butter. He distinguishes instead – and here we can hear the existentialist Tillich – between people who lead lives in touch with the 'depth' dimension in things, who believe something, who believe in something, who affirm something, who are gripped by something of unconditional importance, and people who do not, who lead superficial lives, which sounds a bit like the distinction between authenticity and inauthenticity in *Being and Time*. We hasten to add that this distinction need not become a new binary opposition but one that, in postmodern (deconstructive) style, we understand to be as porous and ambiguous as any other distinction. We all have good days and bad, noble moments and ignoble ones. *We live in the distance between the condition and the unconditional.*

Symbols

One of the central hermeneutical categories employed by Tillich emerges if we ask, what about religion in the strict or common sense – the world religions, like Christianity, Judaism and Islam, Buddhism and Hinduism? Tillich himself was a professional Christian theologian, so what did he think of Christianity in particular? Christianity, he said, like every religion, is a *symbol* of a matter of ultimate concern.[14] Now, since over the years he collected his weekly pay cheques from three famous Christian divinity schools, he tended to say it was the very best symbol. But there is no good reason in his work to think that this meant much more than saying that it was the one that meant the most to him. This was something like offering a toast to your parents on the occasion of their fiftieth wedding anniversary which declares them the best parents in the world. No one in the room takes that to be a factual, testable, propositional claim. It is meant to embarrass them with love's excess.

To the objection immediately raised by the faithful that it is very insulting to be told that religion is only a symbol, Tillich responds that no one who truly understands what a symbol is would ever say 'only a symbol'. You can see this in the passions that are inflamed when someone burns the national flag and then says, well, it's only a flag, only a symbol. People die – and kill – for symbols. Real symbols, living symbols, grab us in the depths of our being. Symbols are living things and they are not refuted; they die because they lose their grip.

The Interpretation of Symbols

With the introduction of the category of the symbol, of the *hermeneutics of the symbol*, the old debates about theism and atheism collapse – they become competing idolatries. The unconditional does not exist *as such*. It is not a particular being but a quality of being itself, and the only way it *can exist* is under certain conditions, which give it symbolic expression. The unconditional is the infinite depth of being in certain finite historical, conditional modes of being – Greek or Jew, West or East, ancient or modern, scientific or artistic, masculine or feminine, religious or secular. These conditions are contingent and historical – we don't get to choose the conditions that precondition us, like our parents or our hometown or our inherited language and traditions. But conditions as such, coming to be under some conditions

rather than others, are necessary; otherwise, the unconditional would be some sort of free-floating abstraction.

So, the challenge is to feel about for – to *interpret* – the
unconditional that is being symbolically expressed *in* the concrete conditions under which it presents itself, and not to
confuse the two. Do not ever, Tillich pleads, *identify* the
symbol (say, Christianity) with what is being symbolized (the
unconditional). That's the idolatry and semi-blasphemy.
That's why we require what Tillich called the 'Protestant principle', that the conditional is never an adequate expression of
the unconditional, and that principle includes both historical
Protestantism and Catholicism in its sweep.[15] It includes
everything; it is a universal hermeneutical principle.

Remember Tillich was German

To understand further what Tillich was saying about a
symbol, we should recall that he was a German – but, I am
happy to say, of the very opposite kind to Heidegger (whose
work Tillich used and admired). He emigrated to the United
States in 1933 after a book he published that same year exposing National Socialism for what it was cost him his job. He
was steeped in the German Idealist idea of *Geist*, of the 'Absolute Spirit', in Hegel and Schelling. Hegel had said that the
Absolute Spirit expresses itself in three ascending ways. In its
most sensuous form, it is expressed in the work of art, and in
its highest intellectual form, in absolute knowledge, which
Hegel identified with philosophy. In between the two is
religion, which shares in the sensuousness of art but is higher
than art inasmuch as it also has a certain intellectual content,

like philosophy, albeit expressed in a distinctively religious mode. This he called a *Vorstellung*, which means an imaginative-pictorial mode, like a parable or a narrative, which is making an important point while still retaining the imagery and sensuous appeal of an artwork. So, Jesus does not only tell parables; Jesus is a parable. *Vorstellung* is clearly the ancestor of Tillich's idea of a symbol.

A *Vorstellung* is like a National Geographic special picturing the Big Bang but without the mathematics – the imagery is sensuous, graspable, but it is both more than an arbitrary graphic design and less than mathematical. The religious symbol has the advantage of being graspable, of grabbing people 'in the gut', people who would not last under the withering abstractions of a lecture in the philosophy department. *Geist* is a hard word to translate, but 'gut' picks up one important part of it. Religion, Hegel said, is how most people get their philosophy, somewhat like the way a lot of people, who have not seen the inside of an art museum since the last time they were dragged there by a teacher, manage to get their art at a football game. So, when Hegel said that Christianity is the absolute truth, the Prussian Minister of Religious Affairs smiled broadly, but then Hegel added: in the form of a *Vorstellung*, that is, of a story. Still, he insists, it is the greatest story ever told, the absolute truth in the form of a story, like a great novel.

Derrida's Quasi-Jewish Principle

If some of this reminds you of what we were saying about Jacques Derrida, it should. Not that Derrida knew anything about Tillich or had any interest in him. As far as I know, he did not. But the two of them were on to something similar, which shows up in their very choice of words: the unconditional. There is a striking analogy between the distinctions they make between the conditional and the unconditional, as well as between Tillich's Protestant principle and what I will hazard to call Derrida's – let's say – quasi-Jewish, slightly atheistic messianic principle. The latter I would formulate as follows: no contingent construction is ever adequate to the undeconstructible. No existing democracy is ever the match for the democracy to come, no work of justice is ever the match for the justice to come. Every time we use a noun in deconstruction, we have to keep it in the lower case and punctuate it with an infinitive, a to-come. The infinitive is not meant to signify an actual infinite, or an Infinite Ideal, an Essence, an Eternal Form, or any sort of everlasting something or other that we are always trying to approximate empirically. It signifies instead a historical, unconditional open-endedness, an unlimited exposure to the future, a promise, which is always a risk.

What's the Difference between Tillich and Derrida?

The difference between Tillich and Derrida goes back to the German metaphysics of *Geist* that still clings to Tillich, even after all those years living in New York City, the notion of an infinite substantial reality that undergirds concrete, finite things. Tillich's post-theistic position is not pantheistic, as it might sound at first blush. It is what came to be known as pan*e*ntheism, a metaphysical theology in which God-is-*in*-all and all-is-*in*-God. That avoids the silliness of saying that God is everything, including the bottle of ketchup on the kitchen table or that ill-tempered old uncle who occasionally shows up for Sunday dinner. But, since it is *in* everything, it also allows Andy Warhol to reproduce something as commonplace as a bottle of ketchup *as* a work of art from which we have something to learn about what is going on in our lives. Nonetheless, as sensible as it is, panentheism is still a *metaphysics*, and hence the sort of overarching (or undergirding) thing from which Derrida regularly excuses himself.

So, it is not the philosophical-theological side of Tillich (the 'ground of being') that converges with Derrida but the existential-experiential side, the hermeneutics of the unconditional, leading an unconditional life – being seized by something of unconditional worth, affirming something of unconditional value, without having a Big Story about the ultimate nature of reality. Derrida, I propose, offers the better of the two versions of the unconditional. Metaphysical debates are like cars up on jacks: you can accelerate to infinity and get absolutely nowhere. We are better off sticking to the slower paths of experience. Better to speak of the hermeneutics of being called upon and responding to – something, I know not what. Let's just call it the event, and not go all metaphysical. Better to isolate an underlying structure of our experience, one that sorts out the things in life of only passing significance from the things of unconditional importance – be they found in art or ethics, theory or practice, science or everyday life, whatever they are and wherever they are found.

Weakening the Spirit into the Spectre

So, instead of an ontology, we once again encounter Derrida's hauntology; instead of the Absolute Spirit, a spectre; instead of Being, a demi-being, a ghost. In a riff on the ponderous tone of Heidegger, Derrida says the *es gibt* (it gives, there is, Being) becomes *es spukt*: the whole place is spooked. What is, what there is, is haunted by the *arrivants*, the ones who are to come, and the *revenants*, the ones who come back from the dead to insist we finish the business of life they left unfinished.

In this way, the Holy Spirit of high Trinitarian theology, first brought down to earth in the Absolute Spirit of Hegelian metaphysics, then further grounded in the ground of being in Tillich, has become a spectre, even a spook. This history – the history of the deconstruction of Christianity, of the Holy Spirit – is the history of what Vattimo calls a *weakening*. If the pious complain that this is the history of a loss, the response is that this loss is nothing to regret, no more than a chap who, after much dieting and exercise, loses a hundred pounds would think he is worse off for the loss. This is the history of a reduction – an ontological, phenomenological and hermeneutical reduction – which trims an overweight metaphysical theology into a form fit for life.

What is gained by the loss is a new vitality, a new spiritedness that preserves the lightness of life, the undecidability of a fluctuating experience. This reduced theology introduces us to what religion would look like in the postmodern world, which takes the form of a post-religion, a post-secular religion of the unconditional. Having passed through the history of strong theology, it emerges all the more vitally and vibrantly in the form of weak theology, trimmed down to the needs of being-in-the-world, turning on a deeper faith, hope and love of life that has shed the excessive weight of supernaturalist beliefs and of religion's powerful institutional interests.

Every Revelation is Special

This explains why postmodern hermeneutics finds something going on *in* religion without quite swallowing religion's own account of what is going on. The name of justice is the name of a promise still unkept – the memory of a promise, the promise of a memory – handed down to us from time immemorial and by who knows what unidentifiable sources and stirrings in a spectral past. The *specifically* Christian symbol – there are indefinitely many other symbols – is constituted by the memory and the promise of Yeshua, a figure largely lost in the fog of history, but the magnetizing point of multiple musings over the centuries, always promising to come again, 'Christianity' being constituted by and opened up as the history of his deferral, of his repeated failure to show up. If he ever showed up, the whole thing would be over.

The hermeneutical mistake I was speaking about at the beginning is this. What Christian revelation reveals is not another world populated with supernatural beings but a specific form of being-*in*-the-world. It is a distinctive and special revelation, the way our parents are special, but it is one of many. A revelation, then, is taken not – as in the mythological and half-blasphemous view – as a supernatural intervention from on high about a world outside space and time. It is not taken as the action of a Superagent who delivers a secret message to mankind – often aided by his messenger angels – the key to the mystery which mortals could never have come up with on their own. Instead, a revelation reveals a form of life; it is the inbreaking of a way to be that lays claim to us unconditionally. The distinctive form of life in the case of the New Testament goes under the name of the kingdom of God, meaning a topsy-turvy and inverted world in which the last shall be first and we are summoned to forgive and love our enemies. Such a form of life looks like madness to what the world calls wisdom and like weakness to what the world calls power (1 Cor. 1:18–31).[16]

From a hermeneutical point of view, a revelation is not taken as a heavenly intervention or a supernatural unveiling but as a *poetic* disclosure. A religious revelation is a poetics – a constellation of parables and paradoxes, of striking sayings and memorable narratives – of what life would look like if God ruled instead of the world, where the name of God is the name of an event. *Every* culture has such a revelatory event, in just the way that it has a language that sings the world in its own distinctive way. What is religious about religion has little to do with dogmas and doctrines, orthodoxies and heresies, clergy and candles. It is found everywhere, in art and science, in ethics and in politics, and all too often it is *not* found precisely in what calls itself religion, which too often is serving up a half-blasphemous and mythological simulacrum of the real thing, which has had the misfortune to fall into the wrong hands.

When people claim to speak with the authority of God, get your hat and head for the door. That is not God speaking but a violently self-assertive will that is prepared not only to die for its take on the truth but to kill for it. But the unconditional is a fragile, precious, priceless something-I-know-not-what in life, an enchanting magic without the mystifications of the supernatural. The unconditional does not require a house of worship and weekly contributions. It requires only a subtle hermeneutic eye, what Rambach called the *subtilitas intelligendi*, to see that it is staring you right in the face.[17]

A Quick Review

WHAT IS POSTMODERN HERMENEUTICS IN A NUTSHELL?

Philosophical Hermeneutics – or Theological?

If I were pressed for a take-away line for my argument in this book, I would say, interpretation goes all the way down, in support of which I would single out the line from Augustine that I cited above, 'I have become a great question to myself.' Augustine sums up the hermeneutic situation, the radical or postmodern one – the endless questionability of lives, which means the endless *interpretability* of our lives. The best answer hermeneutics has to the question of who we are is that we *are* that question. The question *is* the answer. The *next* question for Heidegger was whether we have the where-withal to sustain that questionability, to cope constantly with that interpretability, or whether we will sink back into received opinions and swallow the line served up by the powers that be.

But wait! Augustine *was* one of the powers that be, a famous bishop, arguably the main architect of mainstream Christian theology, who did not suffer 'alternative interpret-ations' gladly. These he denounced, in no uncertain terms, as heresies. True, but that was more true later on, say, in *The City of God*. Notice that Heidegger and Derrida go back to Augustine's *Confessions*, which is a masterpiece of the search-ing soul, of the spiritual sojourner, sometimes called the first autobiography.[1] They found a way to let Augustine speak to us postmodern pilgrims by feeling around for another and more subversive line of thinking, which shows up clearly in *Being and Time*.[2]

So, then, is this a philosophical hermeneutics, as we said at the start, or a theological one? Is Augustine doing philosophy or theology? In what part of the library do we put his books? In which academic department is he to be taught? Augustine would have smiled. He said philosophy is the love of truth and God is truth. Departmentalize that! He lived *before* modernity, and his head was not filled with all the boxes of modernity. That's one of the ways the premodern and the postmodern converge. We postmodern types, too, treat such distinctions with a measured incredulity. So, when I started the previous chapter by saying that my field of specialization is religion and postmodernism, I was also confessing that I myself have never been able to choose between philosophy and theology. Real theology, I think, is just a way 'to regroup before the impossible', as Catherine Keller says,[3] which I think is also exactly what philosophy is. Both philosophy and theology are fed by a deeper spring, by something *pre*-philosophical, *pre*-theological, even *pre*-logical.

What is Postmodern Hermeneutics in a Nutshell?

Accordingly, when the young Heidegger said we have a vague pre-understanding of something, who knows what – Being? God? World? – something very elemental, that we spend our lives trying to articulate, *that's hermeneutics . . . in a nutshell.*

One last time: interpretation goes all the way down. Down where? Into this ever-reinterpretable something or other. But how would we ever gain access to something that elemental? We are already there. That's the hermeneutical circle. We are always going back to where we already are, back to the things that makes us *us*, back to the deep structure of our lives. We are always looking for a way to formulate this primal contact with things. Over the course of our lives, we build up a host of various *beliefs about* this, that or the other thing, most of which has got into our heads because of when and where we are born, but flowing underneath these beliefs is a more primal *faith in* the world itself, in life itself, a faith that precedes the division between beliefs and doubts, philosophy and theology, the sciences and the humanities.

Hermeneutics situates itself precisely there, at that very point where we are plugged into the world, engaged *in* and *by* and *with* the world, and its task is to let that come into words. That is why I count the mystics among our sharpest and most subtle thinkers. Their paradoxes and conundrums ('I pray God to rid me of God!') reflect the delicacy of the double bind we are in. As soon as we speak *about* the world, we have made the world into an object, packaged the pre-propositional into a proposition, objectified the pre-objective, making a pretence that we have somehow found a standpoint outside the world and can speak about it as from afar.

The work of hermeneutics is, to borrow an expression from William James, to turn on the light fast enough to see the dark. Hermeneutics seeks some kind of non-objectifying discourse, some way of speaking not *about* but *from out of* our experience of the world. That is how I read what Derrida called the interpretative imperative, which requires a certain ear to hear, a certain subtlety (*subtilitas intelligendi*). This imperative is not an imperial edict, not a clear and powerful voice, but a more muted and obscure summons, a quiet call, the sort of thing you might hear if, in a moment of genuine silence, you pause to listen to the music of the world. This silence keeps us up in the middle of the night, or sneaks up on us unawares in the middle of a busy day. That is what I love about the early morning, which is when things are clearest to me. That's why some people love the ocean, or a still lake, and why Heidegger loved his cabin in the Black Forest and what worried him about the fast and noisy pace of the technological world. He was always talking about hearing a call – of existential conscience in *Being and Time* and, later on, in a more poetic voice, a call of Being, or of the world. The business of life is to strain to hear what is addressing us, to enter into the dialogue in which the world beckons and we respond.[4] This response is accomplished not in empty talk but in action (*subtilitas applicandi*), not in a single act but in the curve our life cuts as we move through the world, in everything we think or do in life.

It Spooks

So, when I speak of a call, I am not talking about hearing voices in our head, I mean instead this silence. Back in *Being and Time* (§§56–7), when Heidegger is speaking of the call of conscience, he says that it has no content, does not pass on any factual information or words of wisdom, does not give any sage advice about choosing a profession or whom to marry. It does not tell us the secret of life. But instead of leaving everything ambiguous and up in the air, the call produces exactly the opposite effect. For all that silence and nothingness, Heidegger says, 'what the call discloses is unequivocal',[5] even though it may be interpreted differently from one person to the next. There is no mistaking *that* we have been *summoned*, singled out and put on the spot. Furthermore, nothing stops us from turning on the television, or telling ourselves it is just a bit of indigestion and this highly uncomfortable moment will pass, that in the morning we will be feeling much better ('inauthenticity').

If we press Heidegger about who or what is doing the calling, we get the same answer: the caller leaves no calling card.[6] Still, he says, this is nothing negative. In fact, it constitutes the call in the most positive way because it summons up our *responsibility*. If we could identify the author of the call, then the authority of the caller would take over and we would be off the hook. The questionability would cease, the answer would be in and the need for interpretation would halt there. We could be assured that someone – God or Nature, the Program or our DNA, something – is in charge. Instead, Heidegger insists, it leaves us disturbed and uneasy.

He says, 'it calls, against our expectations and even against our will'.[7] 'It' calls, an unfamiliar 'it', a spooky something or other, something 'uncanny', which translates the German *unheimlich*, literally, not-at-home, leaving us with a sense of being a stranger in a strange world. If Heidegger had a better sense of humour, after saying 'it calls', he could have added 'it spooks' (*es spukt*) and then had some fun with *es gibt* and *es spukt*, with ontology and hauntology, all of which had to wait for Derrida, the prankster hermeneut.[8]

So, even if we say, as Heidegger does later on, that this is the call of the world, that does not identify a definite caller. It just means it is not coming from *another* world, beyond space and time. It is more like something that is getting itself called without an active and identifiable caller, something that insinuates itself into the cracks and crevices of everyday life. The situation is very strange: a caller of unknown identity pays an unexpected call upon us, and, by saying nothing and maintaining silence, reduces us to silence and puts us on the spot. Imagine Scrooge awakened in the night by a ghost that simply sits and stares at him.

That, I think, cuts to the nerve of radical or postmodern hermeneutics. It describes the ultimate interpretive situation, where it is the uncanniness that *calls for an interpretation*. It is precisely then that we are asked to decide just what sort of life we want to lead, not in a purely autonomous way but in a responsible way, in *response* to everyone and everything around us which is calling upon us, so that the decision is, as Derrida says, the 'decision of the other in me'. It calls for a decision, one that in the broadest terms we might say consists in a decision to say 'yes' to the world, warts and all, to affirm the world, which is all in all, and to sustain the endless questionability, the irreducible reinterpretability, of our lives.

Life goes on, decisions have to be made. We cannot live in sheer, open-ended suspense, waiting for a Final Word that never arrives. So, we have need of various provisional hermeneutic substitutes – stand-ins, representatives, representations, place-holders, symbols, couriers, envoys, agents, delegates, spokespersons, philosophical and theological nicknames – to give concrete form to the call, to allow the 'unconditional' to take shape in the concrete conditions in which it presents itself. Hermes, of course, was the first symbol we formed of the interpretive imperative, until he lost his job to the biblical angels – while both Hermes and the angels are being put out of work today by Watson. That's the history of hermeneutics – in a nutshell.

Perhaps! – But who is willing to concern himself with such dangerous perhapses! For that we have to await the arrival of a new species of philosopher, one which possesses tastes and inclinations opposite to and different from those of its predecessors – philosophers of the dangerous 'perhaps' in every sense. – And to speak in all seriousness: I see such new philosophers arising.

FRIEDRICH NIETZSCHE[9]

A Conclusion without Conclusion

A GOD EVEN NIETZSCHE COULD LOVE

Now that we have heard from all the big names in hermeneutics today, heard most of their big ideas and observed the way hermeneutics plays itself out in our postmodern and increasingly post-human world, let's listen in again on the dialogue between me and a sceptic about hermeneutics that started us off.

Having reached the end of this book, are not philosophers supposed to say something about the secret of life?

If so, then I would say the secret is there is no Secret, no Secret Truth or Key which unlocks the mystery. That was one of the reasons Derrida avoided the word 'hermeneutics', but in the postmodern interpretation of interpretation cultivated here, we make no attempts to break a code or to find a secret meaning. The secret is a *structural* secret.

And 'structural' here means what?

It means that it's built into the system. It's not like somebody knows the secret and is withholding it from us. It is beyond access, in recess, in principle, withheld from all of us. The ark of the covenant is empty; there is nothing there. Imagine a portrait for which there was no model, a copy for which there was no original. It's portraits, copies, substitutes, supplements, all the way down. The Secret is not hidden somewhere until someone discovers it or until it is revealed to us from on high. It is what is always lacking in every interpretation. So, the best we can do is to stay in play with the ambience and ambiguity, the open-endedness and unprogrammability, that permeates the hermeneutic condition.

That's exactly why a lot of people, hearing all that ambiguity, turn to God.

God is not the Secret but a symbol of the Secret. Still, symbols are important. So, if I don't have a Secret to pass on, I do have something of a surprise – I have not quite given up on God, or, let's say, on the name (of) 'God'. I think it might still have some life left in it, and of that God Nietzsche is the prophet.

Nietzsche? Who said that God is dead?

The very same, and I agree, the God whom Nietzsche criticized is well and truly dead. But Nietzsche once had his Zarathustra ask, If there is a God, what would there be left for me to create?[1] That's a great question. For Nietzsche, the death of God meant the birth of human creativity. Without God, everything is possible. But I take Nietzsche's objection to God and turn it into a great theological breakthrough. What if, I ask in return, *that* is what God *is*? What if the name of God were the name of everything that is *possible*, up to and including the impossible?[2]

And you think Nietzsche could live with this God?

The problem with God for Nietzsche, for a lot of philoso-phers, has always been that God is something of a conversation stopper, a force meant to arrest the play of interpretation, which is why Nietzsche was, let's say, dead set against God. I've been saying that there is an analogy between God's Providence and the Computer Program-to-come, between the Superbeing and the Supercomputer, Yahweh and Watson, so to speak. But my proposal here is to take Nietzsche at his word, take him as the prophet of a new species of theologians – which I would tweak by adding theologians who together foretell a coming God.

And who or what is the coming God?

The God who is taken not as Divine Providence but *as event*; not as the sure hand at the wheel of history but as the promise of the future, which, like any promise, cannot be protected from the threat; not as the enemy of invention but as the very possibility of inventiveness; not as menace to interpretive creativity but its *agent provocateur*; not as the final Why in the sky but as the 'Why not?' This God is not the 'necessary being' of the old philosophers but the may-being of the coming philosophers, new philosophers and theologi-ans of the ultimate 'perhaps' inscribed in things. Then God would be the very thing Nietzsche is calling for in *Beyond Good and Evil*, the very thing prophesied by the 'philosophers of the dangerous "perhaps".'[3] This is a God even Nietzsche could love.

Maybe, but then what would this God have to do with the Bible?

More than you might think. Time and again, the Scriptures say that, with God, everything is possible. The 'kingdom of God' in the Scriptures is full of all kinds of impossible things, miracles and wonders, one amazing turn of events after another. But remember, the Scriptures are 'good news', stories, not newspaper reports. The evangelists are not journalists. The Scriptures are songs of hope, calling for the coming of the kingdom, which is always to-come. They are a *poetics* where the name of God is a stand-in, a trope, a symbol, in Tillich's sense.

A symbol of what?

Of hope. The name of God is a nickname for hope, for hope against hope. The future is always better, not because it is, but because that is our hope. At bottom, religion, if that word is still worth saving (and I am not certain that it is), does not have to do with *beliefs* but with our primal *faith* in the world; it does not have to do with *dogma* but with our deepest *desire*. The name of God is a stand-in for something that we desire with a desire beyond desire. This is not the desire for this or that, but the desire for something, I know not what, which pries open our more particular desires, which maintains the open-endedness of desire itself, of unconditional desire, keeping it always and already exposed to the future. Faith deeper than belief, hope against hope, desire beyond desire, not the possibility of this or that, but the possible, the perhaps *itself* – 'if there is such a thing', as Derrida always adds.

And this is hermeneutics why?

It is a hermeneutics of our primal point of engagement with the world, which we are always trying to wrestle into words, to go back to the young Heidegger. It is a hermeneutics of the 'dangerous "perhaps"', of the promise/threat, in which the name of God functions as a place-holder for the hermeneutical imperative. The name (of) 'God' is an envoy, an icon of the call to interpret the endlessly reinterpretable. That means to think the unthinkable, to conceive the inconceivable, to speak the ineffable, to imagine the unimaginable, to do the undoable, to go where we cannot go. It makes us restless with the present and drives our faculties to their limits. It names a limit state we never reach. It does service for something for which we pray and weep.

Pray? Are you serious?

Perfectly. Part of the perversity of my proposal is that I am not willing to give the old species of theologians exclusive rights to the word 'prayer'. Prayer is part of our elemental condition. To pray is to pay quiet and resolute attention to our elemental condition. We are always praying, with or without religion. Indeed, prayer really only kicks into gear when we pray without any of religion's assurances, without the least assurance that there is anyone to pray to, anyone to hear our prayers, anyone with the power to answer our prayers, and without a precise idea of what we are praying for.

But what would such a prayer look like?

I think the ultimate prayer is to say 'yes' to the world, like Molly Bloom's fetching soliloquy in James Joyce's *Ulysses*, 'and yes I said yes I will Yes'.[4] Even, especially, if this is the last thing we say on earth, as in the example of the string quartet on the *Titanic*. Yes, yes, amen – to the future, to the promise of the world, to the endless interpretability and re-interpretability of the world.

So, in the end . . .

. . . there is no end in sight. The hermeneutic beat goes on, like an infinite improvisation. There is no Final Interpretation that puts an end to other interpretations. Interpretations live on in the plural and the lower case, always exposed to the dangerous 'perhaps'. We pass our lives mingling with the mystery, discerning what is being asked of us, struggling to name the shifting shapes of the clouds, now a man with a long nose, now a horse. Every interpretation is exposed to an interpretation to come, that is always to-come, that never shows up. That endlessness does not discourage us. It lures us on and keeps the future open. It sustains the questionability. Hermeneutics is conducted in the language of the supplement, of the stand-in, of the symbol, of the substitute.

Of the substitute for . . . ?

. . . something, I know not what. It depends upon the interpretation.

SUGGESTIONS FOR

Further Reading

GENERAL

Jean Grondin, *Introduction to Philosophical Hermeneutics* (Introduction, note 1), which has a Foreword by Gadamer, is a superb and compact historical introduction to hermeneutics, with expert summaries of the major figures and movements from classical antiquity to the present. Grondin includes a carefully organized sixty-page bibliography which covers everything of importance through the mid-1990s. For another excellent work of similar scope but with a more literary angle, see Gerald L. Bruns, *Hermeneutics Ancient and Modern* (New Haven: Yale University Press, 1992).

Richard E. Palmer's *Hermeneutics: Interpretation Theory in Schleiermacher, Dilthey, Heidegger and Gadamer* (Evanston: Northwestern University Press, 1969) is an early, readable and reliable guide to these figures that influenced a generation of Anglo-American readers.

There are several helpful anthologies, including:

— *Blackwell Companion to Hermeneutics*, ed. Niall Keane and Chris Lawn (New York: Wiley Blackwell, 2016)
— *The Hermeneutics Reader*, ed. Kurt Mueller-Vollmer (New York: Continuum, 1988)
— *The Routledge Companion to Hermeneutics*, ed. Jeff Malpas and Hans-Helmut Gander (New York/London: Routledge, 2014).

HEIDEGGER

Pöggeler's *Martin Heidegger's Path of Thinking* (Chapter 2, note 17), first published in German in 1963, remains the best overview of the sweep of Heidegger's thought I know. John Edward van Buren's *The Young Heidegger* (Chapter 1, note 6) and Theodore Kisiel, *The Genesis of Heidegger's 'Being and Time'* (Berkeley: University of California Press, 1993), are superb introductions to *Being and Time* and to its hermeneutic innovations. Hubert Dreyfus, *Being-in-the-World: A Commentary on Heidegger's 'Being and Time', Division I* (Cambridge, MA: MIT Press, 1990), is not only valuable in itself but especially pertinent to his phenomenological critique of the limits of AI (Chapter 9). Thomas Sheehan's *Making Sense of Heidegger: A Paradigm Shift* (London: Rowman & Littlefield International, 2014) is a challenging new study by a life-long Heidegger scholar.

There is hardly a better example of the 'conflict of interpretations' than the sea of literature on Heidegger and National Socialism. Gregory Fried, *Heidegger's Polemos: From Being to Politics* (New Haven: Yale University Press, 2000), is an in-depth and balanced reading of the problem; his Introduction compactly summarizes the range of interpretations made of Heidegger and the Nazis. In addition to the writings of Fried, Richard Polt and Thomas Sheehan, I would recommend two up-to-date collections which contain helpful essays by leading scholars representing differing perspectives:

— *Reading Heidegger's Black Notebooks 1931–1941*, ed. Ingo Farin and Jeff Malpas (Cambridge, MA: MIT Press, 2016)
— Martin Heidegger, *Nature, History, State: 1933–1934*, translated and edited, with an introduction, by Gregory Fried and Richard Polt (London: Bloomsbury, 2013). This collection contains a seminar given by Heidegger while he was rector (1933–4).

GADAMER

The study of Gadamer is blessed with a number of excellent works. It is hard to beat Jean Grondin, *The Philosophy of Gadamer*, trans. Kathryn Plant (Montreal: McGill-Queen's University Press, 2003), but for other highly reliable studies, see:

— Donatella Di Cesare, *Gadamer: A Philosophical Portrait*, trans. Niall Keane (Bloomington: Indiana University Press, 2013)
— James Risser, *The Life of Understanding* (Bloomington: Indiana University Press, 2012)
— Georgia Warnke, *Gadamer: Hermeneutics, Tradition and Reason* (Stanford: Stanford University Press, 1987)
— Joel Weinsheimer, *Gadamer's Hermeneutics* (New Haven: Yale University Press, 1985).

There are a number of good collections on Gadamer:

— *The Cambridge Companion to Gadamer*, ed. Robert J. Dostal (New York: Cambridge University Press, 2002), is not to be missed
— *The Gadamer Reader: A Bouquet of the Later Writings*, trans. and ed. Richard E. Palmer, (Evanston: Northwestern University Press), 2007
— *The Philosophy of Hans-Georg Gadamer*, ed. Lewis Edwin Hahn, Library of Living Philosophers, Vol. XXIV (Chicago: Open Court, 1997).

DERRIDA

We could fill libraries with the secondary literature on Derrida. The commentary by Geoffrey Bennington that accompanies Derrida's 'Circumfession' in Geoffrey Bennington and Jacques Derrida, *Jacques Derrida* (Chicago: University of Chicago Press, 1993), is an outstanding guide to Derrida's work as a whole. I highly recommend the works of Michael Naas on Derrida. For current work on Derrida, see the journal *Derrida Today* published by Edinburgh University Press (2007–), eds. Nick Mansfield and Nicole Anderson. The University of Chicago Press is currently publishing the 'Seminars of Jacques Derrida', an English translation of the courses Derrida gave over the years, all previously unpublished.

The 'Roundtable' in *Deconstruction in a Nutshell* (Chapter 4, note 11) is a wonderful introduction to Derrida's work in his own words, speaking in English, which my accompanying commentary is meant to further elucidate. I have always found his interviews to be especially helpful introductions. See:

— *Points . . . Interviews, 1974–1994* (Chapter 8, note 16)
— *Negotiations: Interventions and Interviews, 1971–2001*, trans. Elizabeth Rottenberg (Stanford: Stanford University Press, 2002).

My comparison of Derrida with Hermes the rogue is inspired by Jacques Derrida, *Rogues: Two Essays on Reason*, trans. Pascale-Anne Brault and Michael Naas (Stanford: Stanford University Press, 2005).

The interpretation of the relationship between Derrida and Gadamer I presented is an elaboration of my *Radical Hermeneutics* (Introduction, note 2). For more on this relationship – the main sources are cited in the Notes (Chapter 4, note 10) – see Jacques Derrida, *Sovereignties in Question: The Poetics of Paul Celan*, ed. Thomas Dutoit and Outi Pasanen (New York: Fordham University Press, 2015), 135–40, where Derrida revisits his meeting with Gadamer in 1983.

RORTY AND VATTIMO

Rorty's magnum opus is *Philosophy and the Mirror of Nature* (Chapter 6, note 9). His interpretation of Heidegger is found in Richard Rorty, *Essays on Heidegger and Others: Philosophical Papers*, Volume 2 (Cambridge: Cambridge University Press, 1991). A reliable collection of studies of his thought as a whole, edited by philosophers who are also literate in Heidegger, is Charles Guignon and David Hiley, eds., *Richard Rorty* (Cambridge: Cambridge University Press, 2003).

Rorty's relation with deconstruction is discussed in *Deconstruction and Pragmatism: Simon Critchley, Jacques Derrida, Ernesto Laclau and Richard Rorty*, ed. Chantal Mouffe (London: Routledge, 1996), and in John D. Caputo, *More Radical Hermeneutics: On Not Knowing Who We Are* (Bloomington: Indiana University Press, 2000), Chapter 4.

For more on his collaboration with Vattimo, see Richard Rorty and Gianni Vattimo, *An Ethics for Today: Finding Common Ground between Philosophy and Religion* (New York: Columbia University Press, 2010).

One of Vattimo's most important books is *The End of Modernity: Nihilism and Hermeneutics in Post-modern Culture*, trans. Jon R. Snyder (Baltimore: Johns Hopkins University Press, 1988). Two excellent collections worth consulting are:

— *Weakening Philosophy: Essays in Honour of Gianni Vattimo*, ed. Santiago Zabala (Montreal: McGill-Queen's University Press, 2007)
— *Between Nihilism and Politics: The Hermeneutics of Gianni Vattimo*, ed. Silvia Benso and Brian Schroeder (New York: SUNY Press, 2010). Benso is an Italian philosopher who studied with Vattimo in Milan.

His collaboration with René Girard is found in Gianni Vattimo and René Girard, *Christianity, Truth, and Weakening Faith: A Dialogue*, ed. Pierpaolo Antonello, trans. William McCuaig (New York: Columbia University Press, 2010).

My dialogue with Vattimo is found in John D. Caputo and Gianni Vattimo, *After the Death of God*, ed. Jeffrey Robbins (New York: Columbia University Press, 2007).

EDUCATION

For a philosophy of education taking a postmodern hermeneutic approach:

— Shaun Gallagher, *Hermeneutics and Education* (Albany, NY: SUNY Press, 1992)
— *Journal of Culture and Religious Theory*, 12:2 (autumn, 2012): Special Issue: Pedagogical Exercises and Theories of Practice, ed. T. Wilson Dickinson; www.jcrt.org
— *The Pedagogics of Unlearning*, eds. Aidan Seery and Éamonn Dunne (Punctum Books, 2016; Creative Commons International License)
— Claudia Ruitenberg, *Unlocking the World: Education in an Ethics of Hospitality* (Boulder, CO: Paradigm Publishers, 2015).

Jacques Derrida has written extensively about the contemporary university in *Who's Afraid of Philosophy: Right to Philosophy 1*, trans. Jan Plug (Stanford: Stanford University Press, 2002); *Eyes of the University: Right to Philosophy 2*, trans. Jan Plug et al. (Stanford: Stanford University Press, 2004).

POST-HUMANISM

For an informative and up-to-date commentary, a book written for a distinguished university press, which became a *New York Times* bestseller, see Nick Bostrom, *Superintelligence: Paths, Dangers, Strategies* (Oxford: Oxford University Press, 2014); and John Markoff, *Machines of Loving Grace: The Quest for Common Ground between Humans and Robots* (San Francisco: Ecco/HarperCollins, 2015).

Dominique Janicaud is a phenomenologist whose *On the Human Condition*, trans. Eileen Brennan (London: Routledge, 2005), represents a sensible appraisal of the dynamics of the human and post-human in postmodern times.

Francisco Varela and Manuel De Landa are among the more famous post-humanist theorists.

Bruno Latour is an author worth reading on this topic and most of the other topics mentioned in this book. See his *We Have Never been Modern*, trans. Catherine Porter (Cambridge, MA: Harvard University Press, 1993); *Laboratory Life: The Construction of Scientific Facts*, 2nd edn (Princeton: Princeton University Press, 1986); *Aramis, or the Love of Technology* (Cambridge, MA: Harvard University Press, 1996); *Pandora's Hope: Essays on the Reality of Science Studies* (Cambridge, MA: Harvard University Press, 1999).

Isabelle Stengers, *Cosmopolitics* I, trans. Robert Bononno (Minneapolis: University of Minnesota Press, 2003), and *Cosmopolitics* II, trans. Robert Bononno (Minneapolis: University of Minnesota Press, 2011), offer comprehensive presentations of the post-humanist scene. Jean-François Lyotard, *The Inhuman*, trans. Geoffrey Bennington and Rachel Bowlby (Stanford: Stanford University Press, 1991), is a striking contribution by a leading postmodern theorist.

For more, in addition to M. Kathryn Hayles (Chapter 9, note 4), see:

— Elaine Graham, *Representations of the Post/human* (New Brunswick, NJ: Rutgers University Press, 2002)
— Cary Wolfe, *What Is Posthumanism?* (Minneapolis: University of Minnesota Press, 2010)
— ———. 'Is Humanism Really Humane?' Interview with Natasha Lennard in 'The Stone', *New York Times*, 9 Jan. 2017.

RELIGION

On the postmodern adaptation of Tillich, see George Pattison, *Paul Tillich's Philosophical Theology: A Fifty-year Reappraisal* (Basingstoke: Palgrave Macmillan, 2015), and *Retrieving the Radical Tillich*, ed. Russell Re Manning (Basingstoke: Palgrave Macmillan, 2015).

On Derrida and religion, see, in addition to my own work already cited in the notes (Chapter 10, notes 16, 17), *The Prayers and Tears of Jacques Derrida: Religion without Religion* (Bloomington: Indiana

University Press, 1997). Derrida's own writings on religion are found in *Acts of Religion* (Chapter 7, note 2), and Jacques Derrida and Gianni Vattimo, eds., *Religion* trans. David Webb (Stanford: Stanford University Press, 1998).

The most comprehensive account of the problem of religion and secularism is Charles Taylor's massive *A Secular Age* (Chapter 10, note 6). Fortunately, James K. A. Smith, *How (Not) to be Secular* (Grand Rapids, MI: William Eerdmans Publishing Co., 2014) presents an engaging and remarkable condensation of the book. I have addressed these questions in a popular voice in *On Religion* (London/New York: Routledge, 2001).

In addition to the work of Bultmann (Chapter 10, note 4) and Vermes (Chapter 10, note 7), I think John Dominic Crossan is doing the most interesting work on the historical-critical study of the Scriptures. His *Jesus: A Revolutionary Biography* (San Francisco: HarperOne, 2009) is very readable.

Bruno Latour has also written wisely about religion in the postmodern world in *Rejoicing: On the Torments of Religious Speech* (New York: Polity, 2013), and *On the Modern Cult of Factish Gods* (Durham, NC: Duke University Press, 2010). *Facing Gaia*, his 2013 Gifford Lectures, is currently being prepared for publication.

Blackwell Readings in Continental Philosophy: The Religious, ed. John D. Caputo (Oxford: Blackwell, 2001), is a useful collection of primary and secondary sources.

For more on postmodern hermeneutic theories of religion, see Richard Kearney, *The God Who May Be* (Bloomington: Indiana University Press, 2001), and *Anatheism: Returning to God after God* (New York: Columbia University Press, 2010), and Catherine Keller, *The Face of the Deep* (London/New York: Routledge, 2002), and *Cloud of the Impossible: Negative Theology and Planetary Entanglement* (Chapter 11, note 3).

Notes

INTRODUCTION: A MATTER OF INTERPRETATION: A PRIMER ON POSTMODERN HERMENEUTICS

1. The best account I know of that history is Jean Grondin, *Introduction to Philosophical Hermeneutics*, trans. Joel Weinsheimer (New Haven: Yale University Press, 1994).

2. See John D. Caputo, *Radical Hermeneutics: Repetition, Deconstruction and the Hermeneutic Project* (Bloomington: Indiana University Press, 1987).

3. For the received definition of postmodernism as incredulity about big stories, see Jean-François Lyotard, *The Postmodern Condition: A Report on Knowledge*, trans. Geoffrey Bennington and Brian Massumi (Minneapolis: University of Minnesota Press, 1984), xxiii–xxiv.

4. For a perspicacious and still pertinent presentation of this point, see Richard Bernstein, *Beyond Objectivism and Relativism: Science, Hermeneutics, and Praxis* (Philadelphia: University of Pennsylvania Press, 1983).

5. See 'To Hermes' in *Homeric Hymns*, trans. Sarah Ruden (Indianapolis/Cambridge: Hackett Publishing Co., 2005), 38–56. There is some chance that the name of the god came from the verb *hermeneuein*. That's another interpretation.

6. See Norman O. Brown, *Hermes the Thief: The Evolution of a Myth* (New York: Random House Vintage Books, 1947).

7. Martin Heidegger, *Being and Time*, trans. John Macquarrie and Edward Robinson (New York: Harper & Row, 1962).

8. Hans-Georg Gadamer, *Truth and Method*, 2nd rev. edn, trans. Joel Weinsheimer and Donald Marshall (New York: Crossroad, 1989).

9. Jacques Derrida, *Of Grammatology*, corrected edition, trans. Gayatri Spivak (Baltimore: Johns Hopkins University Press, 1997).

10. Conspicuous by his absence from this list is Paul Ricœur (1913–2005), a major figure and something of a personal mentor to Derrida, whom I omit

because I am following the more radical path of hermeneutics from *Being and Time* through Gadamer and Derrida. In *Freud and Philosophy: An Essay on Interpretation* (New Haven: Yale University Press, 1970), Ricœur referred, in an oft-cited expression, to the 'hermeneutics of suspicion', where meaning is reduced to a manifestation of a subterranean will-to-power (Nietzsche), the unconscious (Freud) or class interests (Marx). This 'hermeneutics of suspicion', Ricœur said, constitutes the negative moment of interpretation, which he then framed within a kind of hermeneutical triad, reminiscent of Hegel: a first moment of uncritical, innocent faith (in an idea, institution, etc.), which passes through the moment of suspicion and critique, in order to be repeated in a higher, post-critical faith. Historically, these three stages could be loosely thought of as premodern, modern and postmodern. For a good account, see Charles E. Reagan, *Paul Ricœur: His Life and Work* (Chicago: University of Chicago Press, 1996). The most interesting hermeneutic work being done in the tradition of Ricœur today is by the Irish philosopher Richard Kearney (Boston College).

CHAPTER 1: HOW HEIDEGGER CHANGED EVERYTHING: READING *BEING AND TIME*

1. The book that drew the headlines was Victor Farias, *Heidegger and Nazism*, trans. Paul Burrell (Philadelphia: Temple University Press, 1989), but the more careful and convincing work was done by Hugo Ott, *Martin Heidegger: A Political Life*, trans. Allan Blunden (New York: Basic Books, 1993).
2. Martin Heidegger, *Ponderings II–VI: Black Notebooks 1931–1938*, trans. Richard Rojcewicz (Bloomington: Indiana University Press, 2016).
3. John D. Caputo, *Demythologizing Heidegger* (Bloomington: Indiana University Press, 1993).
4. See Gregory Fried and Richard Polt, 'Translators' Introduction' to Martin Heidegger, *Introduction to Metaphysics*, trans. G. Fried and R. Polt (New Haven: Yale University Press, 2014; second edition), xxii, fn. 19.
5. Caputo, *Demythologizing Heidegger*, 39–59.
6. This remarkable story is told in John Edward van Buren, *The Young Heidegger: Rumor of the Hidden King* (Bloomington: Indiana University Press, 1994).
7. William James, *The Principles of Psychology* (Cambridge, MA: Harvard University Press, 1981), 462.

8. Martin Heidegger, *Ontology – The Hermeneutics of Facticity*, trans. John Edward van Buren (Bloomington: Indiana University Press, 1999), 5.

9. Heidegger, *Hermeneutics of Facticity*, 86.

10. Heidegger, *Hermeneutics of Facticity*, 8–9.

11. Heidegger refers us to the work of Friedrich Schleiermacher (1768–1834) and Wilhelm Dilthey (1833–1911), the foremost theorists of hermeneutics in the nineteenth century.

12. I follow the usual protocol of translating the verbal noun *Sein* with a capital letter ('Being') to distinguish it from a particular being (*Seiendes*), in lower case.

13. Heidegger, *Hermeneutics of Facticity*, 11–13.

14. The term Dasein should not be mystified. It does not mean an invisible spirit. It is just a technical term for human beings and, unless we discover intelligent life on another planet, the only 'examples' we have of Dasein are the human beings we can see and touch all around us. Heidegger uses the word to stress that his approach to human beings is *ontological*, not anthropological, biological or sociological, etc. Dasein does not signify a particular faculty or force human beings have, but the totality of human life taken *from* an ontological point of view – where the unique thing about human beings is that they put their Being into question and make choices that determine their Being. This in contrast to rocks, which never raise questions, or plants, whose development is dictated by natural causes.

15. Heidegger, *Hermeneutics of Facticity*, 17–22.

16. Heidegger uses the German *auslegen*, the ordinary word for 'interpret', which literally means to lay out or unfold or explicate.

17. Heidegger, *Hermeneutics of Facticity*, 23–4.

18. See the critique of Descartes in Martin Heidegger, *Being and Time*, trans. John Macquarrie and Edward Robinson (New York: Harper & Row, 1962), §§19–21.

19. Paul Tillich, 'The Two Types of Philosophy of Religion', in *Theology of Culture* (Oxford: Oxford University Press, 1959), 10–29.

20. Martin Heidegger, *The Fundamental Concepts of Metaphysics: World, Finitude, Solitude*, trans. William McNeill and Nicholas Walker (Bloomington: Indiana University Press, 1995), 338.

21. Heidegger, *Hermeneutics of Facticity*, 69–70.

22. Heidegger, *Being and Time*, §§12–27.

23. Heidegger, *Being and Time*, §9, pp. 67–8.

24. Heidegger, *Being and Time*, §4, p. 33.

25. Heidegger, *Being and Time*, §27, pp. 126–30.

26. Heidegger, *Being and Time*, §§56–7, pp. 317–25.

27. Augustine, *On True Religion*, trans. J. Burleigh and I. Mink (New York: Henry Regnery, 1991), §39.

28. Heidegger, *Being and Time*, §45, pp. 274–8.

29. Heidegger, *Being and Time*, §62, pp. 349–52.

30. Heidegger, *Being and Time*, §35, p. 213.

31. Heidegger, *Being and Time*, §6, pp. 41–9.

32. van Buren, *The Young Heidegger*, 67.

33. Heidegger, *Being and Time*, §53, p. 311.

34. Heidegger, *Being and Time*, §76, p. 446.

35. Heidegger, *Being and Time*, §74, pp. 434–9.

36. Heidegger, *Being and Time*, §75, pp. 439–44.

37. Heidegger's interpretation of Dilthey is challenged by Günter Figal, *Objectivity: The Hermeneutical and Philosophy*, trans. Theodore D. George (Albany, NY: SUNY Press, 2010); and Rudolf A. Makkreel, *Orientation and Judgment in Hermeneutics* (Chicago: University of Chicago Press, 2015).

38. Thomas Kuhn, *The Structure of Scientific Revolutions* (4th edn, with an Introduction by Ian Hacking (Chicago: University of Chicago Press, 1962, 2012). To be sure, Nietzsche caustically proclaimed that physics, too, is an interpretation, but he did not exactly work that out. Friedrich Nietzsche, *Beyond Good and Evil*, trans. R. J. Hollingdale (New York: Penguin, 1973), 'On the Prejudices of the Philosophers', no. 14, p. 26.

39. Heidegger, *Being and Time*, §3, p. 29.

40. Martin Heidegger, *The Principle of Reason*, trans. Reginald Lilly (Bloomington: Indiana University Press, 1991), 29.

41. The most interesting philosopher of science influenced by Heidegger is Robert P. Crease. For an informative study of Heidegger and science see Trish Glazebrook, *Heidegger's Philosophy of Science* (New York: Fordham University Press, 2000).

42. Jean-François Lyotard and Jean-Loup Thébaud, *Just Gaming*, trans. Wlad Godzich (Minneapolis: University of Minnesota Press, 1985). See Pagan Kennedy, *Inventology: How We Dream Up Things That Change the World* (New York: Houghton Mifflin Harcourt, 2016).

CHAPTER 2: HEIDEGGER STRIKES AGAIN:
HERMENEUTICS AND HUMANISM

1. Martin Heidegger, *On the Way to Language*, trans. Peter D. Hertz (New York: Harper & Row, 1971), 30.

2. Jean-Paul Sartre, *Existentialism is a Humanism*, trans. Carol Macomber (New Haven: Yale University Press, 2007).

3. Martin Heidegger, 'Letter on Humanism', in *Martin Heidegger: Basic Writings*, ed. David F. Krell, 2nd edn (New York: Harper & Row, 1993), 213–65.

4. Compare Martin Heidegger, *Being and Time*, trans. John Macquarrie and Edward Robinson (New York: Harper & Row, 1962), §9, pp. 67–9 and 'Letter on Humanism', 229–30.

5. Heidegger, 'Letter on Humanism', 237–8.

6. Heidegger, 'Letter on Humanism', 247–51.

7. John D. Caputo, *The Mystical Element in Heidegger's Thought* (Athens, OH: Ohio University Press, 1978; rev. edn, New York: Fordham University Press, 1986).

8. Heidegger, 'Letter on Humanism', 253.

9. For more on this conversation, see Tezuka Tomio, 'An Hour with Heidegger', in Reinhard May, *Heidegger's Hidden Sources: East Asian Influences on His Work*, trans. Graham Parkes (London and New York: Routledge, 1996), pp. 61–7.

10. Heidegger, *On the Way to Language*, 1–2.

11. Heidegger, *On the Way to Language*, 15–17, 3, 27.

12. Heidegger, *On the Way to Language*, 29–30.

13. Heidegger, *On the Way to Language*, 30–32

14. Heidegger, *On the Way to Language*, 40.

15. Heidegger, *On the Way to Language*, 51.

16. Heidegger wrote an early version of the *Letter on Humanism* in a short note in 1937 to Jean Wahl, a crucial figure in mediating Kierkegaard and Heidegger to French readers, protesting the reading of *Being and Time* as a 'philosophy of existence'. Wahl replied that he had a hard time believing that. See Jean Wahl, *Transcendence and the Concrete: Selected Writings*, trans. and ed. Allan D. Schrift and Ian Alexander Moore (New York: Fordham University Press, 2017), 185–6, 213–15.

17. Otto Pöggeler, *Martin Heidegger's Path of Thinking*, trans. Daniel Magurshak and Sigmund Barber (Atlantic Highland, NJ: Humanities Press International, 1987), 9–31.

CHAPTER 3: GADAMER'S *TRUTH AND METHOD*:
PHILOSOPHICAL HERMENEUTICS

1. Hans-Georg Gadamer, *Truth and Method*, 2nd rev. edn, trans. Joel Weinsheimer and Donald Marshall (New York: Crossroad, 1989), 86–7, 135.

2. There are today institutions like the Palais de Tokyo in Paris, which push the idea of what an art space means, and small, experimental art galleries which bear witness to the *post*modern turn.
3. Gadamer, *Truth and Method*, 101–10.
4. Gadamer, *Truth and Method*, 166–7, 186–99.
5. Gadamer, *Truth and Method*, 285–90.
6. Gadamer, *Truth and Method*, 163–4, 389–95.
7. Gadamer, *Truth and Method*, 306–7, 374–5
8. Gadamer, *Truth and Method*, 367–9, 383–8.
9. Gadamer, *Truth and Method*, 269–77.
10. Gadamer, *Truth and Method*, 231–42, 340–79.
11. Gadamer, *Truth and Method*, 474.
12. Interestingly, if quantum physics describes a set of quantum possibilities actualized in observation, then the actual world can be said to be their explication or interpretation.
13. Gadamer, *Truth and Method*, 383.
14. Gadamer, *Truth and Method*, 307. See Jean Grondin, *Introduction to Philosophical Hermeneutics*, trans. Joel Weinsheimer (New Haven: Yale University Press, 1994), 60–62, on how Gadamer is adapting Rambach's text.

CHAPTER 4: DERRIDA AND THE TWO INTERPRETATIONS OF INTERPRETATION

1. Edward Baring, *The Young Derrida and French Philosophy: 1945–1968* (Cambridge: Cambridge University Press, 2011), 239–43.
2. Jacques Derrida, *Of Grammatology*, corrected edition, trans. Gayatri Spivak (Baltimore: Johns Hopkins University Press, 1997), 158. All citations of Derrida in this section, 'An Exorbitant Method', are to this page.
3. Derrida, *Of Grammatology*, 158.
4. Derrida, *Of Grammatology*, 159.
5. Jacques Derrida, *Writing and Difference*, trans. Alan Bass (Chicago: University of Chicago Press, 1978), 67.
6. Derrida, *Writing and Difference*, 292.
7. Derrida, *Writing and Difference*, 292.
8. Jacques Derrida, *Edmund Husserl's Origin of Geometry*, trans. John Leavey (Boulder, CO: John Hays Co., 1978), 102–4.
9. Derrida, *Writing and Difference*, 293.

10. The encounter of Derrida and Gadamer in Paris in 1981 – *Dialogue and Deconstruction: The Gadamer–Derrida Encounter*, eds. Diane Michelfelder and Richard Palmer (Albany, NY: SUNY Press, 1989) – was a dud. Derrida's objection to hermeneutics, that 'wanting-to-be-understood' is a kind of Nietzschean will-to-power, seemed quite uninformed about *Truth and Method* and invited the obvious response: what was Derrida doing there, or anywhere else, other than trying to make himself understood? In a reunion, in Heidelberg, in 1988 – Jacques Derrida, Hans-Georg Gadamer and Philippe Lacoue-Labarthe, *Heidegger, Philosophy, and Politics: The Heidelberg Conference*, ed. Mireille Calle-Gruber, trans. Jeff Fort (New York: Fordham University Press, 2016) – they made more sense of each other. This book is also a helpful discussion of Heidegger's National Socialism, based on what we knew in 1988. Jean Grondin, *Introduction to Philosophical Hermeneutics*, trans. Joel Weinsheimer (New Haven: Yale University Press, 1994), 135–9, takes a rather cynical view of Derrida; see John D. Caputo, 'Good Will and the Hermeneutics of Friendship: Gadamer, Derrida and Madison', *Symposium: Canadian Journal of Continental Philosophy*, 8, no. 2 (summer, 2004): 213–25.

11. John D. Caputo, *Deconstruction in a Nutshell: A Conversation with Jacques Derrida* (New York: Fordham University Press, 1997), 8.

12. Augustine, *Confessions*, trans. F. J. Sheed (Indianapolis/Cambridge: Hackett Publishing Co., 1970), Book Four, Chapter. IV, 55.

CHAPTER 5: STRUCTURALISM, POST-STRUCTURALISM AND THE AGE OF THE PROGRAM

1. Ferdinand de Saussure, *Course in General Linguistics*, trans. Roy Harris (Peru, IL: Open Court Publishers, 1986).

2. Jacques Derrida, *Of Grammatology*, corrected edition, trans. Gayatri Spivak (Baltimore: Johns Hopkins University Press, 1997), 48–9.

3. Richard P. Feynman, *The Feynman Lectures on Physics,* Vol. III: *Quantum Mechanics* (New York: Basic Books, New Millennium edition, 2015). These are Feynman's undergraduate lectures.

4. See Johannes Angermuller, *Why There is No Poststructuralism in France* (London: Bloomsbury Academic, 2015).

5. A longer account of the story we are telling here would go into Husserl, who deeply influenced Heidegger; see my *Radical Hermeneutics: Repetition, Deconstruction and the Hermeneutic Project* (Bloomington: Indiana University Press, 1987), ch. 2, 36–59.

6. Derrida, *Of Grammatology*, 30–44.

7. Derrida, *Of Grammatology*, 59, 61.

8. Derrida, *Of Grammatology*, 60–62.

9. Derrida's undecidability principle is not unlike Gödel's: if the system is completely formalized, it is narrowed down; if it is left incomplete, it functions.

10. Derrida, *Of Grammatology*, 6.

11. It was in this connection that Lyotard gave the received definition of postmodernism as incredulity about meta-narrratives; see Jean-François Lyotard, *The Postmodern Condition: A Report on Knowledge*, trans. Geoff Bennington and Brian Massumi (Minneapolis: University of Minnesota Press, 1984), xxiii–xxiv.

12. Donna Haraway, 'Ecce Homo', in *The Haraway Reader*, ed. Donna Haraway (New York and London: Routledge, 2004), 49.

13. Visit www.ibm.com/outhink to see all the ways Watson will 'augment our intelligence' in business, medicine, law, education, and so on, and will change the way the world thinks.

CHAPTER 6: THE ROGUISH HERMENEUTICS
OF VATTIMO AND RORTY

1. *Weak Thought*, eds. Gianni Vattimo and Pier Aldo Rovatti, trans. Peter Carravetta (Albany, NY: SUNY Press, 2013).

2. Friedrich Nietzsche, *The Portable Nietzsche*, trans. and ed. Walter Kaufmann (New York: Viking Press, 1954), 458. See Alan Schrift, *Nietzsche and the Question of Interpretation: Between Hermeneutics and Deconstruction* (London/New York: Routledge, 1990).

3. Friedrich Nietzsche, *The Gay Science*, Section 125, in *The Portable Nietzsche*, 95.

4. Gianni Vattimo, *Nihilism and Emancipation: Ethics, Politics, & Law*, trans. William McCuaig (New York: Columbia University Press, 2003).

5. Gianni Vattimo, *The End of Modernity: Nihilism and Hermeneutics in Postmodern Culture*, trans. Jon R. Snyder (London: Polity, 1988).

6. Richard Rorty and Gianni Vattimo, *The Future of Religion*, ed. Santiago Zabala (New York: Columbia University Press, 2005), 43 ff.

7. Rorty and Vattimo, *The Future of Religion*, 63.

8. See Gianni Vattimo, *After Christianity*, trans. Luca D'Isanto (New York: Columbia University, 2002), and Gianni Vattimo, *Belief*, trans. Luca D'Isanto and David Webb (New York: Columbia University Press, 1999).

9. Richard Rorty, *Philosophy and the Mirror of Nature* (Princeton: Princeton University Press, 1979).

10. Recently, Simon Critchley, a British continentalist philosopher transplanted to the New School in New York City, has been editing *The Stone*, a very successful public forum for philosophy in *The New York Times*. See http://www.nytimes.com/column/the-stone.

11. Richard Rorty, *Contingency, Irony, and Solidarity* (Cambridge: Cambridge University Press, 1989).

12. See Richard Rorty, *Achieving Our Country* (Cambridge, MA: Harvard University Press, 1998), 89–90.

13. Richard Rorty, 'Being That Can be Understood is Language', in *Gadamer's Repercussions*, ed. Bruce Krajewski (Berkeley: University of California Press, 2004), 21–9.

CHAPTER 7: THE CALL OF JUSTICE AND THE SHORT ARM OF THE LAW

1. The proceedings were published in *Deconstruction and the Possibility of Justice*, ed. Drucilla Cornell et al. (New York: Routledge, 1992).

2. Jacques Derrida, 'The Force of Law: "The Mystical Foundation of Authority"', trans. Mary Quantaince, in Jacques Derrida, *Acts of Religion*, ed. Gil Anidjar (New York and London: Routledge, 2002), 234–6. This is the revised version of the lecture.

3. Jacques Derrida, *Specters of Marx: The State of the Debt, the Work of Mourning, and the New International*, trans. Peggy Kamuf (New York: Routledge, 1994).

4. Derrida, 'The Force of Law', in *Acts of Religion*, 243.

5. See Søren Kierkegaard, *Fear and Trembling* in *Kierkegaard's Writings*, VI, *Fear and Trembling/Repetition*, trans. and ed. Howard and Edna Hong (Princeton: Princeton University Press, 1983).

6. Derrida, 'The Force of Law', in *Acts of Religion*, 231.

7. Derrida, 'The Force of Law', in *Acts of Religion*, 249.

8. Derrida, 'The Force of Law', in *Acts of Religion*, 238–9.

9. Derrida, 'The Force of Law', in *Acts of Religion*, 241.

10. Derrida, 'The Force of Law', in *Acts of Religion*, 243.

11. Derrida, 'The Force of Law', in *Acts of Religion*, 243.

12. Derrida, 'The Force of Law', in *Acts of Religion*, 244.

13. Derrida, 'The Force of Law', in *Acts of Religion*, 244.

14. Derrida, 'The Force of Law', in *Acts of Religion*, 247–8.
15. Derrida, 'The Force of Law', in *Acts of Religion*, 249.
16. Derrida, 'The Force of Law', in *Acts of Religion*, 252.
17. Derrida, 'The Force of Law', in *Acts of Religion*, 252.
18. Derrida, 'The Force of Law', in *Acts of Religion*, 253.
19. Derrida, 'The Force of Law', in *Acts of Religion*, 254.
20. Derrida, 'The Force of Law', in *Acts of Religion*, 255.
21. Derrida, 'The Force of Law', in *Acts of Religion*, 255.
22. Derrida, 'The Force of Law', in *Acts of Religion*, 255.
23. Derrida, 'The Force of Law', in *Acts of Religion*, 254.
24. Derrida, 'The Force of Law', in *Acts of Religion*, 257.

CHAPTER 8: GADAMERIAN NURSES

1.   John D. Caputo, *Deconstruction in a Nutshell: A Conversation with Jacques Derrida* (New York: Fordham University Press, 1997), 8.
2.   Caputo, *Deconstruction in a Nutshell*, 8.
3.   Hans-Georg Gadamer, *The Enigma of Health: The Art of Healing in a Scientific Age*, trans. Jason Gaiger (Stanford: Stanford University Press, 1996).
4.   Nancy J. Moules, Graham P. McCaffrey, James C. Field and Catherine M. Laing, *Conducting Hermeneutic Research: From Philosophy to Practice* (New York: Peter Lang, 2015), 78.
5.   Jacques Derrida, 'The Force of Law: "The Mystical Foundation of Authority"', trans. Mary Quantaince, in Jacques Derrida, *Acts of Religion*, ed. Gil Anidjar (New York and London: Routledge, 2002), 252.
6.   *Conducting Hermeneutic Research*, 58.
7.   *Conducting Hermeneutic Research*, 11, 49–50.
8.   Nancy Moules, David W. Jardine, Graham P. McCaffrey and Christopher Brown, 'Isn't All of Oncology Hermeneutic?', *Journal of Applied Hermeneutics* (2013). *JAH* is an online open-access journal: http://jah.journalhosting.ucalgary.ca/jah/index.php/jah/index.
9.   'Isn't All of Oncology Hermeneutic?', 3.
10. 'Isn't All of Oncology Hermeneutic?', 6.
11. *Conducting Hermeneutic Research*, 58.
12. Jean-François Lyotard, *The Differend: Phrases in Dispute*, trans. Georges Van Den Abbeele (Minneapolis: University of Minnesota Press, 1988), 86–106.

13. Gerard Manley Hopkins, 'Spring and Fall', available online at https://www. poetryfoundation.org/poems-and-poets/poems/detail/44400.

14. Nancy J. Moules, 'Suffering Together: Whose Words Were They?', *Journal of Family Nursing* 5:3 (1999): 255.

15. *Conducting Hermeneutic Research*, 99–114.

16. Jacques Derrida, *Points . . . Interviews, 1974–1994*, ed. Elisabeth Weber, trans. Peggy Kamuf et al. (Stanford: Stanford University Press, 1995), 152.

17. Edmund Husserl, *Philosophy as a Strict Science*, trans. Quentin Lauer, in *Phenomenology and the Crisis of Philosophy* (New York: Harper Torchbooks, 1965).

18. Moules, 'Suffering Together', 251–3.

19. Hans-Georg Gadamer, *Truth and Method*, 2nd rev. edn, trans. Joel Weinsheimer and Donald Marshall (New York: Crossroad, 1989), 17.

20. Moules, 'Suffering Together', 253.

21. Moules, 'Suffering Together', 256.

CHAPTER 9: THE SPECTRE OF THE POST-HUMAN: HAVE WE EVER BEEN HUMAN?

1. Robert J. Gordon, *The Rise and Fall of American Growth* (Princeton: Princeton University Press, 2016).

2. Donna Haraway, 'A Manifesto for Cyborgs', in *The Haraway Reader*, ed. Donna Haraway (New York and London: Routledge, 2004), 7–46.

3. Ray Kurzweil, *The Singularity is Near: When Humans Transcend Biology* (New York: Penguin, 2005); Hans Moravec, *Robot: Mere Machine to Transcendent Mind* (Oxford: Oxford University Press, 2000).

4. This is the argument of M. Katherine Hayles, *How We became Posthuman: Virtual Bodies in Cybernetics, Literature, and Informatics* (Chicago: University of Chicago Press, 1999).

5. Maurice Merleau-Ponty, *The Phenomenology of Perception*, trans. Colin Smith (London/New York: Routledge & Kegan Paul, 1962). This is also the point made by Hubert Dreyfus – to simulate human intelligence, computers would need bodies – in *What Computers Still Can't Do: A Critique of Artificial Reason*, rev. edn (Cambridge, MA: MIT Press, 1992). The original 1972 edition, which created quite a stir, was first attacked then carefully studied by the AI people.

6. Jacques Derrida, *The Animal That Therefore I Am*, ed. Marie-Louise Mallet, trans. David Wills (New York: Fordham University Press, 2008).

7. Donna Haraway, *The Companion Species Manifesto: Dogs, People, and Significant Otherness*, ed. Matthew Begelke (Chicago: Prickly Paradigm Press, 2003).

8. They even have a certain religion, according to Donovan Schaefer, *Religious Affects: Animality, Evolution, and Power* (Durham, NC: Duke University Press, 2015).

9. Jacques Derrida, 'Plato's Pharmacy', in *Dissemination*, trans. Barbara Johnson (Chicago: University of Chicago Press, 1981), 95–117.

10. John Markoff, 'Synthetic DNA is Seen as Way to Store Data for Centuries', *The New York Times* (14 Dec. 2015).

11. David Brooks, 'Intimacy for the Avoidant', *The New York Times* (7 Oct. 2016).

12. Greg Milner, 'Ignore the GPS', *The New York Times* (14 Feb. 2016); Mart Vella, 'People Shouldn't be Allowed to Drive', *Time Magazine* (7 Mar. 2016).

13. Joel Stein, 'Why We're Losing the Internet to the Culture of Hate', *Time Magazine* (29 Aug. 2016).

14. See Steve Lohr, 'Fulfilling Watson's Promise', *The New York Times* (19 Feb. 2016).

15. Dina Fine Maron, 'The Right Pill for You', *Scientific American*, 315:4 (Oct. 2016): 38–45.

16. Nicholas Wade, 'Scientists Seek a Moratorium on Editing of Human Genome', *The New York Times* (4 Dec. 2015).

17. Dean H. Hamer, *The God Gene: How Faith is Hardwired into Our Genes* (New York: Random House Anchor Books, 2005).

18. See Alice Park, 'Life, the Remax', *Time Magazine* (4 Jul. 2016).

19. Steve Lohr, 'Don't Fear the Robots', *The New York Times* (25 Oct. 2015).

20. This was also pointed out by Dreyfus, a philosopher steeped in Heidegger and Merleau-Ponty, in *What Computers Still Can't Do*.

21. Catherine Malabou, *Before Tomorrow: Epigenesis and Rationality*, trans. Carolyn Shread (Cambridge: Polity Press, 2016).

22. Derrida, 'Plato's Pharmacy', 125.

23. There is of course another interpretation of Plato. While I generally give Plato, and especially the Platonists, the aftermath of Plato, a hard time for his dualism, in historical context Plato was arguing against Parmenides, who was even harsher with time and change and images than was Plato. Plato was trying to 'save the appearances' and to show that, while sensible images could lead us astray, they were, if *interpreted* well, our path to the upper world of Absolute Truth, about which he said we find ourselves reduced to telling stories.

24. As Brian Greene points out in *The Hidden Reality* (New York: Vintage Books, 2011), 272, Plato could be right in an even stronger sense. According to the 'holographic principle', everything (including us!) we encounter in ordinary experience could be a three-dimensional holograph being generated by the activity taking place on a 'distant boundary surface', at a 'thin and remote locus'.

CHAPTER 10: POSTMODERN, POST-SECULAR, POST-RELIGIOUS

1. Gianni Vattimo, *Belief*, trans. Luca D'Isanto and David Webb (New York: Columbia University Press, 1999), 69–70, 93.

2. Jacques Derrida, 'Circumfession: Fifty-nine Periods and Periphrases', in Geoffrey Bennington and Jacques Derrida, *Jacques Derrida* (Chicago: University of Chicago Press, 1993), 155–6.

3. See Christopher Hitchens, *God is Not Great: How Religion Poisons Everything* (New York: Hachette Book Group, 2009); Richard Dawkins, *The God Delusion* (Boston: Houghton Mifflin, 2006); Daniel Dennett, *Breaking the Spell: Religion as a Natural Phenomenon* (New York: Penguin, 2006); and Sam Harris, *The End of Faith: Religion, Terror, and the Future of Reason* (New York: Norton, 2004).

4. Rudolph Bultmann, *Jesus Christ and Mythology* (New York: Charles Scribner's Sons, 1958).

5. See Samuel Freedman, 'Secular, but Feeling the Call to Divinity School', *The New York Times* (17 Oct. 2015).

6. Charles Taylor, *A Secular Age* (Cambridge, MA: Harvard University Press, 2007).

7. See Geza Vermes, *Christian Beginnings: From Nazareth to Nicaea* (New Haven: Yale University Press, 2014).

8. See Carlo Rovelli, *Seven Brief Lessons on Physics*, trans. Simon Carnell and Erica Segre (New York: Riverhead Books, 2016), for an insightful, short and readable account of exactly what I mean.

9. Simone Weil, *Gravity and Grace*, trans. Emma Crawford and Mario von der Ruhr (New York/London: Routledge, 2002), 114–15.

10. *Meister Eckhart: The Essential Sermons, Commentaries, Treatises and Defense*, trans. Edmund Colledge and Bernard McGinn (New York: Paulist Press, 1981), 200.

11. Paul Tillich, *Theology of Culture* (Oxford: Oxford University Press, 1959), 25.

12. Paul Tillich, *The Courage to Be* (New Haven: Yale University Press, 1952), 186–90.

13. Paul Tillich, *Dynamics of Faith* (New York: Harper & Row, 1957), 1.

14. Tillich, *Dynamics of Faith*, 47–62.

15. Tillich, *Dynamics of Faith*, 33.

16. I explore this at length in *The Weakness of God: A Theology of the Event* (Bloomington: Indiana University Press, 2006).

17. I have worked out this view of religion in a number of my books, the most accessible of which is *The Folly of God: A Theology of the Unconditional* (Salem, OR: Polebridge Press, 2016).

CHAPTER 11: A QUICK REVIEW: WHAT IS POSTMODERN HERMENEUTICS IN A NUTSHELL?

1. It is fascinating to see how many postmodern authors, even the most atheistic, are interested in Augustine's *Confessions*. See *Augustine and Postmodernism: Confessions and Circumfession*, eds. John D. Caputo and Michael Scanlon (Bloomington: Indiana University Press, 2005).

2. See his 1920 lecture course on the *Confessions* in Martin Heidegger, *The Phenomenology of Religious Life*, trans. Matthias Fritsch and Jennifer Anna Gosetti-Ferencei (Bloomington: Indiana University Press, 2004).

3. Catherine Keller, *Cloud of the Impossible: Negative Theology and Planetary Entanglement* (New York: Columbia University Press, 2015), 16.

4. The call is our 'vocation', from *vocare*, to call.

5. Martin Heidegger, *Being and Time*, trans. John Macquarrie and Edward Robinson (New York: Harper & Row, 1962), §56, p. 318.

6. Heidegger, *Being and Time*, §57, p. 319.

7. Heidegger, *Being and Time*, §57, p. 320.

8. See my 'Proclaiming the Year of the Jubilee: Thoughts on a Spectral Life', in *It Spooks: Living in Response to an Unheard Call*, ed. Erin Schendzielos (Rapid City, SD, Shelter50 Publishing Collective, 2015), 10–47.

9. Friedrich Nietzsche, *Beyond Good and Evil*, trans. R. J. Hollingdale (New York: Penguin, 1973), no. 2, p. 16; for a commentary, see Jacques Derrida, *Politics of Friendship*, trans. George Collins (London & New York: Verso, 1997), 34–45.

A CONCLUSION WITHOUT CONCLUSION:
A GOD EVEN NIETZSCHE COULD LOVE

1. Friedrich Nietzsche, *Thus Spoke Zarathustra*, trans. Walter Kaufmann (New York: Viking Press, 1966), 'Upon the Blessed Isles', 87.

2. I have proposed such a postmodern version of God in John D. Caputo, *The Insistence of God: A Theology of Perhaps* (Bloomington: Indiana University Press, 2013).

3. Friedrich Nietzsche, *Beyond Good and Evil*, trans. R. J. Hollingdale (New York: Penguin, 1973), 16.

4. Available online at: https://archive.org/stream/MollyBloomMonologEnd/ MollyBloomMonologhyEnd_djvu.txt.

Index